Never too old to backpack

A 364-mile walk through Wales

Tracy Burton

DEDICATION

Our long hike through Wales might never have happened had it not been for Harri's long-time obsession with the Cambrian Way. For that reason, this book is dedicated to the late Tony Drake and all those who are equally passionate about the Welsh landscape.

CONTENTS

PREVIOUSLY

Harri first told me of his intention to walk through Wales in March 2007, the month we started dating.

I wonder now if he mentioned his lifelong ambition so early on in our relationship as a test of kinds; if I'd thrown my hands up in horror at the prospect of covering such a distance on foot he would have known immediately that I wasn't the one for him.

Fortunately, the idea excited me enormously. Long-distance hiking was definitely my thing… in my dreams anyway. I still remember standing on the beach near Merthyr Mawr at the point where the Ogmore estuary prevents you walking any farther along the water's edge and announcing to my bemused father that one day I intended to walk around the entire British coastline.

That was in 1976 and while the intervening decades saw me tucking many happy hiking miles under my belt, family and work commitments meant there was never sufficient time to undertake a long-distance walk.

Harri had unwittingly ignited a long-buried ambition. Though secretly, I wondered if at 45 I'd left it a little late to take up backpacking; my regular running meant I was now fitter – a lot fitter – than I'd been in my 20s or 30s, but was I really up to weeks of hard hiking with a heavy rucksack on my back? And then there was the camping. No getting out of that and I hated it.

It was the late Tony Drake's Cambrian Way that particularly piqued Harri's interest; at 18, he had picked up the slim volume outlining the route in Hay-on-Wye and, ever since, had been eager to complete the high-level route himself. In November 2007, Harri sent an email to the great man himself, suggesting some changes to the route in the no-longer-industrialised South Wales valleys. Harri was delighted to receive a response. The timing of his correspondence, however, couldn't have been worse.

'What a joy to have some suggestions for route improvement on the Cambrian Way,' Tony wrote. 'I get very few suggestions. What a shame, however, that you didn't write back in the summer when I and my friend John Coombe were actively checking the guide book for amendments.' The man who in 2001 was awarded the MBE for his services to public rights of way added generously, 'You were not of course aware of my revision programme.'

Sadly, Tony Drake died in March 2012. In its obituary, the Guardian newspaper describes the Cambrian Way as his 'magnum opus' – a route 'traversing Wales at its wildest and highest'.

Eighteen months into our relationship, Harri decided to abandon local government and embark upon a career as an outdoor writer. He was therefore delighted when a well-known outdoor publisher showed an interest in publishing a comprehensive, step-by-step guide to the Cambrian Way illustrated with photographs of Wales's stunning landscapes.

And so began our protracted attempt to complete Tony Drake's 275-mile route across the highest and wildest parts of Wales in snatched weekends and the odd (frequently wet) extended break. Our somewhat unorthodox approach to walking the 'Mountain Connoisseur's Walk' was relatively easy at first – we live near Newport and Drake's route travels south to north, from Cardiff Bay to Conwy. Public transport links – if not always great – at least existed in some form, and if the fare prices frequently caused us to flinch, we were at least able to make steady progress towards the Brecon Beacons.

As we travelled deeper into Wales, the practicalities of end to end walking became starkly apparent. Faced with buses that ran several times a week – and frequently not at all – our progress was hampered by the need to return to our car each day. Always creative with a map, Harri devised a series of circular routes which saw us edging several miles up country on any given day only to do an about turn halfway through the day to make our way back to our starting point.

It was on some of these long, arduous and frustrating yomps that I started questioning what exactly it was that I liked about hiking – certainly not the continual squelching through peat bogs with the heavens emptying down on us and definitely not the nights spent shivering in a tent high above sea level.

One day in August will be forever engrained in my mind for being spectacularly miserable (and this coming from someone who is well-versed in Wales's always inclement and frequently very wet weather). We left our campsite at Devil's Bridge in steady drizzle, our destination the nearby Dyffryn Castell. Stick to the road and it's a four mile journey, follow the undulating route of the Cambrian Way in torrential Welsh rain and it feels as though you're walking to the earth's end the long way.

Suffice to say, we were soaked to the skin from head to toe pretty much from the word go, which meant we couldn't face stopping for elevenses or even lunch. (It's not as hard as you'd imagine to ignore a rumbling stomach when you're stood knee-deep in a swamp.)

Harri tried to raise our spirits by conjuring up images of us warming ourselves in the cosy bar of the Dyffryn Castell Hotel. Located on the busy A44 to Aberystwyth, it would provide shelter for two very bedraggled – and cold – walkers for an hour at the very least. At last, the building materialised, a beacon of hope in the drenched, colourless landscape. Seeing it, we increased our pathetic pace, squelching across the sodden moorland; in just minutes now we'd be warming our icy feet in front of a roaring fire and sipping glasses of ruby port. But like the mirage in a desert, as we grew closer our hopes were cruelly dashed. The once strategically located hotel was closed and, judging from the various building works that were underway, it was unlikely to be offering liquid refreshments to hikers in the near future.

Fast forward a year and we were still meandering through Wales, edging a few miles forward before turning to trek back to our car. By now I'd taken voluntary redundancy from my own job; with both Harri and I temporarily free from the fetters of the day job we were keen to complete the Cambrian Way.

Once again – and despite it being August – the weather soured and Harri had an awful experience when he attempted to traverse the Rhinogs in torrential rain and poor visibility. Knowing he was at risk of becoming disorientated, he wisely decided to abort the day's walking. When I picked him up near Dyffryn Ardudwy on the Barmouth–Harlech road, Harri was soaked through and shivering uncontrollably.

Still we persevered; after all, there was a publisher waiting in the wings. By late April the following year, we had reached Snowdonia and the highest peaks on the Cambrian Way yet. By now, the mountainous landscape was making it impossible for us to employ our former circular walk method while adding any worthwhile miles to the project. I was delegated to the role of chauffeur for the high-level sections, joining Harri only when the walking was relatively straightforward or confined to the valleys. I wasn't with him when he walked across the Glyders to Ogwen and became seriously disorientated in an unexpected white–out, but I recognise terror in a voice when I hear it.

The final section of the Cambrian Way meanders down the majestic Conwy Mountain with stunning views across the Conwy estuary and beyond. Though for logistical reasons I was unable to join Harri for the day, I climbed from Conwy and walked the last mile or so with him.

We'd reached the end of the Cambrian Way – Harri had walked the entire route while I'd covered all but the toughest terrain. Unfortunately, however, the whole experience had been so disjointed – and was spread over such an extended timescale – neither of us had any sense that we'd completed an end to end walk through Wales. Moreover, our scariest experiences had occurred at the end of April and in two successive Augusts, making us question if there can ever be a safe time of year to complete the highest sections of the route.

Harri agonised. We'd walked the Cambrian Way and had enough material to write a comprehensive guidebook. Deep down, however, he felt Tony Drake's route was at best, unnecessarily demanding and at worst, downright dangerous. We hadn't been backpacking or aiming to finish the route in one continuous walk, which meant we had the luxury of remaining in our comfortable Beddgelert cottage or Barmouth bed and breakfast accommodation when the weather conditions were too atrocious to carry on. Harri was concerned someone travelling to Wales for the sole purpose of completing the Cambrian Way in three weeks might be faced with climbing the Rhinogs or Snowdonia's high peaks in extremely dangerous conditions – or bailing out.

Gradually an idea took root. The Cambrian Way would always be popular with serious mountaineers – experienced hikers who were confident in their navigation skills and who had faced similar (or worse) conditions before – but we felt certain there were many other backpackers looking for a long-distance challenge who might prefer a lower-level route across Wales.

And so the idea for 'O Fôn i Fynwy' was born – an end to end through Wales suitable for someone of reasonable fitness to walk in normal weather conditions (and in Wales, that probably means some rain and mist) without undue difficulty or danger.

In June 2014, I heaved a hefty rucksack onto my back and set off to Anglesey with Harri.

I'd waited a long time for this moment and, finally, on the day before my 53rd birthday, I found myself joining the ranks of the backpacking community.

JUNE 2: SETTING OFF

After years of dreaming, months of planning and weeks of worrying, the big day at last arrived.

And after much deliberation about what constituted the 'ends' of Wales, Harri finally opted for the traditional ends as coined in the Welsh expression 'O Fôn i Fynwy' ('From Anglesey [Ynys Môn] to Monmouthshire'). Starting at Holyhead and finishing in Chepstow, the route will take in some of Wales's most stunning landscapes, including the Anglesey AONB (Area of Outstanding Natural Beauty), Snowdonia National Park, the Cambrian Mountains, the Brecon Beacons National Park and the Wye Valley AONB.

If everything went as planned, we hoped to complete 'O Fôn i Fynwy' in one continuous hike, stopping overnight at campsites and B&Bs, with even the occasional night of wild camping to keep the costs down, but we needed to be realistic.

The weather would make a huge difference to our success or otherwise – and it was one thing that was out of our control. There were other perils too: potential sprains, blisters, sunstroke (well, it's *possible* even here in Wales) or just sheer exhaustion.

I was more than a little nervous about what we were about to take on, particularly after May's 'reconnaissance' trip along the soon-to-be England Coast Path. Our original plan was to walk from Chepstow to Minehead in five days; in the event, we ran out of time and were forced to finish at Watchet – eight miles short of Minehead.

So, what did we learn from that ill-fated trip? First, it's not a great idea to use Google directions to estimate walking distances (the coastline tends to follow a rather more convoluted route than major roads!). This rather vague measuring method (utilised by me because Harri was too busy with 'O Fôn i Fynwy' planning and other freelance work to properly plot the route) was the reason for us completing several marathon-distance days, one after the other.

Next, don't ever, *ever* pre-book overnight accommodation when the above method of distance-calculating is used. If you do you're likely to discover – as we did – that your hotel rooms are roughly 30 miles apart. Unless you're prepared to wave goodbye to lots of money, you have no choice but to do the distance.

Thirdly, avoid combining chunky socks and snugly fitting trail shoes. If the sock/shoe combination doesn't feel 100% comfortable when you're setting off, you can be sure it's not going to improve 20 miles into the hike. I made this mistake on day one, opting for the nice new *thick* socks I'd bought in an Asda sale instead of my usual threadbare, but tried and tested, pair. And paid the cost when *four* excruciating blisters had appeared on my little (hammer) toes by nightfall, three of which were jostling for space on the one toe. Poor judgement and sock vanity meant I hobbled the biggest part of 70 miles in *absolute agony*.

Next, be sure to remember there's just one person carrying all those extra tee shirts, thick and thin fleeces (you can never know which you'll need), novels, toiletries, socks, food supplies … you! Last time I checked there weren't an awful lot of working Sherpas in the UK. Believe me, it's easier to live without most things than to carry them.

Finally, it's worth giving some attention to the issue of wild camping, specifically where you're going to do it. Few people would choose a nuclear power station as the backdrop to their first *ever* wild camping experience, but that's what's likely to happen when you leave your hunt for 'the perfect place to pitch a tent' until nightfall is imminent. Far better to stop a little early in a great spot than have security patrols trailing you around the perimeter fence of Hinkley Point and then be forced to pitch within a stone's throw of high-level CCTV cameras.

Yep, there's nothing like the good old 'recce' to highlight what's wrong with almost everything you planned to do on the expedition proper.

And though I didn't want to dwell on it, there was also this niggling worry at the back of my mind that perhaps I was being a little unrealistic taking on such a big challenge at my age. Everyone knew that backpacking was something youngsters did in their gap year, the holiday of choice for young people with more energy than money. As far as I was aware, none of my contemporaries – certainly none of my friends – had the inclination to do anything so energetic. All-inclusive holidays in the Caribbean, cruises in the Bahamas, European city ... count them in. But walking for four weeks in unpredictable British weather with a heavy pack strapped to their back? No way. I was on my own with this one.

And so, with much excitement – and more than a little trepidation – I prepared to face the biggest hiking challenge of my life.

After our England Coast Path experience when we pre-booked our train tickets home (last-minute or open rail fares are *ridiculously* expensive) and were consequently unable to finish the route, we decided to allow a whole month for our expedition. It seemed unlikely we'd need quite that long – unless the weather let us down *really* badly – but we felt it best to err on the side of caution. Realistically, we hoped to complete our walk of around 400 miles in around 26-28 days.

We left Newport on June 2, one day after I took part in Fairwater Runners' annual relay race, the Rack Raid. At eight miles, my leg from Hen Gwrt to Monmouth was one of the shorter ones, but the country lanes were undulating and I could feel the tiredness in my legs as I crossed from the bus stop to Newport railway station.

Unfortunately, yesterday's gorgeous blue skies were nowhere to be seen, and it was already drizzling when we boarded the two-carriage train for our journey to Anglesey; the low-lying grey clouds weren't the best omen for a long, hot spell of weather but I tried to be optimistic.

I've always enjoyed travelling by train. When I was in my early twenties I worked in Cornwall and travelled from Truro for long weekends at home. That my student nurse salary allowed me to do this regularly says a lot about rail fare inflation over the past three decades.

You can relax completely and absolutely on a train journey. A four-hour car journey (to an open day at Nottingham Trent University for instance) invariably involves a frantic thirty minutes of switching to and from Google Directions and my (preferred) large-scale road map trying to memorise the route. There are decisions to be made about distance times, routes and parking. If, like me, you must slavishly follow a printed route planner to have any chance of reaching your intended destination, there's the continual fear of ending up trapped between articulated lorries in the wrong motorway lane from whence you inevitably find yourself sailing off to Folkestone (believe me, it's happened).

All the stresses and tribulations of travel disappear instantly when you choose the train. Rather than spend four long hours teetering on the edge, you are able to relax in the knowledge that someone else is in charge of transporting you from A to B. If you end up in the wrong place, it's their fault and not yours.

Rather than devouring our precious reading material so soon into our trip (we'd limited ourselves to just one novel each), Harri and I chatted and enjoyed the changing scenery as we first passed through the familiar Cwmbran, Pontypool and Abergavenny before heading upcountry, where we chugged through the border country of Herefordshire and Shropshire. A disjointed voice on the tannoy reeled off the stations we had yet to reach.

Years ago I travelled to York by train and was disappointed by the lack of iconic Yorkshire scenery discernible from my window seat. If I'd imagined rolling dales, valleys and drystone walls, what I got was a grim and unprepossessing landscape filled with grimy towns and factory chimneys. Fortunately, York itself made the tedious journey worthwhile.

Heading from south to north Wales on tracks is much the same. Not that the countryside whizzing past isn't lush and green; it just feels too flat to qualify as authentic Welsh soil. And there's the added peculiarity that travelling from south-east to north-west Wales by train involves a lengthy detour into England.

As the inimitable environmentalist and journalist George Monbiot, a former resident of Machynlleth, once wrote in a piece entitled 'The Open Veins of Wales': 'It is also bleeding ridiculous. As far as I can discover, this is the only country in Europe which you cannot traverse by rail without spending most of the journey passing through another.'

It's not until you leave Chester and its impressive-looking racecourse behind and start heading west towards the North Wales coast that the landscape becomes more mountainous and you get a sense of being in Wales *proper*.

The railway is squeezed in between mountain and sea and passes through Rhyl, Colwyn Bay, Llandudno Junction and Bangor. On a brighter day the scenery would have been quite spectacular, but the combination of slate-grey skies and heavy rain lashing against the windows made the towering mountains to our left appear foreboding rather than alluring.

Back in 2007, I walked from Rhyl to Prestatyn on a wet and blustery spring day while Harri took part in a Welsh learners' competition in Flint. The visibility wasn't great, but I remember being mesmerised by the line of huge wind turbines far out in the distance. North Hoyle began operating in 2003 when it became Wales's first – and the UK's most powerful – offshore wind farm with the capacity to produce enough energy to power 50,000 homes. (North Hoyle no longer holds the latter record; it's been claimed, in August 2013, by the London Array in the outer Thames Estuary.)

I'm an enthusiast of offshore wind farms – what a crime to allow the blustery gales of the British coastline to go to waste. The wind turbines of Liverpool Bay perform a stoic task out there in those murky, salty waters, benignly embracing the elements and transforming a cold, miserable day into something ethereal and magical.

A few months after my stroll, construction work began on an adjacent wind farm. Rhyl Flats officially opened in December 2009, a year after planning consent was granted for what will be Wales's largest wind farm, the neighbouring Gwynt y Môr. When the latter's 160 turbines become operational in 2015, they will bring the total number of wind turbines off the North Wales coast to 215, collectively providing power for over half a million homes and massively reducing carbon emissions. A far safer source of energy than fracking in my humble opinion.

Casting aside the environmental benefits of renewable energy, North Wales's wind farms also provide Wales Coast Path walkers with a vista that's infinitely more aesthetic and interesting than Rhyl's faded promenade, although in today's worsening weather those views were completely obscured by heavy rain and mist.

Once we'd crossed the Menai Strait (not as exciting as I'd anticipated), I popped to the toilet. When I emerged minutes later, we'd stopped at the first 'request' station on Anglesey, Llanfairpwll – or to give it its full name Llanfair–pwllgwyn–gyllgo–gery–chwyrn–drobwll–llanty–silio–gogo–goch (fortunately for tourists and non-Welsh speakers like me, it's a shorter version – Llanfairpwllgwyngyll – which is used on the station plaque). I doubt many non-Welsh speakers would attempt to say it aloud; however, if you're hell-bent on having a go, Wikipedia helpfully suggests the approximate English pronunciation might be something along the lines of *Llan-vire-pooll-guin-gill-go-ger-u-chwurn-drob-ooll-llantus-ilio-gogo-goch*.

And before anyone wonders how any landmark on earth could have acquired such a tortuous place name, you have a Victorian to curse for the seemingly endless string of syllables: some nineteenth-century wisecrack cobbler with his/her eye on boosting commerce and tourism in the village. (Incredibly, it's not even the longest place name in the world, coming second after an 85-letter Maori name for a location in North Island, New Zealand.)

The Welsh translates roughly into English thus: 'Saint Mary's Church in a hollow of white hazel near the swirling whirlpool of the church of Saint Tysilio with a red cave'.

Needless to say, locals tend to abbreviate the village's name to *Llanfairpwll* or even just *Llanfair*.

There wasn't too much time to dwell on the ethics of renaming a historic village because we were immediately off again. The train slowed to a pleasant Sunday drive pace lest anyone be waiting at one of several 'request stops' with snappy and authentic names: Ty Croes, Rhosneigr and Valley.

From the train window, inland Anglesey looked more enticing than I'd anticipated, with lots of open grassland and craggy outcrops. The weather, too, was improving now that we'd crossed the Menai Strait and put some distance between ourselves and the cloud-magnets of Snowdonia.

Just over four hours after our train journey began, our train finally ground to a halt in Holyhead, and we heaved our rucksacks, stuffed full with clothes, maps, emergency rations and a whole load of other imagined necessities onto our backs. We were off …

Our first impression of Anglesey's largest town – the birthplace of comedian Dawn French – was that it looked a little run down, though in fairness we saw very little of the busy port, other than its station, a street full of small shops (and pubs), and the beautiful St Cybi's Church. Perched high above the port, the original church was built on the site of a monastic settlement dating back to AD540. The present building was erected between the thirteenth and sixteenth centuries within a three-walled Roman fort (the fourth wall was the sea, which used to come up to the fort).

Over the centuries, the church has survived attacks by the Vikings, Henry IV (whose men stole St Cybi's shrine and relics and installed them in Christ Church Cathedral in Dublin where they disappeared during the Reformation), and Cromwell's Roundheads. Yet, despite the violent assaults and frequent looting, St Cybi's survived.

Holyhead port is one of the main sea routes from the UK to Ireland; huge ferries arrive and depart regularly from Admiralty Pier. I've always been fascinated by, and drawn to, ports – perhaps in part because I was born in one – however, there's also something intriguing and authentic about a busy, working port. Whether it's the pull of the ocean, the promise of the unknown, of exotic places and people just a stone's throw away across the waves ... I've always been captivated by seaports, places like Plymouth, Fishguard, Penzance.

I was loathe to leave Holyhead without having made the slightest attempt to get acquainted with the place, but we needed to start walking if we were to reach our overnight accommodation before nightfall. Harri had booked an idyllic barn conversion for our first night away, thinking it would be nice for me to wake on my birthday in lovely surroundings. It was a lovely, romantic gesture; there was just one snag. Our bed for the night was fourteen miles away in Porth Swtan and we were travelling there on foot. It was time to get going.

Taking a quick shortcut through the railway station we'd left half an hour earlier, we bade farewell to Holyhead and left town via the dramatic Celtic Gateway footbridge. The £6.2m steel bridge – which opened in 2006 – links the port with the town centre and was built by the same Italian company (Cimolai) that supplied the arches for the roof of the Olympic stadium in Athens. As is often the case with large public construction projects, not everyone thought it was money well spent, but we rather liked the futuristic bridge with its huge arches.

The 125-mile Anglesey Coast Path predates the Wales Coast Path by six years (it was officially opened in June 2006), and so we were expecting a high standard of path maintenance and signage. Not so. We'd barely crossed the bridge before we were confused by a sign which appeared to be pointing us back to town centre. That couldn't be right.

Fortunately, Harri's unparalleled map-reading skills came to the fore and within minutes, we were following the correct route (I do wonder how people manage without the wonderful OS maps because we'd barely gone more than a few more yards before we reached another junction where this time the Wales Coast Path sign was missing).

At this point, perhaps I should explain that Holyhead is itself located on an island (Holy Island) off the coast of Anglesey (a larger island separated from the Welsh mainland by the Menai Strait). This Russian doll-like geographical quirk meant we had to walk several miles before we left our first island to join the second.

That first hour or so had a decidedly 'doggy' theme: dead and alive. We'd barely left the port when a growling mongrel who clearly thought a grassy headland was its own personal fiefdom approached us menacingly, fangs exposed … his owner made a half-hearted attempt to call him off then wandered indoors again to leave us to our fate. Like so many canines, thankfully this one was all bark and no action, but encounters like this can be really frightening.

Fortunately (for us, not them), the numerous dogs we passed in Penrhos Country Park were a little less lively, many of them having been dead for decades. There's something particularly poignant about a pet cemetery, and the idea that an animal should touch its owner's life so deeply that they'll go to the considerable expense of purchasing a burial spot and erecting a tombstone. We love our 14-year-old cat Tabitha dearly, and will miss her terribly when she's no longer with us, but a marked grave in a designated cemetery? Probably not.

We could see Stanley Embankment (known locally as the Cob) from a fair distance as it stretches for over a kilometre across the inlet. By the time we reached it, the tide was right out, giving the impression that the bay is a large, still lake rather than the open sea. I'd place money on the views being better from the road/railway than our lower level cycle path, but that's the price you pay for staying safe.

The Cob was designed by Thomas Telford and named after local benefactors, the Stanley family. Astonishingly, it was constructed in just over a year, opening in 1823. The rubble and raw building materials needed for this massive building project were dug from earth on the Anglesey side and created an artificial valley. The village which grew up on the spot was hence known as Valley, a name it has retained to this day despite the disappearance of the dip. Despite being damaged in a storm in 1824, Stanley Embankment was significantly widened in the 1840s to carry a new train line. In 2001, the construction of the A55 nearby took much of the road traffic from the embankment; the railway line still runs across the Cob.

At the far side, we were surprised to see the Anglesey Coast Path signpost directing walkers onto the pebble beach below Valley. It shouldn't seem odd for a coastal path to follow the coast, but experience has shown us that even when there's a perfectly good sandy beach available, the Wales Coast Path route frequently directs people away from it, as occurs at Oxwich on the Gower peninsular and at Pendine in Carmarthenshire. Yet here, when the beach was pebbly and uneven underfoot, and likely to disappear completely at high tide, the official route stuck rigidly to the coast. I've given up trying to understand officialdom!

It was late afternoon and I was starting to feel weary. The previous day had been packed with physical and social activity; we'd had an early start this morning. The weight of my rucksack was getting to me. It's one thing carrying a backpack for a few minutes from bus stop to railway station but quite another staggering under its weight for hours, straps digging deeply into your shoulders. We'd bought the lightest packs we could afford but mine wasn't designed for a woman's smaller frame; even when I tightened the straps it didn't fit as snugly on my shoulders as I'd have liked. While Harri's rucksack was larger (and heavier), it fitted his larger frame much better.

Generally, I'd find fourteen miles of flat, coastal walking a doddle. Today, however, we hadn't starting walking until gone 2 pm. Three hours on the road. Eight miles tops, maybe less. We wouldn't reach Porth Swtan by nightfall unless we speeded up but the load on my shoulders was becoming unbearable. I needed to off-load something – and soon. Harri was a little way ahead when I heaved my rucksack off my back and onto a rock. I hauled out some of the (considerable) food supplies and crammed everything into two spare carrier bags I'd brought with me. The relief when I strapped my backpack on. I lifted the plastic bags and called out for Harri to wait. I guessed I looked more like a regular shopper than a long-distance walker but right then I was past caring.

Feeling slightly cheered, I checked our progress. We weren't as far up the coast as I'd hoped and there was a dreaded estuary coming up. As we learnt in Somerset, estuaries can feel endless when you're fast running out of energy. It's tough accepting that all the stomping and

14

effort has got you precisely to … the opposite riverbank! Estuaries should be tackled in the morning when you're fired up, energetic and positive, and not towards the end of a long day when there's a strong temptation just to toss your rucksack onto your head and wade across!

Fortunately, this evening's estuary (the Afon Alaw) had nothing in common with the wide and windy River Parrett. The route was well signposted, the footpath surface reasonably dry and, this being the official coast path route, we eventually traversed the now narrow river via a nice new footbridge.

I generally love coastal walking: the undulating footpaths linking high cliffs and beaches, tiny fishing villages and tawdry seaside resorts, a constantly changing landscape with the constant presence of the sea. On a coastal route, you feel as though you're going somewhere … except when the coastline is so fractured, the rocky inlets and various estuaries so numerous that you get the sense you're walking around in circles.

For hours it seemed we'd been approaching then walking away from the single chimney stack of Anglesey Aluminium (one of the biggest employers in North Wales until it closed in September 2009); on the far side of the estuary this vast landmark (it stands at over 90 metres) still appeared depressingly close. Holyhead's ferry wharfs, too, were refusing to blend into the distant scenery.

Suddenly I was filled with resentment. It was madness for Harri to schedule a 14-mile section on this our first day, especially when we hadn't started walking until mid-afternoon. On day one, we should have been taking things easy, strolling around Holyhead and acclimatising ourselves to the unaccustomed weight of our rucksacks. Instead, here we were charging along the coast path with a very real possibility of nightfall arriving before we'd reached Porth Swtan. Had we learned nothing from the impossible schedule we'd followed when walking from Chepstow to Minehead in May? Clearly not.

I was simmering inwardly when Harri suddenly asked, 'How would you like to live there?' At the water's edge stood a large estate with a gorgeous conical tower; with the sea glimmering in the evening sunshine, you couldn't have found a more idyllic spot. 'I think I could probably cope,' I muttered, before realising that Harri didn't seem to be looking at my perfect home. Instead, he was admiring a static caravan to our right!

Onwards we trudged (and what a trudge it was with my aching back, sore feet and plummeting spirits). I'm guessing most people would have prepared for a long-distance hike across Wales with a few days' rest beforehand – not me! Instead, I'd spent the previous day running through the undulating country lanes between Llantilio Crossenny and Monmouth (giving the whole walk a wonderful sense of synchronicity as we'd be spending our last night in Monmouth before the homeward stretch to Chepstow). At 8.1 miles, my 'leg' of Fairwater Running Club's infamous 'Rack Raid' was one of the shorter ones; however, it was hilly from beginning to end and stiflingly hot on the hard metalled surfaces. It's fair to say my legs were probably not at their most rested as we headed along the Anglesey coast with an increasing sense of urgency.

Finally, as the sun disappeared on the horizon, we left the coast path and approached our overnight accommodation at Porth Swtan. Once again Harri had chosen well. The Loft at Pen-y-Craig is described as 'cosy and romantic', and it is both. The internal quarry tiled steps to the rooms are original and steep, but rather than being a nuisance, they simply add to the charm of the lovely open-plan accommodation. We were warned about the low doorways but at 5 foot 4 inches I was well within safety limits. Of all the historic buildings we've visited and stayed in, I think there's only been one place (a converted mill near Machynlleth) where I've managed to bang my head on the door frame and that was more likely to be due to me rushing and bouncing around than the shortcoming of the timbers (Harri's four inches taller and he managed to emerge from our four-day stay unscathed).

The price included a cooked breakfast, which owner Victoria carries across from the farmhouse at an agreed time, all bundled up in a miniature quilt (the food, not Victoria). It's a really clever slant on the whole B&B package and means that you can eat in the comfort of your room, in your PJs if you wish.

The simplicity of the Loft reminded me of the wonderful converted stable block in Porlock, Somerset, where Harri and I enjoyed a romantic week's holiday during our first year together. It was February and we were just setting off to walk the South West Coast Path having completed the Pembrokeshire Coast Path the month before. There's an alluring simplicity about living in a small space with few personal belongings; I often think we'd all be a lot happier with fewer possessions.

It's a shame our stay was too brief to really appreciate the lovely accommodation; still, Harri gets awarded ten out of ten for taste and for being determined that I would wake up somewhere beautiful and comfortable on my birthday. I'd also survived the first day of backpacking with no sign of a blister, which had to be good news!

For photographs visit uk.pinterest.com/thewalkerswife

JUNE 3: CHURCH BAY TO BULL BAY

It's my birthday! Maybe I'm unusual in believing my 53rd birthday is something to celebrate but, hey, I'm still here, and who cares about a few wrinkles when you consider the alternative?

Since my best friend Lynne died of cancer at the age of 44, I've tried harder than ever to count my blessings, not in any kind of religious way but acknowledging that life has generally been good to me – I was born to loving parents in a forward-thinking era in a relatively rich and democratic country. At an age when many of my contemporaries are dealing with long-term illness and/or disability, I'm running relays alongside 20-somethings and backpacking through Wales. By anyone's standards, I'm not doing badly.

I've always enjoyed having an early summer birthday. Though my plans have often been cruelly thwarted, at least there's the possibility of celebrating outdoors. You can't even breathe the word 'barbecue' if you're born in January. Last year, we spent the day researching and walking a circular route from Caldicot Castle for our *Castle Walks in Monmouthshire* book. After some pretty appalling weather in the spring, it felt like summer had finally arrived, with an abundance of wild flowers everywhere. Yes, June is a good month to be born.

We slept like a pair of logs in The Loft's Spartan but surprisingly cosy stonewalled bedroom.

After cereals and a filling cooked breakfast (full English for Harri, scrambled egg on toast for me) delivered straight to our own private breakfast table by Victoria, it was time to return to the coast. We mentioned to our host that we'd received text messages welcoming us to Ireland that morning and she said it happened a lot (my middle daughter has since explained to us that transmitter signals travel much better across water than land and she knows about these things).

While Harri was occupying the bathroom, I browsed the bookshelf. I have a love/hate relationship with other people's bookshelves. On one hand, who knows what treasures you're going to find; on the other, what could possibly be worse than finding that one book you never realised you needed to read on the last day of your stay?

On the final morning of a stay in Machynlleth a few years back, I was dismayed to stumble upon some amazing 1950s hardback journals about the then Hollywood stars and upcoming starlets. There were interviews with young actors like the fabulous Mitzi Gaynor (who would later play Ensign Nellie Forbush in the 1958 film *South Pacific*). I spotted several familiar faces and would have been perfectly happy to spend an entire day wading through the various editions had we not had a busy day's hiking and long drive home ahead of us.

The Loft's bookshelf didn't disappoint. Almost immediately, I spotted a copy of *We Bought An Island* by Evelyn E Atkins. I borrowed a copy of the book from the Carnegie Library on Corporation Road when I was in my teens; Evelyn E Atkins might never have known it, but it was the author's account of her move to Cornwall that ignited my lifelong love affair with Cornwall – and islands generally.

Evelyn's new home was Looe Island, just off the Cornish coast. I couldn't resist rereading the first chapter when Evelyn talks about her early retirement and subsequent new career as a potter. A retired (through ill health) middle-class professional woman (clearly) with money to spare, Evelyn's *joie de vivre* and willingness to take a chance and act on a mad whim, emphasises everything we seem to have lost in the twenty-first century. I doubt anyone would buy an island nowadays unless there was an economic incentive to do so or a profit to be made. Evelyn appears to have wanted nothing more than to live on her island and make pots. I made a promise to myself that I would reread the book sometime soon, if only to feed my soul.

As soon as we stepped outside, all thoughts of reading left me. What perfect weather for a birthday and how glorious to have nothing to do all day but to walk and soak up the sunshine.

Feeling a little bit livelier this morning, I took more interest in my surroundings than I'd done the previous evening. Church Bay acquired its name from English-speaking sailors who identified places along the coast for their maps using obvious landmarks. The high steeple of Llanrhuddlad Church is easily visible from the sea, so Church Bay it was.

The Welsh seemed to have taken the opposite vantage point when bestowing their name on the village. Standing on land and looking towards the sea, they were inclined to call it after a breed of fish which was caught there, a 'swtan'.

We'd hoped to have a quick look around the Swtan Heritage Museum, but unfortunately it didn't open until 10 a.m., long after we needed to get going. The museum, housed in a gorgeous seventeenth century thatched cottage, gives visitors the chance to see what rural life would have been like in Wales at the turn of the twentieth century.

The scenery was stunning the instant we reached the coast – and very different from yesterday's relatively flat terrain. From the cliff tops of Carmel Head, we found ourselves gazing across the waves to the Skerries. We'd been able to see these sparsely vegetated islets, with their distinctive lighthouse, since we set off from Holyhead yesterday afternoon, but they were lying almost within touching distance now.

Staring across the waves, I was reminded of our lovely seal-spotting boat trips to the eastern and western islands back in the early 1980s when I lived on St Mary's in the Isles of Scilly. It seems unthinkable that those amazing – and sometimes quite choppy – boat trips were more than thirty years ago. When you're young you never imagine that one day you'll be looking back down the years and clinging onto memories gathered by your younger self – or that they'll remain so vivid.

The Skerries are actually just under two miles offshore and cover an area of around 42 acres; like most islands devoid of human habitation, they attract breeding seabirds. More ominously, the waters around the islets are popular with divers, who explore the numerous shipwrecks deep below.

Outside the relative calm of Holyhead Bay, the rugged coastline and turbulent waters of the Irish Sea have been the stuff of nightmares for many a sea captain. Those same jutting rocks which draw thousands of hikers every year make the north Anglesey coast a treacherous place for shipping (as the presence of the Skerries lighthouse, the white beacon on West Mouse (Maen-y-bugail in Welsh, meaning the Shepherd's Stone), and several day markers near Carmel Head testify.

In 1823, the sailing ship *Alert* was travelling from Ireland to Holyhead when she was driven off course during a gale. The wind dropped, but the strong tide between Carmel Head and the Skerries drove her onto rocks where she quickly sank. The lifeboat was launched and seventeen people scrambled on board before that too capsized. Of the passengers and crew on board, only three made it safely to shore.

Shipwrecks were a part of life in these rough waters and many of those rescued went on to live out the rest of their lives in North Wales. One such individual was a boy who, with his brother, was washed up in Anglesey sometime between 1743 and 1745. His brother died soon afterwards, but the boy was adopted by a local doctor and went on to revolutionise the ways bones were set. Evan Thomas, as he became known, introduced new techniques to orthopaedic surgery, including using traction and splints. His remarkable bone-setting talents were passed on to no fewer than eight generations, including Hugh Owen-Thomas, considered to be the father of orthopaedic surgery in Britain and the first of the clan to be formally trained as a doctor, and Sir Robert Evans, the first doctor in the world to use X-ray in the diagnosis of fractures.

It was hard to believe the ocean was capable of wreaking such devastation on days like today when the water appeared benign and enticing; however, tragedies like the sinking of the *Alert* are a sobering reminder of the power of the sea.

While the scenery and weather certainly lifted our spirits, Harri and I were still struggling under the weight of our rucksacks. Though we'd offloaded last night's late supper of chicken and Thai green curry couscous into our bellies, we were still carrying a ridiculous amount of food.

If the England Coast Path had been all about agonising blisters on my toes, it was starting to look as though our long walk through Wales would be about aches and pains in my neck and shoulders. Though taller and stronger, Harri, who was carrying our lightweight Vango tent and (almost) his entire collection of OS maps for Wales, was similarly struggling. You can kid yourself you're reasonably fit but the moment you start using a new set of muscles … oh boy!

I wondered if those blisters had actually served a useful purpose in distracting me from the heavy load on my back. Certainly, when you're having to summon up every ounce of courage to put one painful foot in front of another (so I'm a coward), you do overlook dull aches in other parts of the anatomy.

Anyway, I was determined to avoid a repeat performance of 'blister-gate', so for this expedition I'd abandoned my long-time summer hiking favourites, Salomons, in favour of new Brooks running shoes (with my well-worn Brasher sandals packed should I need 'relief' at any point). Before setting off, I had extracted a promise from Harri that he'd replace them pronto on our return if necessary.

Feet problems are the bane of every hiker's (and runner's) life. Which shoes to wear for different terrains, distances and weather conditions? And what if the terrain is mixed – road, mountain and marshland? Or the forecast is wrong (don't even start me on that one)?

Decisions. Decisions. Given the choice (and a mule), I'd have brought along Karrimor hiking boots (comfortable, solid, keep out water in all but the very wettest conditions but so, so heavy), Salomon trail shoes (usually comfortable, flexible on rocky surfaces but, as I'd discovered, need to be paired with the right socks), and my wonderful amphibious Teva shoes (unbeatable when there's a shallow river to wade across or a pebble beach to stroll along but have a tendency to remove sections of my skin over long distances). And if there was any room left, I'd probably also throw my Brasher sandals in too. But, I had no mule so I probably spent longer deliberating over my footwear than Harri spent planning the route.

I eventually opted for the Brooks simply because they are well-ventilated and have lovely wide feet. I realised they wouldn't keep my feet dry but being lightweight, neither would they remain sodden for days. Anyway, with 'blister gate' still fresh in my memory, I'd opt for wet feet over pain any day.

Not that I needed to worry about wet feet on this glorious June day, just the incredibly tough and undulating terrain of the north Anglesey coast.

Somewhere just past Carmel Head, we paused briefly to chat to a couple heading in the opposite direction. They'd walked to the top of Holyhead Mountain the previous day but said the mist was too thick to appreciate the views.

As well as being a walker and birdwatcher's paradise, the highest point on Anglesey (the summit stands at 720 feet) is scattered with the remains of ancient settlements. On a clear day, it's apparently possible to stand high above Holyhead itself and gaze across the Irish Sea at the Wicklow Mountains or even to watch the numerous ferries departing and arriving at the port below.

We were surprised to learn that Holyhead's breakwater is the longest in the UK. Unsurprisingly, the 1.7 mile breakwater took an awful long time to build; construction began in 1845; however, it wasn't until 28 years later that Prince Albert (then Prince of Wales) declared it officially open.

The construction of breakwaters, promenades, bridges, piers and such, is something that's always fascinated and, yes, hugely impressed me. When you consider the unimaginable power of the ocean, the tides, currents and gale-force winds that have to be factored into both the design and the actual building of these enormous structures, you have to be inspired by mankind's indomitable determination – or perhaps his arrogance – to control the elements.

Looking back, it appears the Victorians were unstoppable when it came to embarking on wildly ambitious construction projects. This was an era when the railway network was increasing dramatically and the opening of the Chester and Holyhead Railway in 1848 had dramatically increased the number of sailings between the port and Ireland.

Holyhead breakwater enclosed the existing harbour and an additional 400 acres of deep water to create a safe area for ships to wait at anchor. The tragic pay-off for the safety of sea passengers was the death of more than forty of the 1,300 men who were employed on its construction.

In 2014, a Wales transport think tank mooted a proposal to link Holyhead and Dublin via a 74.8-mile rail tunnel. Such a massive underwater project would dwarf the 31.4-mile Eurotunnel and put Holyhead in the rare position of being closer to two other country's capitals – in terms of travelling time – than its own in Cardiff. It's not like it's going to happen anytime soon … the timescale mentioned was the end of this century.

As with any long-distance route, we inevitably had to make choices when determining the places 'O Fôn i Fynwy' would pass through. We'll save Holyhead Mountain and the breakwater for another trip … perhaps when walking the Anglesey Coast Path or, better still, the entire 870 miles of the Wales Coast Path!

Farther along the north coast, just short of Wylfa nuclear power station (more on that later), we came upon Cemlyn Bay, where several families were enjoying the sunshine.

The beach here is crescent-shaped, steeply sloping and pebbly; lying behind it is a lagoon fed by several small streams and regulated by a weir at the western end. This lagoon provides a breeding ground for around 1,500 pairs of sandwich terns (the third largest colony in the UK). The on-site warden encouraged us to take a look through her telescope, and it was fascinating to watch so many birds landing and taking off in a relatively small area (like an airport in miniature).

Terns aside, the lagoon also attracts wintering wildfowl and a number of vagrant birds. I don't know a whole lot about birdwatching but one thing's for sure, Cemlyn Bay appears to be a popular (and very noisy) place with our feathered friends.

The lagoon and surrounding land – the Cemlyn estate – is leased from the National Trust by the North Wales Wildlife Trust, which itself has an interesting history having been set up by wealthy pioneering aviator Captain Vivian Hewitt. In April 1912 – and just days after another pilot (Damer Leslie Allen) had disappeared attempting the same feat – Hewitt successfully flew 75 miles from a field near Rhyl to Dublin. Although his success came four days after another successful Wales–Ireland flight (Goodwick, Pembrokeshire, to Enniscorthy), Hewitt's flight was generally deemed to be the more difficult and dangerous.

While the lagoon was pretty, it was the house itself which intrigued me most. As far as we could establish, Bryn Aber currently stands empty, its last owner having died in 2009 and probate allegedly taking an eternity. It's a strange place, more like a fortress than a home, with massive walls around it. The wall was apparently constructed with a walkway in between the layers of brick so visitors could view nearby birds without disturbing them.

From where we stood, the weir created the impression that a moat surrounded at least part of the house. I really do hope that the probate issues are resolved soon and that the house can once again become a home to someone who appreciates the wildlife on its doorstep as much as Vivian Hewitt did.

The site was designated a Site of Special Scientific Interest in 1958, and is part of the Anglesey Heritage Coast and the Isle of Anglesey Area of Outstanding Natural Beauty.

After the beauty of Cemlyn Bay and its lagoon, we headed towards Wylfa nuclear power station with heavy hearts. We're sufficiently realistic (yes, even me) to know that not every step of a long-distance route is going to be picturesque and beautiful, but our Hinckley Point experience was still fresh in our minds and the last thing we wanted to do was get lost on another inland detour around a nuclear power station.

So what did we do? Get lost on another inland detour around a nuclear power station. To be fair, the original signage was probably quite clear, but a new station is proposed for the peninsula (imaginatively called Wylfa Newydd) and, while formal public consultation was not starting until the latter part of 2014, ground investigation studies have been taking place since 2011.

The first hint that we'd gone wrong was when we emerged from a diverted footpath onto a minor road heading in the wrong general direction. Now if it had been me map-reading, in all likelihood we'd have been wandering around Anglesey for the rest of the summer; however, Harri's a stickler for his contours and directions and he wasn't happy, not one little bit. When the wiggles on the OS map don't correspond with the land around you, topographically speaking, there's nothing for it but to turn around and retrace your steps. So that's what we did.

It wouldn't have been so bad but I'd just squeezed myself and my rucksack through the tiniest metal kissing gate ever erected. From the outset, it was clear Anglesey has some of the smallest kissing gates on the planet, but this one really did take the biscuit. It's not like I'm some enormous person – I wear a size 12 very comfortably – yet I was having trouble squeezing my combined rucksack and womanly curves through every kissing gate we encountered.

We changed direction and quickly spotted where we'd gone wrong; Harri had led us along a footpath going the wrong way. Confident now that we'd soon be supping my promised birthday drink at Cemaes, we strode off and somehow managed to miss a second diversion sign. Now we were following Wylfa's Nature Reserve trail which took us into woodland – where all signage abruptly stopped.

We were hot and sticky (we chose our days for walking around in circles carefully) and all we wanted to go was to reach the other side of Wylfa. Eventually Harri managed to get us back on track and we arrived in the lovely little seaside resort of Cemaes just after 5 pm for our first proper rest (and drink) of the day.

As we sat outside The Stag enjoying a bottle of cider, Harri casually mentioned that so far today I'd walked through three fields with a bull in each. I'd been aware of one of these (and had bowed my head and stepped up my pace accordingly); however, now I was being informed that I'd strolled through another two fields blissfully ignorant of any male bovine presence.

We don't have a dog so I tend not to be too concerned about walking through fields of cows (we always stay well away from calves and take care not to walk between mother and calf). I am far more nervous around bullocks, however, and admit to becoming a gibberish wreck when I spy a bull. On occasion, I've sized a bull up, decided it looked 'frisky' and refused to put one foot into the field, necessitating a fairly long detour. When a bull is giving you the evil eye, it's always best to err on the side of caution. On one occasion, a weathered farmer in mid Wales actually suggested we seek an alternative route to the one on our map … which his bull was guarding. Detours like this become much more difficult when you're walking the coast, which was why Harri had kept quiet.

Out of curiosity, I checked the advice *Farmers Weekly* offers its members. The general rule (in law) is that it *is* an offence to allow a bull in a field crossed by a public right of way.

There are exceptions, however. Bulls under 10 months old *are* allowed, as are bulls which do not belong to a recognised dairy breed (Ayrshire, British Friesian, British Holstein, Dairy Shorthorn, Guernsey, Jersey and Kerry). All other bulls older than 10 months are *banned*, unless accompanied by cows or heifers.

Farmers Weekly advises farmers to put up a sign informing people, e.g. bull in field, but warns that signage will not suffice if the bull is known to be aggressive or unpredictable (when it should not be in field crossed by a right of way).

Harri is not as perturbed by the presence of a bull as I am because he grew up on a small dairy farm. He loves reminding me of the time he noticed a young bull was pawing the ground with its forefoot and he thought it wise to quietly mention the fact. Instead of proceeding calmly (as he'd hoped), I did exactly what you shouldn't do: I panicked and ran. Without so much as a backwards glance, I galloped across the field and charged straight into a metal gate (somewhere at the back of my mind I must have imagined myself vaulting over it, until I got there and discovered it was just that little bit too high). I was bruised for days. And the bull? After a few seconds' interest, it put its head down and calmly continued grazing.

And now we were heading to Bull Bay for the night. Fortunately, Wales's most northerly village is not named because it's a popular gathering place for bulls; its English name is derived from the Welsh Pwll y Tarw ('the bull's pool').

After Cemaes, the going got tougher still, with frequent rocky climbs followed immediately by a descent. On stretches like this, I'm certain coast path walking is more demanding than, say, walking up Cadair Idris or Pen y Fan. With a mountain, you're faced with a steady climb and know that each hard pull is taking you closer to your destination. Undulating coastal landscapes have you clambering up a rocky path one minute, walking along a grassy headline the next and plunging down to sea level again round the next bend. The cider that had been so cool and enjoyable when it went down, was now making me tired and lethargic. Once again, Harri had booked ahead so we had no choice but to keep going.

Fortunately, there was plenty of visual interest along this strenuous stretch, quite apart from undeniable spectacular coastal beauty.

One of the highlights of the early evening was Llanbadrig Church. Most likely the oldest Christian site in Wales (it dates back to at least AD440), the church perches on the headland of the same name, on rocky cliffs high above the waves.

Like many other Welsh landscapes, Llanbadrig headland appeared as someplace other than itself on film; it was briefly transformed into a Scottish peace camp in the 2006 movie *Half Light* starring Demi Moore.

The coast path runs right past the entrance to the churchyard and then alongside the cemetery wall. It really is one of the prettiest spots for a church and I wish we'd had time to explore it, but if we were to reach Bull Bay before darkness we needed to press on.

Not long after, we reached Wales's most northerly point – the headland of Porth Llanlleiana – where little remains of the old porcelain works except the ruins of a once three-storey building, a surrounding wall built to provide protection from the sea, and, a little way off, the chimney which directed fumes away from the areas where people worked. The works closed in 1920 after a fire.

As was often the case with secluded and stunning locations, the creek attracted interest from a religious community, and around the seventh century a nunnery was established there (Llanlleiana means 'church of the nuns').

This morning Victoria had mentioned that one of her favourite spots along the coast was the old brickworks near Bull Bay. We were exhausted by now, but perhaps we'd have mustered up the energy to clamber down to the towering red brick chimneys had a circle of brightly-coloured tents not been set up on the flat grassy area in front of them. Wafts of smoke floated up from a campfire, and we could hear people calling out to one another. We'd have felt like intruders stomping down there into this little impromptu community; besides, we barely had sufficient energy left to reach Bull Bay without introducing a detour (however intriguing) at this late hour.

Setting the tone for many days to come, we eventually arrived at our overnight accommodation – Trecastell Hotel – weary and ready for bed. The smells wafting from the dining room might have tempted us downstairs for a birthday meal had we not been exhausted. Instead, we made ourselves at home in our sumptuous room, with its red and white furnishings, and I prepared a cold meal of sorts from the squashed offerings in my rucksack. We shared a pot of tea and then turned our attention to laundry.

Harri, who is much better at colour co-ordinating his outfits than me, kept things simple with two bamboo tee-shirts (one black, one blue) and two pairs of shorts (one black, one blue). He added a third tee-shirt for sleeping and emergencies and one ribbed long-sleeved top plus a minimal amount of underwear.

I, on the other hand, had packed an assortment of aertex tops (one far too large) garnered from various running events, a silk patterned vest, one pair of shorts (too loose, too long) and a pair of full-length trousers. Just in case the weather turned nippy, I'd also packed my lovely new zip-up hoodie fleece (a birthday gift from Harri's parents), a long-sleeved aertex top and my own ribbed long-sleeved top. Oh, and a floaty evening top (just in case!) and a satin nightdress for the sleeping bag. I won't spell out my underwear requirements here but clearly there were certain items that I needed and the flat-chested Harri didn't.

It wasn't absolutely crucial for us to launch ourselves into a laundry session, but with all the essentials on hand – hot water and one of those wooden rack contraptions that many hotels still provide – it would have been foolhardy not to get washday rolling.

Around ten o'clock, with our room suitably strewn with damp clothing, we settled down in a large comfortable bed with its crisp, white bedding and fell into a deep, deep sleep.

For photographs visit uk.pinterest.com/thewalkerswife

JUNE 4: BULL BAY TO MOELFRE

After all the anticipation and excitement of a birthday, the next day often feels something of an anti-climax. You wake with the realisation that you're a whole year older and, if you don't get a move on, you're in danger of never doing all those things you planned to do.

Today's schedule didn't sound too bad on paper; we were aiming to reach Moelfre on the island's eastern coast. Just 14 miles to cover and a whole day to do it; nothing more than a stroll in the park for a pair of seasoned hikers like us.

The only blight on the landscape was that after two nights of gorgeous accommodation we were going to be camping for the first time tonight. And there'd be none of your Caravan Club or Camping and Caravanning Club luxuries either; we'd be staying at a farm campsite, where the facilities were likely to be pretty basic. Happy days! Still the sun was still shining and we were out in the fresh air doing what we loved best.

Despite the Trecastell Hotel's remarkably comfortable bed, Harri had been woken in the night by a bad dream. He had the strong sensation that something was pressing down on his chest but wasn't prepared for the sight that greeted him when he did open his eyes. Just inches away from his face a plump tabby cat was purring contentedly. We later learned our trespasser was Holly, one of the hotel's four resident cats, who had sneaked into our room through the open window and decided to share our bed. Holly stayed in our room companionably while we showered and dressed, leaving the same way she'd entered only when I turned the hairdryer on.

When we mentioned the incident to the hotelier, he was mortified and very apologetic despite our insistence that as cat lovers we didn't mind at all and had really enjoyed Holly's purring presence. We just hope we didn't get poor Holly into trouble!

Over breakfast, we chatted to two fellow guests at a neighbouring table. Long-time friends and passionate hikers, they shared their plans for the day and seemed amazed at the distance we'd covered in less than two days. Like many hikers, they viewed 8-10 miles as a reasonable day's walking and viewed our 31 miles since Monday afternoon as pretty tough going, even without the heavy rucksacks.

Listening to their comments brought my own doubts flooding back. Perhaps I was deluded in thinking myself fit enough to tackle nearly four hundred miles of frequently very tough terrain. My shoulders were already complaining and our first two nights had seen us luxuriating in sumptuous holiday accommodation, enjoying hot showers and cooked breakfasts. In contrast, tonight we'd be sharing washing facilities with strangers and snuggling down in separate sleeping bags. Knowing me, I'd toss and turn all night, unable to get comfortable on my lightweight but very basic foam mat. By morning, I'd be a complete wreck. Who was I kidding? I was never going to make it to Chepstow. I looked across the breakfast table at Harri, knowing I was about to let him down but saying nothing.

Despite Anglesey's popularity as a holiday destination, this part of the island seemed oddly devoid of campsites. The farm on the other side of Moelfre was the only campsite in the vicinity; if we pushed ahead after that, it would be wild camping for us.

I pushed the thought to the back of my mind. Wild camping would be a necessity at some point over the next few weeks (if only to keep our costs down), but I intended to delay the inevitable for as long as possible. We had a relatively short day to look forward to with plenty of interest en route. Anglesey had been something of a revelation to me, and I was keen to explore more of its dramatic and varied coastline.

This section of coastline doesn't have endless sandy beaches; it is, however, full of fascinating rocky inlets with the sort of natural pools that every kid on the planet loves poking around in, looking for crabs and anything else that moves. We passed steep stone steps leading down to a tiny sandy cove, which would vanish altogether at high tide.

We'd barely got into our stride when we arrived at Amlwch Port just after 10 a.m. These days, the main town is set back from the actual coast, but it's the historic port and harbour area where it was all happening in the eighteenth century.

Amlwch's heyday came as a result of its proximity to Parys Mountain, at that time the world's biggest copper mine. The harbour

31

was extended and a shipbuilding industry developed. It's hard to imagine now, but back then Amlwch had a population of around 10,000 (more than three times its current population) and was the second largest town in Wales.

The decline of copper mining in the mid-1850s saw Amlwch turns its attention to shipbuilding, brewing and tobacco. With several breweries in the town (drawing their water from St Eleth's well), there were ale houses everywhere in Amlwch. The Beerhouse Act of 1830 saw some of these small establishments close, but by the end of the nineteenth century, over 70 licensed premises existed. What a great place for a pub crawl it must have been.

It was too early to go hunting for a pub, so instead we meandered along the restored port area, jiggling our rucksacks around to find the most comfortable position but failing miserably. We'd covered barely two miles and already our shoulder muscles were aching badly – not a great omen for the much tougher walking (in terms of terrain and distance) yet to come. Vowing to learn from our Somerset Levels experience – when we had (out of necessity) covered around 28–30 miles on two consecutive days – we weren't covering such enormous distances – yet. We had plenty of time to get to Moelfre so we decided to make use of an empty bench overlooking the waterless harbour.

Harri pointed out to sea where a heavily loaded cargo ship was passing. I was reminded of a Radio Four programme I'd listened to a few months ago when shipping experts were talking about the ever-increasing size of these vast container ships, which transport everything from white goods and furniture to food and clothing across vast oceans to satisfy our seemingly insatiable consumerism.

In 2013, six shipping containers were built in Denmark, each measuring 1,306 feet – right now, they are the longest ships in the world but probably not for long.

The trouble with taking rucksacks off, even briefly, is that they have an uncanny knack of gaining weight in the few minutes you're resting. If the Anglesey Coast Path was proving tough going, how on earth would I cope with Snowdonia?

We passed Copper Kingdom where the staff were putting out billboards; the man seemed keen to engage us in conversation – and despite having walked no more than a few hundred metres, I was equally keen for an excuse to stop walking. It transpired he was an ex-military man who'd done many a long-distance hike in his day. His advice for preventing blisters? Talc and tights. So now we know. Next time I see a group of tough-looking soldiers undertaking training exercises in the Brecon Beacons, I'll know that underneath their macho khaki kit, they'll be wearing women's underwear and smelling of babies' bottoms.

Upon our arrival on Anglesey, we'd amused ourselves with 'Spot the house where Will and Kate lived' (I should say here and now – or he'll kill me – that Harri was far less enthusiastic about this game than me). We had little to go on except the fact that Prince William had been based at RAF Valley, but we sort of reasoned that he'd prefer a commute to somewhere a little bit scenic than Holyhead itself.

The game proved much more difficult than we'd anticipated (who'd have realised that Anglesey was quite so wealthy? Or dotted with so many properties that wouldn't look out of place in London?). We passed many contenders: detached properties in large gardens with plenty of outbuildings (to house the security people, we reasoned). Not that we could see much of the actual properties; they were typically hidden behind towering walls and/or mature woodlands.

We passed my own 'favourite' yesterday: a stately hilltop property with wonderful sweeping lawns, yet clearly displaying too casual an approach to privacy to be a serious contender. (We later learned the Royal couple's first home was actually inland at Bodorgan and was a far more modest abode than the properties we'd been speculating about.)

Talking of posh, sprawling properties, as we approached Point Lynas we spotted a For Sale sign. It seemed the lighthouse itself was on the market (we later learned the price tag was a cool £1.37 million). I could definitely imagine myself living in a lighthouse and, being located on the mainland and close to civilisation, this one was better suited to being a permanent home than many.

The lighthouse is still in operation, but if it's the thought of the electricity bills that's worrying you, it's leased back to Trinity House who generously pay for the 1,000-watt lamp to shine for nine seconds out of every ten, 24 hours a day.

Actually, the price tag isn't all that bad when you consider it includes three keepers' cottages, the freehold of the lighthouse, and 17 acres of grazing land. As I write, it's still on the market so, if you're interested, check out the details on Lighthouses for Sale.

Dreaming about living in a lighthouse kept us occupied for the next few miles until, at Traeth Dulas, we found ourselves with a wide tidal lagoon to cross starting with an inland detour around the Llys Dulas Estate (the owners of the estate haven't granted access rights to walkers).

If you have seen Douglas Ray's chilling short film 'Get off my land', which shows what happens when a landowner catches a young couple straying from the footpath, you will understand why I wasn't prepared to risk any shortcuts. In the event, the detour was long and involved a steep climb through several fields (and a tantalising glimpse of the ever-so-private property in a copse surrounded by mature trees). We headed past a church and Great Gatehouse before joining – and then abandoning – a very wet footpath alongside the lagoon's edge.

Though the route was pleasant enough in terms of scenery, it just feels inherently wrong that landowners are able to flout the spirit of the Wales Coast Path and force harmless walkers (because let's face it, most of us are too busy fretting about maps, food and where the next pub stop might be to cause any problems) so far from the shore.

Rather than get our feet soaked traipsing along above sea level, we chose to walk on the relatively solid surface of the sea bed (we were a little perplexed about how the official higher-level route works at high tide).

I'd been promised lunch on the beach, but at low tide, sitting on the silt that was Dulas Beach would have resulted in a very wet and muddy bottom; I wasn't even tempted! We pushed ahead, Harri promising that we'd stop at the very first opportunity, me wondering if we were likely to eat before bedtime given the increasingly unfriendly picnicking terrain.

The lagoon marked a distinct change in the coastal landscape. Now the rugged high cliffs were replaced by low-lying lands, with the sweeping, white sand beaches that Anglesey is best known for. Lying towards the mouth of the estuary were several old boat wrecks; however, investigating them close-up would have involved us heading towards the mouth of the estuary (in other words, backtracking) so we decided against it.

Instead, we headed inland – the only route unless you're willing to risk life and limb and attempt crossing the estuary. We passed a car park which looked like it might disappear at high tide, but there were no wooden benches here. In desperation, we perched on a damp log; not the comfiest of places to eat lunch but better than mud.

With the Red River alongside us and our onwards route there on the opposite bank, I started suspecting we'd be wading across at some point soon. Not on your nelly. The Wales Coast Path has been a catalyst for investment in footpaths and, like an oasis in the desert, a spanking new wooden footbridge appeared.

Back on the 'right' side of the estuary, there was another steep climb and then at last we were back on the coast, meandering above two of the sweeping, white-sand beaches – Traeth yr Ora and Traeth Lligwy – which are the reason for so many flocking to Anglesey's east coast. Not that we were tempted onto the beach; since we'd been inland, the wind had picked up and the sky was looking decidedly overcast and stormy.

The 'perfect storm' of the turbulent Irish Sea and the treacherous rocky shoreline has resulted in these waters seeing more than their fair share of nautical tragedies, the most famous being the mid-nineteenth century wrecking of the Royal Charter off rocks at Porth Helaeth.

The steam clipper – one of the fastest of her day – was on the final leg of her voyage from Australia to Britain in October 1859 when she found herself at the mercy of one of the biggest storms to hit the Irish Sea that century (it was subsequently named the Royal Charter Storm). The Royal Charter had among her passengers a large contingent of gold miners who were bringing their booty home; gold worth over £320,000 (tens of millions today) was stashed in the hold alone.

Rendered powerless by the hurricane-strength winds, the ship was eventually grounded on a sandbank just 25 yards from the shore. When daylight came, a rescue operation was immediately launched by local people. All might have ended well had the incoming tide not lifted the Royal Charter off its sandbank and tossed it onto rocks, breaking it in two.

The passenger list was lost in the tragedy, but it's believed that around 450 lives were lost that night, the highest number of deaths for any shipwreck on the Welsh coast. Around 40 passengers and crew survived, none of them women or children.

The hero of the day was a Maltese sailor called Giuseppi Ruggier (subsequently known by the anglicised name of Joe Rogers). When the ship was in distress, Mr Ruggier showed great courage in volunteering to swim to the vessel with a rope; his efforts undoubtedly saved many lives, but he was ultimately powerless against the elements.

Another local 'hero' was the Reverend Stephen Hughes, who dedicated many, many weeks to identifying the bodies, contacting and consoling bereaved relatives and burying the dead (including those who remained unidentified). Charles Dickens was intrigued and arrived on Anglesey two months later. Dickens writes of what he found and the Reverend's great compassion in *The Uncommercial Traveller*.

A memorial stone stands above the cliff tops where the Royal Charter was lost. In 2009, the 150th anniversary of the disaster, a sculpture was commissioned from sculptor Sam Holland. 'Hither and Thither' comprises two reliefs facing one another: one depicts the ship being engulfed by huge waves, the other, Giuseppi Ruggier climbing up a cliff face with a rope.

Situated just a few yards away is another of Ms Holland's sculptures: a bronze memorial to the lifeboat hero Dic Evans (1905–2001), which was unveiled by Prince Charles in 2004. The huge likeness of the man, who was twice awarded the RNLI's gold medal for bravery, towers over the waves he spent a lifetime battling. It was erected as a tribute to the bravery, sense of duty and purpose of all lifeboat crews.

Still on the subject of memorials, there is another rather unusual one alongside the road in Moelfre. Simply headed 'Rhyfel' (Welsh for war), a plain commemorative stone in the town reads: 'Our street lighting was installed as a memorial to the men of this district who made the supreme sacrifice in the 1939–1945 war.' While no one could argue with the sentiment, I can't say I've ever come across commemorative street lighting before.

We arrived at Moelfre too early to head straight for the campsite. By now, the weather was decidedly grey and miserable (and cold) so we popped into the Pilot Boat Inn for a drink or two (in the event, we opted for two … and chips from a nearby cafe).

One of the hardest things about long-distance hiking is getting the daily distances just right. Ideally, you arrive at your destination early evening, allowing plenty of time to eat and settle down for the night. We chose June for this trip because of the long daylight hours, but there are drawbacks, like trying to get to sleep while it's still light.

Having delayed heading to the campsite as long as possible, we were eventually faced with a choice: get wet or set up camp for the night. And much as I hate tents, I couldn't see much point in wandering around Moelfre in the rain, even if there were still hours until nightfall.

Just to set things straight, I feel I should emphasise here how much I hate camping. I don't just dislike spending a night under canvas, I absolutely loathe it. Memories of my first (and only) camping trip with the Girl Guides are the stuff of nightmares: ten prepubescent girls sharing a bell tent, revolting food, and a midnight walk to Weston. I parted company with the Guides soon after, lest my mother pack me off again.

Of course, there are times when it's nice to sit outside on a summer's evening enjoying a drink, but you don't need to put up a tent to do that... just locate a nice beer garden.

It definitely wasn't beer garden weather tonight – or camping weather. The overhead sky was growing darker and darker and the wind was gusting across the open cliff top.

We knocked tentatively on the farmhouse door. The lady who answered was friendly enough and explained that they'd been too busy with lambing to mow the grass on the camping field, hence it being two-foot high. The cost was £14 per tent per night, which sounded quite steep until I glanced down at the bookings ledger and saw that four people in a caravan (or campervan) had been charged £60 per night that week. Their fee covered electricity, of course, which we wouldn't be requiring, but as our tiny Vango 300 requires so little space and there were only two of us (and no facilities on the overgrown field other than a shower and toilet block), £14 did seem a tad expensive.

Not that we had a choice, of course; it was disappear into the swaying, wet grass or continue wandering along the cliffs in the hope of finding a wild camping spot.

Other would-be campers must have felt the same because it was the quietest campsite we visited on our entire walk – just two tents (including ours), two caravans, and two of those massive recreational vehicles.

The fish and chips (one portion between us) hadn't been cheap either, and we'd been charged an additional 30% on the advertised price to sit inside out of the rain (a practice I find quite peculiar). We were beginning to realise how long-distance walking costs can add up when you're passing through popular tourist areas! Still, even Anglesey isn't as expensive as Cornwall in August. Harri's still recovering from the shocking price of lunch in St Ives!

The tent up, we had several hours of daylight left but no inclination to venture outside again. As a result, we spent an unhappy evening cramped inside, shoulders hunched, listening to the rain hitting the canvas (and praying tomorrow would see the return of the sun).

Even worse than the sound of heavy rain were the mournful calls from the calves in the barn behind. It's an apparently common, though in my view cruel, farming practice to separate new-born calves from their mothers. Hearing their young close by, but unable to reach them, the frustrated cows waited on the other side of a gate; the continual bellowing was heart-rending.

Harri assured me the desolate noises wouldn't go on all night. He was wrong, and the combination of wind, rain, discomfort, and grief-stricken bovines made for an awful night's sleep.

On such nights, it's difficult not to get camper van envy. Imagine … sitting within four solid 'walls', probably with a cuppa in front of you, reading or playing cards, then yawning and saying 'I'm off to bed' before shuffling over to a *proper* bed, or at least some sort of person-sized shelf. I'm not greedy, my camper van wouldn't have to be very big; in fact, given the narrowness of some of Wales's country lanes, the smaller the better. But it would feel like home, albeit a small home, whereas a small, cold tent just feels like … well, a small, cold tent!

For photographs visit uk.pinterest.com/thewalkerswife

JUNE 5: MOELFRE TO PENMON

All things being well, today would be our penultimate day on Anglesey. While I was sorry to be leaving the coast, I understood what Harri meant when he said he wouldn't feel we were on our way proper until we'd crossed the Menai Strait and were back on the Welsh mainland.

The prospect of leaving Anglesey and its gorgeous coastal scenery so soon made me a little despondent. Having spent a lifetime without exploring this most northerly part of Wales, this was my second visit in three months. And I really liked it here.

My first time on the island was back in March. Harri was commissioned to update several walks in the AA's popular guidebook *50 Walks in Snowdonia & North Wales* (and contribute some new routes); the Anglesey walk a new nine-mile route that he wanted to add.

We parked at Llyn Rhos-ddu car park, near Newborough on the south-west coast. It was one of those cloudy days when the weather hasn't quite decided whether to embrace spring or retreat to winter. Still, despite the lack of sunshine, there was no rain forecast. I was excited because the day's destination, Ynys Llanddwyn, is allegedly the most romantic place in Wales.

We followed the edge of the forest for a mile or so until we reached the 'dogs are allowed' end of Traeth Penrhos. It's a wonderful stretch of coast, with simply stunning views back across the Llŷn; from this angle the peninsula's 'spine' is clearly visible.

Ynys Llanddwyn has long been associated with romance, a result of it being home to Saint Dwynwen, who lived here in the fifth century. Dwynwen rejected love for herself, choosing to live the life of a hermit on Llanddwyn; however, she prayed for all true lovers to find happiness. Saint Dwynwen's Day on 25 January is celebrated in Wales in much the same way as Valentine's Day.

I was instantly enchanted with Ynys Llanddwyn, the island that's not really an island (it only becomes inaccessible at very high tides). As well as the ruined sixteenth-century church dedicated to Saint

Dwynwen, there is a gorgeous white-washed lighthouse (built in 1845) and, perched on a tiny island just yards from the coast, the original beacon (Twr Bach), which was constructed in 1819, taken out of service when the new lighthouse was built, and eventually returned to service with an automated modern light.

Nearby, the wonderfully quaint row of stone cottages provided homes to the men (and their families) who manned the old lighthouse and guided ships safely through the treacherous waters of the Menai Strait. The cottages have been renovated and two are open to the public (though unfortunately not on the day we visited). Peering through the window of these tiny abodes, it's hard to imagine whole families lived and slept in them. Standing just a few yards from them is the small cannon which was used during the nineteenth century to summon the lifeboat and its voluntary crew (made up of the nearby pilots).

Ynys Llanddwyn definitely worked its magic me that day, and I fell in love with Anglesey right there and then. It was certainly no hardship to be returning less than three months later.

Interestingly, the island's powers that be were way ahead of the rest of Wales when it came to the concept of creating a long-distance coastal path. The Isle of Anglesey Coastal Path was officially opened on 9 June 2006, and it was at the official launch event that Rhodri Morgan, then Wales's First Minister, announced plans to create a path around the entire coast of Wales by 2012.

The Welsh Government delivered on that pledge and now we have the Wales Coast Path – 870 miles of splendid coastal walking, much of which might have remained inaccessible to hikers had it not been for the vision and determination of that small team of visionaries in Anglesey.

On our end to end walk across Wales, we could, of course, have chosen to follow Anglesey's western coast. This would certainly have been quicker (62 miles rather than the 70 we walked). However, after examining his OS maps for hours, Harri decided that the eastern coast looked to be the more interesting route. He was probably right – the scenery has been stunning throughout – and yet, to my mind, we've passed nowhere quite as magical (or romantic) as Ynys Llanddwyn.

We'd awoken at around 6.15 a.m. to a much brighter day, which immediately lifted our spirits. The poor heartbroken cows and their calves were still creating a cacophony nearby, causing us to reflect on the cruel farming practices required to fill our supermarket shelves, in this case with cheap milk. There are blogs on the internet which argue that it is in a calf's best interests to be separated from its mother at birth, but having spent a night listening to the obvious distress of both, I refuse to believe this inhumane practice benefits anyone other than the cost-conscious consumer.

Keen to leave this disagreeable place, we wolfed down a quick breakfast of banana chips and uncooked porridge oats (those individual packs of porridge oats with golden syrup make a really tasty, if rather tiddly-sized breakfast), packed our camping gear and quickly rejoined the coast path.

The morning's destination was Benllech, a small town (though its population of almost 3,500 makes it the fifth largest on Anglesey) with a supermarket!

The tide was out, so it would have been possible for us to walk along the beach at Traeth Bychan; however, Harri needed to establish accurate instructions for the high tide alternative so off we trekked through more fields until finally we reached Benllech.

Once again, we (and one of us in particular) were having trouble with the narrowness of Anglesey's kissing gates. Each time we squeezed through one, we had to stop and check everything attached to our rucksacks was still there. I wondered how many people had been forced to abandon their coastal walk simply because they couldn't wriggle through Anglesey's kissing gates, or whether rescue operations were regularly mounted to free walkers from the vice-like clutches of these (un)hinged parts. Getting wedged in a kissing gate certainly wasn't a risk we'd identified during the planning stages of our expedition. I was greatly impressed with Anglesey's natural beauty and I'd like to think everyone could enjoy it, not just the stick-thin.

We were barely two hours into day four and Harri was already becoming a little concerned that he wasn't getting sufficient time to type up notes. He uses a digital voice recorder to dictate directions, but it's an older model and doesn't possess a huge amount of memory (a bit like me). Our original plan was that he would transcribe his recorded instructions onto our iPad each evening, but two late finishes and a cramped night in a tent meant he was already falling behind.

It was a beautiful morning, sunny and quite warm, so we came up with what we thought was a great idea. Harri would settle himself down on a bench on Benllech's seafront with our luggage, while I set off for the supermarket unencumbered by my rucksack.

Our plan sort of worked, except it transpired that the town's three small supermarkets were nowhere near the seafront and we weren't sure of the best route inland (while OS 1:25 000 maps are fantastic guides to walking, they're less useful for locating shops). Spying some steep steps, I headed up them, only to arrive on a street of very expensive-looking houses. The only way was up, so up I went … until I reached the top of the hill and had to head downhill again. I eventually found a small Co-op, but was somewhat disappointed with its offerings. A Tesco Express was located a little farther along, so I popped in there; again, there was little to get excited about, and the prices seemed much higher than I'm used to paying down south.

Clutching two carrier bags filled with crusty bread, Pringles, pâté and a few other delicacies, I thought it time I headed back to Harri. I spotted a sign for the beach pointing in the opposite direction from where I'd come. Not wishing to retrace my steps unnecessarily, I decided to give it a try. I rounded the first bend and, miraculously, the sea was there right in front of me. Without a map (or any sense of direction) I'd managed to circumnavigate most of Benllech's residential areas when I could have just nipped around the corner!

From the little I did see of Benllech's wide, crescent-shaped beach and promenade, it looked like a lovely place to while away a sunny day. The beach is very clean and has consistently won European Blue Flag awards, making it perfect for families and sun-lovers, or even walkers like us who enjoy wandering along the water's edge.

Unfortunately, we needed to cover 15–16 miles today so sticking around wasn't an option; besides, by the time I'd returned from my lengthy wander around Benllech, the weather had again turned sour and poor Harri was getting rather cold on his sea-facing bench.

A little farther along the coast and the views towards north Wales were beginning to open out. Across the waves we could see one of my favourite places, Great Orme.

For anyone who hasn't had the pleasure of visiting the Llandudno area, Great Orme is the limestone headland which towers above the wonderful Victorian seaside resort. Its English name is derived from the Viking word for sea serpent, Great Orme being the creature's head, the low-lying isthmus upon which Llandudno lies its body, and (presumably) the smaller headland of Little Orme (on the eastern side of Llandudno Bay) its tail. Great Orme has long been used for sending and receiving messages; during World War Two the hotel became an RAF radar station and was used for signalling purposes.

I first visited Great Orme back in the late 1980s and instantly fell in love with this rugged mountain rising straight from the sea. At 679 feet, it is tiny by north Walian standards; however, its diminutive size has the advantage of making it very accessible. Someone of average fitness should have no problem reaching the summit by foot, and even if you couldn't manage the walk, there's a cable car (the longest of its type in the UK) and the 112-year-old cable-hauled Great Orme Tramway to get you there (I'm pretty certain my first ascent to the top was via cable car). Otherwise, you can drive or catch a bus.

I visited Great Orme again in April 2012. At that time, Harri was still trying to complete the Cambrian Way, despite his growing misgivings about the route. I'd joined him for most of the journey; however, as we made our way farther north, there were occasions when the lack of public transport made it impossible for us to continue walking the linear route together. I was necessarily demoted to chauffeur, dropping Harri off in one remote location and picking him up at a pre-arranged place at the end of the day (it's safer never to rely on mobile phones in mountainous regions of Wales).

This arrangement worked well because it allowed me time to explore some of the most beautiful areas of mid and north Wales which weren't on the route, places like Ynys-las, Borth, Llandudno and Great Orme. Occasionally, when I'd be regaling Harri with stories of my day, I'd detect a look of envy on his face; while I'd had plenty of company and entertainment, he'd have spent hours trekking across the tough terrain of the high peaks, alone and exhausted.

Llandudno and Great Orme were definitely among the highlights of that April trip. Having dropped Harri off in the middle of nowhere (I suspect there was a grid reference/pass name on the map but I'm afraid it's long forgotten), I headed straight to my favourite Welsh Victorian seaside resort. As is usually my way, I had no definite plans other than to walk, find a fudge shop and amuse myself for seven to eight hours. Unlike Lewis Carroll, who began writing *Alice in Wonderland* in the town, I had no intention of writing a novel.

I parked on Llandudno's sheltered western beach and headed straight to the Great Orme, clambering up a steep zigzagging footpath to emerge on the summit near the cable car station. There's a visitor centre up there (located in an old tram), plus the full complement of food, drink, gifts and a play area (it's not as bad as it sounds, probably because all the facilities are housed in an old whitewashed inn, later rebuilt as a hotel). Descend on the opposite slope and you'll reach the twelfth-century St Tudno's Church.

I returned to Llandudno past the impressively landscaped ski slope and toboggan run, dropping down into Happy Valley, on the eastern side of Great Orme. After a pleasant sojourn at Grumpy's Sweet Shop (where I'm pleased to confirm the owner was very *ungrumpy*), I set off again, this time following the four-mile scenic walk around the base of the headland (it's a toll road but there's no charge for walkers).

But what really gets me excited about Llandudno is its location right there on an isthmus. Ever since I lived on St Mary's, in the Isles of Scilly, back in the early 1980s, I've adored isthmuses. The word comes from the ancient Greek and simply describes a narrow strip of land connecting two larger land areas; there's usually water on both sides but not always.

Isthmuses come in all sorts of sizes. One of the largest (and most famous) is the Isthmus of Panama, which was formed about 4.5 million years ago and links North and South America. It's so vast – hundreds of miles long and up to 110 miles wide – that you'd never know you were standing on an isthmus at all.

Llandudno's isthmus is tiny in comparison, which makes it far more exciting. One moment you can be enjoying a stroll along the main promenade overlooking the Irish Sea, and just minutes later paddling on the West Shore and gazing up the Conwy estuary. Just a brisk stroll separates two very different coastlines – how thrilling is that?

Delighting in Great Orme and the surrounding area as I much as I do, it was tough being so close and yet so far away; knowing our path would be taking us inland and towards Snowdonia long before we reached Llandudno.

But that's enough about Llandudno. Today's challenge was crossing another expanse of sand, this time Red Wharf Bay. Though not actually an estuary, this wide bay feels very much like one when you're walking the coast path and faced with traversing its considerable perimeter. We pulled up at low tide when almost ten square miles of sand is exposed; we'd loved to have been able to sit around and watch the waves rushing back into the bay but, as is always the way on these long-distance walks, we had to push on, even resisting the temptation to stop for a drink at the Ship Inn.

The path circumnavigating the estuary is almost entirely flat (after a brief initial climb); however, after a while I started to feel we were getting nowhere fast. Certainly, the other side of the estuary didn't seem to be getting any closer. The terrain changed frequently, from wet and muddy underfoot to a firm gravel track, sand and boardwalks. There's one section where the path becomes rather vertiginous as it follows the old sea wall with drops either side. We could have avoided it altogether and walked along the beach, but Harri wanted to make certain his high tide instructions were accurate.

Sheer drops aside, this is a really lovely stretch of coast path. At one point we passed the campsite where Harri once spent two weeks of one of the wettest Julys on record in an extremely leaky trailer tent.

At the far end of Red Wharf Bay, we climbed steeply towards the flat-topped prehistoric hill fort of Bwrdd Arthur. We reached the crest of the hill, and found ourselves gazing across the Menai Strait at the towering peaks of Snowdonia National Park. Nothing can prepare you for the sudden and breath-taking spectacle of Wales's highest mountains; we've walked in Snowdonia before, and yet the craggy summits looked so much more impressive – and imposing – when beheld from the relative flatness of Anglesey.

With the weather vastly improved and spectacular views to feast upon, we marched ahead with renewed enthusiasm. We had no firms plans for the evening's 'accommodation' but knew the chances of finding a campsite were remote (there were none marked on the OS map).

It's easy to underestimate the kindness of your fellow human beings so we were taken aback when, on hearing of our plans to wild camp that evening, a local man offered us the use of the large field behind his walled garden. It was an incredibly kind gesture; however, it was barely 4 p.m. and far too early to set up camp for the night. We thanked him and continued, following a line of high walls as we again headed towards the coast.

The weather had been steadily improving all afternoon, and by the time we reached the eastern tip of Anglesey facing Puffin Island it was wonderfully clear and sunny. This is a popular spot with tourists; there is car parking and a proper cafe selling ice creams.

From where we were standing, Puffin Island looked pretty small; yet it lays claim to being the ninth largest island off the coast of Wales. It's privately owned and uninhabited; there are boat trip around the island and landing is allowed with special permission. Like most small islands without human residents, Puffin Island attracts an abundance of birdlife alongside the puffins, namely guillemots, razorbills, terns, shags and gannets.

St Seiriol established a monastery on the island in the sixth century and is said to be buried there. The ruins of several ecclesiastical buildings, including a twelfth-century church, are apparently still evident, but from our vantage point across the waves we could only just make out what might have been some sort of tower poking over the top of the island's highest point.

Slightly to the left of Puffin Island (from our perspective) stood the attractive Trwyn Du lighthouse on the low-lying Perch Rock. The circular stone lighthouse with its distinctive three black bands was built in the late 1830s at a cost of £11,589 to warn sailors not to pass between Puffin Island and the main island. Trwyn Du has been unmanned since 1922 and in 1996 it was converted to solar power.

Against the backdrop of the north Wales coastline, Puffin Island and the lighthouse create a stunning landscape that attracts lots of tourists. Seduced by the lovely scenery and late afternoon sunshine, Harri wondered whether this might, in fact, be an ideal spot to set up camp for the night. There was already a campervan (bizarrely advertising tropical fish for sale) parked in such a way as to suggest it was staying overnight, yet I hesitated.

Agreed, it was an idyllic spot for wild camping – and a huge improvement on the perimeter fence at Hinkley Point Power Station in Somerset (where we'd been forced to set up camp when we ran out of daylight and energy back in May) – but there were a lot of people around and on such a lovely evening (and with the prospect of an amazing sunset) it seemed unlikely they would disappear anytime soon.

Plan B was to remain on the headland but wander slightly off the beaten track. This sounded great in theory, but when we headed left the footpath quickly led us to a disused and fenced-off quarry. The coastline to our right was no better suited to a clandestine camp as the obvious path appeared to lead directly onto private property. Despite our enchantment with this lovely spot, we realised we had no choice but to retrace our tracks and see if we could find somewhere slightly further inland.

We hadn't walked far when Harri spotted a narrow gap in the overgrowth. Intrigued, we weaved our way through the spiky vegetation and found ourselves clambering up a lovely little hillock looking out on the lighthouse and island, and in a few hours' time, the sunset. We doubted our low-level green tent would be visible to passers-by, but even if it was, it seemed unlikely anyone would go to the trouble of fighting their way through the undergrowth in the night just to disturb us.

Besides, there was evidence that others had camped here before (some charred marks on the grass), which suggested it was the perfect place to spend the night.

I must have had too much sun (or was perhaps feeling the after-effects of last night's lack of sleep) because I was feeling decidedly sleepy by the time Harri had put up the tent (for some reason he always rejects my offers of help). With the tent up, he sat outside enjoying the wonderful evening light and transcribing route instructions onto the iPad, while I lay inside dozing contentedly. At some point, I think I was persuaded to produce something to eat, but to be truthful my memory of that evening remains rather hazy.

I was thinking about the girl who'd served me earlier in the cafe. I was wearing my Newport Half Marathon 2014 tee shirt and she asked me about the race, telling me 'running was my life before I had children' (hers were very young). Our conversation had made me realise how much I was missing my running. Four days into our hike and there were some aspects of being 'on the road' that I was really enjoying, but some things I missed. My girls (three daughters and two granddaughters) were top of the list, of course, but after my close family, it was my running and running mates that I was missing most of all.

In my semi-delirious state I told Harri I didn't like backpacking. He agreed, probably because it's easier, or maybe he was tired himself, or perhaps it's actually true, right then anyway. I don't know. What I do know is that it's tough work walking all day over undulating ground with a heavy rucksack strapped to your back – and we hadn't even stepped foot in Snowdonia yet!

With a clear sky and only sea on the horizon, tonight's sunset promised to be a spectacular occasion, and one I'd normally want to capture on film. Unfortunately, tonight the designated expedition photographer just couldn't keep her eyes open. Snuggling up in my sleeping bag, I muttered my last words of the day to Harri. 'I hate camping,' I snarled at him. 'I really do hate it!' And with that, I promptly fell asleep.

For photographs visit uk.pinterest.com/thewalkerswife

JUNE 6: PENMON TO BANGOR

The world always seems a better place after a good night's sleep. When we unzipped our tent just before 7 a.m. it was to look out onto a scene so enchanting I had the urge to compose another verse to Louis Armstrong's classic song 'Wonderful World'. Something along the lines of:

> I see sparkling waves, and sea birds fly
> The distance peaks against blue sky
> And I think to myself
> What a wonderful world.

Everything – the lighthouse, Puffin Island, the north Wales coast, the Carneddau Mountains – was bathed in that crisp, bright light which is unique to early mornings. It's no wonder keen photographers are out there at dawn; by the time the rest of the population has emerged, yawning and making coffee, the most magical time of day has passed. The previously bustling Trwyn Du headland was completely deserted, heightening the sense that we really were camping in the wild.

My eyes feasted on the scenery and I thought I'd explode with happiness. Wales was the most amazing, beautiful place, full of stunning scenery and incredible views (which it is, of course, but this morning I was overly ecstatic to the verge of seeming unhinged – giving further credence to the sunstroke theory).

Despite our early finish, Harri calculated that we'd walked between 15 and 16 miles yesterday. No wonder I'd been dead beat!

With no toilets, showers or even breakfast to delay us, we were on the road by eight o'clock, relishing in the morning's peace and tranquillity and filled with an incredible sense of freedom.

Who needed bed and breakfast? A hotel room? A campsite? Not us. We'd had a lovely, undisturbed night's sleep on our little hillock and it hadn't cost us a dime. As a result of roughing it, we were able to set off early, listen to birdsong and walk on blissfully quiet lanes which hadn't yet become busy with holidaymakers in cars.

'I love camping,' I beamed at Harri. 'I really do love it'.

Our first stop of the day was the historic site of Penmon (three miles short of Beaumaris) where there is a priory, a church, a dovecot and, probably the oldest structure of all, St Seiriol's Well.

It's a pretty area with a fascinating past. The original church on the site was constructed in wood and was destroyed by Viking raids in 971. St Seiriol's priory church was rebuilt in stone in the twelfth century and the oldest remaining parts date back to 1140.

The monastery was dissolved in 1537; however, its huge, roofless refectory is still standing. There are interpretation boards inside explaining more about monastery life and the adjacent sixteenth-century priory house is privately owned.

Penmon dovecote was built round 1600 by the Bulkeley family of Beaumaris, who had converted Penmon Priory into a residence after the dissolution. These days we tend to think of dovecotes as places where doves and pigeons can nest safely away from predators, but back in the seventeenth century, their eggs and the young birds were a prized source of food. The birds, blissfully unaware they were destined for some rich man's dinner table, readily entered (and left) via a small cupola in the roof.

The dovecote is unsecured so we poked our heads inside. There are reputedly 930 nesting holes (we didn't count them) which would have been reached by means of a (long gone) revolving ladder supported by the central stone pillar.

We were intrigued (and amused) to spot a bottle high on a ledge above our heads. It was standing upright so presumably hadn't been tossed up there, leaving only one possibility: some prankster must have risked life and limb and somehow clambered those steep walls to plonk it there.

We moved on, still pondering the conundrum, and soon reached St Seiriol's Well, probably the oldest structure at Penmon. The well itself is enclosed by a small building, believed to be eighteenth century in origin. There's not really much to see; however, we felt obliged to wander over to peer down. We really needed to refill our water bottles but thought better of eliciting water from a centuries-old well.

The small building next to the well purports to be the remains of St Seiriol's cell, but evidence is thin on the ground and the shape is apparently wrong for a sixth-century hermitage.

It's a lovely spot, Penmon, but our rumbling tummies were reminding us it was breakfast time, so we pushed on, revelling in the magnificent views of Snowdonia across the Menai Strait. Our aim was to reach Bangor by teatime.

We were wondering where we could stop for breakfast (more dry porridge oats) when Harri spotted a bench in front of a property. There was a sign on it saying you could use it at your own risk so presumably the house owners originally put it there out of kindness, but were later warned they could be liable if anyone fell off, through or over it! Sometimes I think this world has gone mad! If I managed to fall off a bench, I'd assume it was my own hapless self who was to blame and not the kindly person who'd placed it there.

Whatever, we were very grateful for the bench with its open views over the Menai Strait. The weather had grown so warm I wriggled out of my long trousers and into my shorts, the first time I'd bared my legs this year ('ne'er cast a clout till May be out').

By the time we reached Beaumaris, the tide was almost completely out, revealing pebble beaches and extensive mud flats. Harri pointed out Bangor, clearly visible on the distant bank. I was surprised the university city was so close to the coast and said so.

Sometimes I wonder if I should voice my geographical ignorance so readily as it inevitably leads to a bombardment of questions from Harri, all fired off in that incredulous, professorial tone he reserves for occasions like this. Harri: '*Where did you think it was?*' Me: '*Somewhere up north.*' Harri: '*Where up north?*' Me: '*I don't know, somewhere to the east of Snowdonia.*' He looked bewildered. *Really* genuinely bewildered. Because to Harri, maps are like books; there to be read and reread, devoured and pored over. When you've studied a map of Wales as often as he has, the location of every town and city is imprinted on your mind. And you know that Bangor is coastal and faces Beaumaris across the Menai Strait. It is most definitely *not* somewhere to the east of Snowdonia.

All morning, I'd been looking forward to seeing Beaumaris Castle, that great unfinished castle of Wales. The aerial shots look amazing, but Beaumaris was not built on a hilltop and from our low vantage point, its magnificence was marred by a recycling lorry, a myriad of signposts and the steady stream of traffic passing in front of its walls. We could, perhaps should, have gone inside, but it would have cost £10 for the two of us and we couldn't spare the time for a proper look around.

Beaumaris itself felt very well-heeled and doesn't feel particularly Welsh despite the dazzling views of Snowdonia (maybe the ghost of Edward I still lingers; after all, he did build his castle to subdue the Welsh). Almost as impressive as the castle is the elegant and Grade I listed Bulkeley Arms Hotel overlooking the Strait. Built in 1832 by Sir Richard Bulkeley, it helped transform Beaumaris into a middle-class resort. The hotel might never have been built had Sir Richard not received a request from Buckingham Palace in 1829 asking if a future Queen of England could be accommodated on a state visit to Beaumaris Royal Eisteddfod.

At the time, no property existed in Beaumaris that was grand enough for royalty, but that didn't deter the rich landowner. He promised to build the young Princess Victoria a house specifically for her one-night visit. He was true to his word. The 'house' was designed by architect Joseph Hansom, inventor of the Hansom cab (a kind of horse-drawn carriage) and built from local stone from Penmon. So single-minded was Sir Richard in his quest to build a residence fit for a future queen that he demolished 450 houses to improve the view.

Unfortunately, he hadn't counted on the devious scheming of Lord Anglesey, who was so peeved at being excluded from the arrangements that he intercepted the Royal Party as they reached Anglesey with news of a (fictional) smallpox outbreak in Beaumaris and an offer of hospitality at his own home, Plas Newydd. The royal party had no reason to doubt his story and did not venture any farther.

Thus, Room 104, with its spacious layout and three windows boasting panoramic views of the Menai Strait and Snowdonia, never did get to play host to Princess Victoria in 1832.

Yet life has its own sweet way of righting wrongs. Nearly two decades later (by which time Victoria had long learned the truth), the royal party returned to Beaumaris and did stay at the Bulkeley Arms Hotel. Sir Richard was able to cock a snook at his duplicitous neighbour because this time round, his royal guest was none other than Queen Victoria.

More than a hundred and sixty years later, there remained an air of gentility about Beaumaris, a sense that one should mind one's Ps and Qs and keep one's voice down.

As you'd imagine in a town named by a monarch (Edward I gave it the name Beaumaris, meaning 'beautiful marsh'), there were plenty of contenders for the Royal residence here, though when I helpfully suggested the castle itself might have been refurbished to house the newlyweds, Harri pooh-poohed the idea.

We strolled along the wide seafront promenade towards the pier, enjoying the mid- morning sunshine, before wandering into the narrow streets tucked behind the main thoroughfare.

Harri was ready to mail his first OS map home. It didn't take us long to locate the post office, but there was quite a queue. While we were waiting to be served, we got into conversation with another customer who asked where we were from. It turned out that the last time he'd visited south-east Wales in his caravan, he'd stayed at Pentre Tai Farm, less than a mile from our home.

Our chores sorted, we headed off again, me (not unreasonably I feel) expecting the Wales Coast Path to follow the coastline all the way to the Menai Suspension Bridge.

I'd forgotten that in this day and age, the car driver is king. Meaning that whenever there's a conflict of interest, i.e. not sufficient room for both to travel alongside one another, it's an inconvertible rule that it should be the slower-moving pedestrian who is inconvenienced and whose journey is subsequently lengthened.

We left Beaumaris, me simmering inwardly. How unfair that motorised vehicles got to follow the nice, flat coastal road, while the Wales Coast Path sign directed walkers inland, up a long, steep lane. When I finally managed to muster enough breath to splutter a few words, it was to have a rant about car drivers generally (of which I'm one) and car drivers on Anglesey specifically (of which I'm not). I'm not convinced that the officials who determine waymarked routes like the Wales Coast Path have ever walked significant distances with heavy rucksack straps digging into their shoulders.

Right then, the climb from Beaumaris felt unnecessarily cruel and sadistic. Hours later, staring across the water from the other side of the Menai Strait, we could see that the coastal road itself eventually left the seafront to weave behind numerous opulent properties, so I suppose we couldn't have escaped the climbing altogether.

After briefly losing the path on the wooded Baron Hill estate (seat of the Bulkeley family), we finally reached the elongated Llandegfan, a commuter village for many of those working in nearby Bangor and the childhood home of the television presenter Aled Jones (a choirboy who shot to fame with his recording of 'Walking in the Air' in 1985).

With a good chunk of today's mileage completed (we'd already decided it made sense to stop overnight at Bangor where there were plenty of accommodation options), we paused to enjoy our pâté and rolls lunch on a picnic bench under the Menai Suspension Bridge. We'd barely settled down before the biggest, fattest tortoiseshell cat we'd ever set eyes on waddled over to join us. She made it abundantly clear that she expected an invitation to eat with us, so soon we were sharing our pâté with this roly-polyest of creatures. If she's as persistent with everyone who eats at that picnic table, it's no wonder she's not as svelte as she should be.

Lunch over, it was time to say goodbye to Anglesey and cross the Menai Suspension Bridge. Just to clarify, there are now two road bridges over the Menai Strait. The one we were walking over was the first of the two, the 1826 suspension bridge designed by Thomas Telford (there is no pedestrian footway on the Britannia Bridge, designed by Robert Stephenson and originally opened exclusively as a railway bridge in 1850).

On the Anglesey side of the bridge, we stopped to read a bilingual memorial plaque which reads in English: *Menai Suspension Bridge/Constructed 1818–1826 to complete the London to Holyhead Road/Thomas Telford 1757–1834 Engineer*, but somehow managed to miss a memorial to the terrible Aberfan disaster of 1966 that killed 116 children and 28 adults.

From the bridge, we had an excellent view of that 'other' crossing – the Britannia Bridge. When he built his bridge, Telford had chosen the 'easiest' point at which to cross the water, a span of 1,007 feet. Over twenty years later, Robert Stephenson planned to erect his railway bridge across a much wider stretch of water (1,475 feet). Isambard Kingdom Brunel had his doubts about the tubular design and the idea that trains would run through the middle of eight separate tubes rather than on top of them.

Britannia Bridge opened in 1850 and was hailed an engineering triumph until disaster struck over a hundred years later. A group of teenagers, trespassing on the bridge as they made their way home from a cancelled party, were using a piece of burning paper as a lamp when they accidentally set the bridge alight. The flames spread rapidly, helped by strong winds, the tar on the wooden sleepers, and the bridge's tubular shape.

The fire burned for nine hours and could be seen from as far away as Holyhead and Llandudno. Despite the best efforts of more than sixty fire fighters, the damage was devastating. The wooden roof was completely destroyed and the tubes sagged between the towers. After 120 years of service, Stephenson's engineering triumph had been annihilated by a group of careless youths. There's an interview on YouTube where one of them talks about the incident, concluding ruefully, 'I wish we hadn't gone to no party now.'

Within days, it was clear the bridge – a vital communication link – would have to be rebuilt, but it was eighteen months before trains were running between Anglesey and mainland Wales again, and a decade before a new road deck opened to vehicles. As traffic (and congestion) has worsened, civil engineers have been looking at options for turning the single-lane road deck into a dual carriageway. Interestingly, the Britannia Bridge is the only section of route E22, which links Ireland and the UK to Europe – and ends in Ishim, Russia – which is not dual carriageway. Despite its single-lane status, pedestrians aren't allowed to cross.

We meandered across the Menai Suspension Bridge, stopping frequently to look down at the infamous Swellies (one of the most treacherous sections of the 16-mile Menai Strait). Theoretically, it's possible to ford the Swellies at the lowest of spring tides when the water depth falls to around a foot and a half; however, the strong currents make it difficult (and dangerous). Personally, I think I'd prefer to take Telford's high (and dry) road!

Coincidentally, my middle daughter was in Bangor that day, being interviewed for a job with Bangor University (which she subsequently got). I got it into my head that it would be nice to meet up with her, even if it was only for a few minutes. Thus, I quickened my pace as we walked first along a busy main road and then through pretty fields and woodland. Unfortunately, by the time we rolled into town, she was already on a train bound for Cardiff.

Bangor was a pleasant surprise. We emerged near Garth Pier, the second longest pier in Wales after Llandudno; Garth is 1,500 feet (460 metres) long against Llandudno's 2,295 feet (700 metres). It is also the ninth-longest pier in England and Wales (Llandudno being the fifth). I really like piers, and this one only cost 50p to walk along (officially it's free but there's an honesty box suggesting a 50p donation per person), but Harri wasn't interested and you absolutely need a dashing man on your arm for pier strolling.

Shockingly, this impressive Victorian structure was almost demolished in the early 1970s by the now defunct Arfon Borough Council; fortunately, Bangor's own city councillors had more foresight and objected. They obtained Grade II listing for the pier and bought it for 1p in 1975. It took years and funding from various public bodies, but eventually the renovated pier reopened in 1988.

It's hard to imagine what the view across the Menai Strait might have looked like had the short-sighted Arfon councillors got their way (though as is generally the case with historic structures, the pier now needs even more money spent on it).

We booked ourselves into the nearest decent-looking hotel, the Eryl Môr (two nights' consecutive camping was enough for both of us and, besides, the weather was set to change for the worse overnight).

The trouble with walking most of the day is that when you do have some unexpected leisure time, you don't want to do anything that involves walking; instead, we tend to spend our evenings being lazy in pubs or lazy in hotel rooms. There's also the small issue of writing up the directions (for Harri) and the day's notes (for me). Then there are laundry duties and (for me) the challenge of feeding two people without access to any cooking facilities. While we occasionally share a takeaway, we rarely eat out, simply because we're usually too exhausted to do justice to a decent meal.

Our hotel room was on the third floor but directly overlooked the pier and the views across to Anglesey were wonderful. It was lovely-sized accommodation with a fabulous shower (we probably got our money's worth from the time we stayed under the shower alone). But, best of all, if we stood close to the window and gazed down the estuary past Beaumaris, we could still see Puffin Island

After five glorious days walking the Anglesey Coast Path, we were about to embark on the next stage of our long-distance hike – a journey that was about to take us across Wales's highest mountains, the peaks of Snowdonia.

For photographs visit <u>uk.pinterest.com/thewalkerswife</u>

JUNE 7: BANGOR TO THE FOOTHILLS OF THE CARNEDDAU

Our intention was to get a good night's sleep in a nice hotel to prepare ourselves mentally and physically for the challenge ahead: the mountains of Snowdonia. Not only was the weather going to be pretty awful until mid afternoon, but the terrain meant we'd probably be faced with no option but to wild camp again that night.

Unfortunately it wasn't to be. We were woken at 3.28 a.m. by the raucous and drunken antics of the men staying in the next room. Not that there's anything wrong with having a good time, but we so needed our sleep. And that becomes impossible when people are bellowing at one other in the room next to yours.

It took us ages to get back to sleep and then, at 5.20 a.m., we were woken again, this time by cackling female laughter. Exhausted, we did eventually get back to sleep, only to be woken by our alarm at 6.40 a.m. It was hardly the fault of the hotel, but so much for a good night's sleep!

As predicted, the weather had taken a turn for the worse. Outside it was raining hard and I showered to the sound of thunder rumbling immediately above us. Garth Pier, so exquisite in the evening sunshine, was barely visible in the mist. The thought of heading into Snowdonia in this dire weather was pretty depressing. Harri reminded me that it was due to brighten up later in the day, but was quick to add that we couldn't wait around until then.

Over breakfast, we couldn't help overhearing other guests' conversations; it seemed we weren't the only ones who'd been woken by the late-night revellers. Of course, in true British fashion, we all preferred to sit there grumbling to one another rather than confront the culprits at the time.

When we're at home in Newport, Saturday morning means only one thing: parkrun! I first stumbled upon this amazing running community back in September 2011, and to say I'm an enthusiast is understatement of the year. Two days before we caught the train to Holyhead, I'd been presented with my coveted 100 tee shirt, awarded to runners who have completed 100 of the 5k parkrun events which take place across the UK and many other parts of the world. Almost all my own runs have been at Newport – a wonderfully scenic route around the grounds and lake of Tredegar House. I'd heard on the grapevine that a parkrun was imminent in Bangor. Although it wasn't up and running yet, today's route would take us past the Penrhyn Estate, the proposed site of the course. Not quite parkrun tourism, more sort of looking at the brochure.

I'd accepted I wouldn't be running for a few weeks, but it was *Saturday* after all. I decided to don my 100 tee shirt (which I'd stuffed into my rucksack because it was lightweight and new… and, okay, because I was too proud to leave it behind). North Wales was rather barren in terms of parkrun events, so I figured perhaps a little marketing wouldn't go amiss.

Not wanting to get soaked the minute we left the hotel, we hung around in our room eating oranges (me!) and writing up notes (Harri). Just after 10 a.m., there was a brief interlude, so we grabbed our rucksacks and hit the road.

What a difference a day makes! Yesterday, we'd strolled into a Bangor of blue skies, warm sunshine and people; this morning, it was wet, grey and deserted. Which was a shame as it was carnival day, and a funfair had been set up around the port area. Harri reassured me that the townsfolk of Bangor would get their sunshine from 2 p.m.

Unfortunately, there are no rights of way through the Penrhyn Estate, so we didn't actually get a glimpse of the enormous nineteenth-century mock castle. It was built by the wealthy George Hay Dawkins Pennant at an estimated cost of £150,000 (around £49.5 million today) and designed by architect Thomas Hopper. The castle was constructed using slate from the family's own quarries at nearby Bethesda, and every attention was paid to detail – the main staircase alone took ten years to build.

Slate quarrying may well have contributed to the Pennant family's great wealth (they also owned sugar plantations in Jamaica), but the grey rock wasn't to everyone's liking. On her visit to Penrhyn in 1859, Queen Victoria refused to sleep in the one-ton slate four-posted bed that had been crafted for her, commenting that doing so would be like sleeping in a mausoleum.

A cycleway now runs along the old railway line, built in the 1850s to transport slate from the quarry at Bethesda to Porth Penrhyn. The lovely wooded route through the Cegin Valley eventually emerged close to the sprawling Parc Bryn Cegin Business Park on the outskirts of Bangor. It's a strange white elephant of a place – 90 acres of land which have been awaiting the arrival of the promised cutting-edge industries since the year 2000. Fifteen years later, those businesses – and the much-needed jobs that were promised – have never materialised. Instead, the site remains deserted and its wide roads and roundabouts are eerily devoid of traffic.

We'd managed to stay dry for over an hour, but the torrential rain finally caught up with us in the village of Tal-y-bont. We huddled under tall trees, doing our best to avoid the frequent tsunamis thrown up by cars whooshing past but our makeshift 'shelter' proved hopeless; we couldn't have been wetter if we'd been deep-sea diving. The downpour was showing no sign of abating, so it seemed madness to hang around, soaked to the skin and getting colder by the minute, when we could be walking and warming up).

Before setting off, we'd done our best to 'waterproof' the contents of our rucksacks, packing everything in individual resealable freezer bags before piling them into the rucksack's waterproof liner. We'd done everything within our power to stop our clothes, map, and, most importantly, our new iPad getting soaked, but now we were wondering if even these precautions would be enough in the torrential rain.

My camera and Harri's digital voice recorder were vital to our trip, yet both were susceptible to water damage. We'd taken to tucking them inside our coats when we weren't actually using them, but with our clothes now saturated, they offered little protection.

When you're hiking in heavy rain, there comes a point when you're so drenched you stop worrying about getting wetter. It actually came as a relief to realise that the rain had done its worst. The relentless rain meant we'd stomped along at speed, pausing only to take one photograph: Harri had spotted a signpost informing us we were splashing through Lôn Ddŵr, Welsh for watery lane.

Still, it's unlikely anyone could complete a long-distance walk through Wales without at least the occasional drenching, so, fingers crossed, this was the worst Mother Nature was going to throw at us ... for the time being.

We covered several miles quickly, our morale strengthened by the promise of a brighter afternoon. We joined the North Wales Path, and climbed steadily into the foothills of Snowdonia, all the while scanning the sky for that first tiny pocket of blue, which would widen until there was sufficient blue sky for the sunshine to break through.

It was just as the weather was brightening up that disaster struck. When we'd decided to push on in the rain, Harri had been left with no choice but to continue using his five-year-old digital voice recorder. Now the on/off button was stuck ... on. If he couldn't turn it off again, the batteries would quickly drain. Harri carried spare batteries, but only the one set.

The timing couldn't have been worse. Bangor was at least three hours behind us, and we were now heading into the mountains. It was almost certain we would not pass a shop for the rest of the day, and anyway, with the device permanently switched on, the number of batteries we'd need over a couple of days would be phenomenal.

We ran through our limited options. We could, of course, retrace our steps to Bangor and buy a new device there; however, Harri was reluctant to lose a day's walking. Another option was to could leave the North Wales Path and descend to one of the coastal towns, Llanfairfechan perhaps? We'd still lose a day, but there wouldn't be that sense of backtracking. But Llanfairfechan had fewer than 4,000 residents ... would any of its shops sell digital voice recorders?

Another worrying thought had occurred to Harri. If the voice recorder was left without batteries for too long, it was possible (even likely) that he'd lose the instructions he'd already recorded. The past five days' walking would have been in vain in terms of writing his Wales end to end guidebook.

We walked in silence, convinced that all was (soon to be) lost. Harri had been writing up instructions on the iPad whenever he could but two successive nights in a tent had resulted in him falling behind. While he could write instructions on paper from this point on if absolutely essential, it didn't resolve the problem of what to do about the previous days' notes.

And then a miracle happened. Just as the first tiny glimmer of blue sky appeared above, Harri managed to slide the on/off button to the off position. To say we were relieved is the understatement of the year. We were positively punching the (now much brighter) sky.

By now, we were enjoying extensive views along this exposed stretch of the North Wales Path. Ahead, the north Wales coastline stretches all the way to Llandudno and Great Orme. Behind, Garth Pier was still visible and, across the Menai Strait, we could pick out all the places we'd passed through yesterday, including Puffin Island, now shrouded in mist.

Just before Abergwyngregyn, we left the coastline and headed up a narrow valley into the foothills of the Carneddau range of mountains where our route took us to the wonderful Aber Falls (Rhaeadr Fawr in Welsh), a waterfall which plunges 120 feet over an igneous sill (thank you Wikipedia).

The well-surfaced paths provide easy access to the bottom of Aber Falls and the valley's indisputable prettiness makes it really popular with visitors. After hours without seeing a soul and with the promised sunshine finally here, we suddenly found ourselves at a busy tourist attraction.

It wasn't as bad as it sounds; this being rural Wales there was plenty of room for everyone. Unlike almost everyone else (who'd walked up to the falls from the car park), we'd approached from the west, passing just one other walker, meaning we had our side of the falls all to ourselves.

After a quick stop for elevenses/lunch, we crossed the Aber Goch on a nice solid wooden bridge and headed down the valley and through Coedydd Aber Nature Reserve.

Knowing we'd be wild camping that night, we amused ourselves by looking for the perfect spot to pitch our tent. It was a shame it was too early in the day to think about setting up camp, because there really were some beautiful spots where you could tuck a little tent completely out of sight. Harri thinks the apparent abundance of 'perfect' pitches early on in the day is more to do with our frame of mind than actual location; it's strange how when you're tired and daylight is fast fading, most of those idyllic places lose their appeal as overnight stops.

Having walked down one valley, we were immediately faced with climbing its neighbour (don't you just love the Welsh mountains?). And though it was nice to be warm and dry again, the sun's rays were exactly what we didn't want as we trekked up one of the steepest lanes we'd encountered so far. We'd hoped to refill our water bottles in the toilets in the car parking area at Bont Newydd (marked on the OS map *and* interpretation board); however, it appeared the toilet block had *disappeared* from the landscape. Oh, we could work out where they'd been situated alright, it was just that they were no longer there.

The lack of public toilets in Wales is one of my bugbears. Everywhere we went in Anglesey the toilets were closed (though still standing so maybe there is some hope) and here, in the hugely touristy Snowdonia National Park, the toilet block had clearly been bulldozed. Just what are people supposed to do when Mother Nature calls? Coopy down behind the bushes? Cross their legs for the next two or three hours in the – let's face it – vain hope that somewhere (anywhere) they might stumble upon an open toilet block?

By now, the weather was glorious and it was hard to remember how miserable we'd been just hours earlier. We were heading for the Bwlch y Ddeufaen pass, after which we'd be descending to Llanbedwr-y-cennin, where there was a pub. Harri gave me the option of stopping sooner, but once I'd got it into my head that we could have a much-needed drink, I was determined to carry on.

Now the scenery was magnificent. To our right, basking in the early evening sunshine, were the magnificent Carneddau Mountains, home to the second highest mountain in Wales. Our route wouldn't be taking us over the towering Carnedd Llywelyn, which was a relief because at 3491 feet, the summit is only 69 feet lower than Snowdon's own.

Our pace picked up again as we meandered along a lane flanked by the high drystone walls that defined this bleak and empty landscape.

So enticing was this mountain landscape, Harri suggested we clamber over a gate and pitch our tent behind one of the walls. I might have been persuaded had I not spent the last hour fantasising over the cold cider waiting for me on a bar in Llanbedwr-y-cennin.

Gradually the Conwy Valley came into view. From a distance, it looked lush and enticing; I mentally added it to the (long) list of places I hoped to one day visit. Conwy itself is absolutely gorgeous, with a well-preserved medieval castle, town walls and a beautiful quayside area with stunning views across the estuary towards Llandudno and Great Orme.

Conwy also boasts the smallest house in the UK, which is still owned by the descendants of the last resident, a fisherman called Robert Jones who (allegedly) stood at 6 feet 3 inches and only moved out in 1900 when the house was declared unfit for human habitation. The sixteenth century house is just 6 feet wide and 10 feet tall. Only four people can enter at a time and the low entrance fee (£1 adults/50p children) reflects the fact that there's not an awful lot to see. As someone who aspires to minimalist living, I must say I'm rather drawn to a home where there's simply no room to accumulate clutter; in fact, no room for anything much at all, including visitors!

We were tiring by the time we reached Ye Olde Bull, which won lots of Brownie points for offering a choice of draught cider other than the ubiquitous Strongbow.

Worryingly, my little toe had started bothering me. Nothing serious (yet) but the memories of multiple blisters and my agonising limping across the Somerset Levels were too recent for me to ignore the warning signs. This time I was taking preventative action in the form of a posh (read expensive) blister plaster, kindly donated to the cause by my running mate, Roni.

Feeling nicely cheered by alcohol, we set off optimistically to find somewhere to camp. It was at this point that the day began to go seriously downhill (spot the synchronicity … terrible start, terrible finish).

After a false start in the wrong direction, we headed uphill on a badly overgrown footpath. We stumbled through endless brambles and clambered over several fallen trees before finally emerging in the most vertical field imaginable.

If its topography wasn't bad enough, this dry-ski slope of a field was so badly rutted it made walking almost impossible. There were thistles everywhere, along with a liberal scattering of sheep poo. There was also the small detail of the missing footpath … we'd emerged at one side of this monstrous land but had no clue as to how we should proceed across it.

'This is the worst field I've ever walked across,' I announced tearfully, as Harri strode ahead searching for clues as to where the footpath was.

See, this is what happens when I've walked twenty miles, had a thorough soaking, and knocked back two halves of good cider in twenty minutes. I get overly melodramatic. Harri's used to it and tends to ignore me, which makes me even rattier. My feet were again soaking, my trouser legs wet and, as the warm glow created by the cider wore off, I was exhausted – in body and spirit. My little toe was hurting too.

We trooped up, down and then finally to the top of this green grass of nightmares – and came face to face with a barbed wire fence. Time was ticking on and the route clearly wasn't up to scratch so Harri did what he's so good at: he studied his map for a good few minutes and devised an alternative route.

Why is it that when things are going badly, they tend to get worse before they get better? As we hurried along a minor road, with the light rapidly fading, we found ourselves staring at a construction site linked to Dolgarrog Power Station, complete with sign announcing that the way ahead was closed. Talk about last straws!

With daylight and our options fast running out, Harri decided the best and only course of action was to head for the nearby foothills as fast as we could (our meandering route had taken us to the far side of the Carneddau summits we'd passed earlier).

Wild camping sounds so romantic in theory yet it's nothing of the kind in practice. First, contrary to popular opinion, there are very few wild places in Wales which: a) are not overlooked or privately owned, b) are sufficiently secluded to be safe from troublesome passers-by, c) are flat enough to pitch a tent – and actually get any sleep, d) are not covered with sheep poo, thistles or rocks, e) provide at least some shelter from the elements, and f) are located close to clean water for washing, refilling bottles, etc.

Our eventual camping spot ticked just one of the above. At around 1,250 feet above sea level, the place we finally pitched our tent was overlooked only by the towering Carneddau and was certainly on common ground. It was just yards from a quiet lane which became unnervingly busy after dark, was very uneven underfoot, was covered with rocks, thistles *and* sheep poo, was exposed to the considerable gusts that blasted us all night and was nowhere near a stream.

It was almost dark when Harri spotted the flattish hillock just off the undulating mountain road along which we'd been trudging for what felt like an age. Within 15 minutes, it would be pitch dark (or 'bible black' as Welsh poet Dylan Thomas would undoubtedly have written) and near impossible to erect our tent or even see it.

We'd unknowingly chosen the worst possible spot to set up camp as our subsequent lack of sleep was to prove. We had barely zipped up our sleeping bags and closed our eyes, when a car's headlights lit up the mountainside, causing us considerable consternation. Had someone followed us, I wondered nervously? Were they planning to plunder our tent once we were asleep? Now I remembered that a vehicle *had* passed us just before we joined the mountain lane. Had its occupants they guessed our plans? Returned under the cover of darkness to ... to what? A second set of passing headlights had us both alert, our hearts hammering in readiness for flight.

There were gates positioned at regular intervals along the lane so this definitely wasn't a case of boy racers taking advantage of the night. Anyway, judging from the stationary headlights, one or more vehicles appeared to have parked up nearby – too nearby for comfort.

'It's probably young couples looking for a secluded spot to canoodle in the car,' I whispered. But I didn't really believe that and knew Harri didn't.

Desperate to calm our growing nerves, we consoled ourselves in the knowledge our tent was so tiny (and green to boot) someone would have trouble finding it on a mountainside if they were *looking* for it. In the mountain blackness, no driver would notice us as they drove past.

Minutes passed and we tried to doze without success. Outside the wind was growing ever stronger and our aluminium tent pegs hadn't exactly sunk easily into the hard, stony ground. I sought reassurance from Harri that no tent had ever blown away with its occupants still inside, *Wizard of Oz* fashion.

To make things worse, it was now raining; the cacophony outside was hardly conducive to a good night's sleep, with or without the possibility of Viking intruders (see how your imagination runs away with you when you're lying in a sleeping bag, tired and scared, on top of a mountain?).

It was then that I heard footsteps next our tent. 'There's someone outside,' I whispered urgently to Harri, who was lying wide awake alongside me. To be fair, he didn't try to fob me off with talk of the wind and rain or an overactive imagination, but immediately grabbed our torch and clambered outside. Of course, there was nobody there, not even a curious sheep, but the experience only added to our feelings of agitation and unease.

Eventually, after what felt like an eternity of listening to noises real and imagined, we fell into a fitful sleep.

For photographs visit <u>uk.pinterest.com/thewalkerswife</u>

JUNE 8: FOOTHILLS OF THE
CARNEDDAU TO DOLWYDDELAN

When we woke at 4.15 a.m. it was already getting light, but it was too early to set off again, so we snuggled down and managed a few more hours' sleep.

Never again, we vowed, as we packed away our stuff a few hours later. Never again would we leave it so late to start looking for a camping spot. And never again, I vowed silently, would I agree to wild camp in the Welsh mountains. Hinkley Point – a nuclear power station with its perimeter fence under constant surveillance – had proved an oasis of peace and calm compared to the Carneddau.

We were on the road before eight o'clock, forsaking breakfast to put some distance between ourselves and that hillock. We were even more spooked when Harri checked the OS map; the spot where we'd spent our sleepless night was the site of an ancient settlement, most likely Bronze Age. We're not the least bit superstitious, but there's no denying we'd both had a severe dose of things-that-go-bump-in-the-nightitis. A Bronze Age settlement? It makes you wonder …

Regardless, we were relieved to be on the move again. Mountains look magnificent and alluring in certain lights, but grim and foreboding in others. Unfortunately, the sparsely-vegetated Carneddau looked anything but alluring this morning, and I couldn't wait to reach something like civilisation again.

We climbed steadily on a gravel path, soon passing Llyn Eigiau on our right. Eigiau was a natural lake until it was dammed across part of its eastern side in 1911 to supply water for Dolgarrog Power Station (the original contractor pulled out, alleging corner cutting). Fourteen years later, on November 2, 1925, after heavy rainfall, the dam wall broke. Water flowed down to Coedty Reservoir, causing its embankment dam to burst. Subsequently, millions of gallons of water flowed into Dolgarrog, three miles away, resulting in sixteen deaths. (Old film footage from the disaster can be viewed online.)

Undoubtedly, more people would have died had they not been watching a film in the local theatre. The tragedy led to the introduction of legislation regulating the safety of reservoirs.

Llyn Eigiau is now just half the size it was before the tragedy, but the towering dam walls remain, the wide breach in its line and nearby deep gully ugly reminders of man's desire – and frequent failure – to control the elements.

Soon we were squelching past a long-abandoned stone farmhouse, marked on the map as Eilio. How anyone could have lived in such a remote location before central heating, cars, telephones and internet access were commonplace is beyond me. The winters must have felt endless, with Eilio's inhabitants seeing no one for weeks on end.

This morning's theme was water, both in reservoirs and underfoot. As I moaned about wet feet, Harri explained that the igneous (volcanic) nature of much of Snowdonia's rock face means that rainfall doesn't quickly soak away like in the Brecon Beacons where there is an abundance of limestone. While this makes sense geologically, it doesn't diminish the unpleasantness of walking through bogs. My choice of lightweight walking shoes didn't help either … the first hint of dampness and my feet were soaked, aggravating the threatened blister.

Llyn Cowlyd loomed into view soon after we'd climbed through a pass. This two-mile long (but narrow) lake, 1,164 feet above sea level, provided our immediate views for the next hour or so, as we meandered along its (occasionally) rocky and (frequently) muddy bank.

This natural lake owes its record depth to the man-made dam at one end. The average depth is 108 feet, but it's actually an awful lot deeper in some places. Just one look into those murky waters and you just sense the bottom is a long, long way down. I took special care not to get too close to the edge.

There is little vegetation on these steep hills (and no trees at all). Harri was concerned that the colourless landscape was perhaps not sufficiently scenic to be included in his 'O Fôn i Fynwy' route. Briefly uncertain, we turned and gazed back at the dam, at this magnificent expanse of water which just seemed to topple off the edge of the horizon like the original infinity pool. The menacing slate-coloured clouds above merely added drama to what was already an incredibly atmospheric view. We looked at each other and nodded – Llyn Cowlyd was definitely staying on the route!

We hadn't passed anyone at all since we'd set off that morning, but as we reached the far end of the lake we spotted a group heading towards us. We didn't stop to talk but did the usual walker thing of nodding and saying hello to each person as they passed. In the Welsh mountains, this use of individual greetings doesn't pose much of a problem as we rarely see more than two to four people at any one time.

It can become rather onerous, however, when you're confronted with walker after walker, passing with the frequency of M25 traffic and all determined to do the polite thing and say hello. It happened to us a few years ago when we travelled to the stunning Picos de Europa in May. The walking was good and the scenery spectacular with meadows, mountains and gorges; everything was going fine until we decided to walk through the Cares Gorge on a glorious sunny Sunday afternoon … in the opposite direction to every member of the local population. It's a route which attracts around 300,000 walkers a year and, I'm hazarding a guess here, but it's probable that the majority choose to walk it on gloriously sunny Sundays. As a result, we found ourselves smiling and murmuring '*Hola*' every two or three seconds for hours on end until we became quite hoarse. It's wonderful to visit a region where hiking is such a big part of many people's lives; however, it can become quite demanding on one's vocal cords.

Fortunately, we rarely encounter such high numbers of walkers when we're walking in Wales, with perhaps the exception of the popular peaks of Snowdon, Cadair Idris and Pen y Fan. Elsewhere, you can usually walk for hours without passing a soul – all day, if it's raining.

We were so accustomed to having the mountains to ourselves, we were at first a little surprised to suddenly find ourselves confronted with a steady stream of walkers heading in our direction, until we realised our proximity to the tourist honeypot of Capel Curig.

The weather had been improving rapidly for the past hour and the grey clouds were at last lifting, revealing the isolated summit of Moel Siabod (at 2,860 feet it's the highest peak in the Moelwynion mountain range). We climbed this mountain in March 2014, setting off from Capel Curig on what promised to be a warm spring day and reaching the summit cairn in gusting winds and poor visibility. Far from enjoying incredible views across neighbouring ranges, we struggled to see each another; on the descent, we inadvertently wandered from the footpath because we couldn't see it in the mist. An hour or so later, we were sitting alongside the river's edge in Capel Curig enjoying lunch in the sunshine.

At no point had we put ourselves at risk (our meandering descent followed gentle mountain slopes with no sheer drops); however, the experience was a sombre reminder of how changeable mountain weather can be. It's never worth taking risks just to bag a summit; far better to turn back and be safe (we always remember it's not just our own lives we'd be risking but those of the Mountain Rescue Teams who'll come out looking for us).

The clouds lifted suddenly, exposing the mighty Yr Wyddfa. Soaring 3,560 feet above sea level, the highest mountain in England and Wales is better known by its English name, Snowdon.

We were silenced by the stark beauty around us, humbled by the towering peaks which dominate the north Wales landscape. We were reminded, if we needed reminding, of how frail and transient the human experience is when compared to these massive geological wonders, created by erupting volcanoes and widespread glaciation millions of years ago.

This is the wonder of Snowdonia, the reason millions of people visit the National Park each year (it is the third most visited national park in England and Wales). Like us, they come to be bowled over by the outstanding beauty of the natural world, to stand quietly and witness something special, something awesome. They won't be disappointed.

One of the things that surprises me is that almost 70% of the National Park's 823 square miles (2,131 km^2) is privately-owned land. Of the remainder, Natural Resources Wales (formerly the Forestry Commission and the Countryside Council for Wales) owns 17.5%, the National Trust 8.9%, the National Park Authority 1.2%, and water companies 0.9%. 1.6% is described as being owned by 'other'.

It was this preponderance of private landowners which led to Wales being held to ransom in the late 1990s. Farmer Richard Williams revealed his intention to sell his 4,000-acre estate in Snowdonia, which included one-third of the summit of Snowdon itself and the nearby 'Welsh Matterhorn', Cnicht (deliciously pronounced with a hard 'c').

Following a high-profile 100-day public appeal, to which Oscar-winning Welsh actor Anthony Hopkins not only lent his support but started the ball rolling with a cool £1 million donation, the 'ransom' was raised. The Stereophonics played a concert, the Chris Brasher Trust donated an entire year's income, and (it's reputed) Prince Charles also made a personal donation.

At the time it was reported that over a quarter of a million people had pledged donations and, ten days before the deadline, the National Trust announced the amount raised had reached £4.16 million.

Mr Williams eventually secured £3.65 million for the land, which has remained in National Trust ownership.

According to newspaper reports at the time, Richard Williams's family had farmed the land for fourteen generations, so it was a fluke of birth that resulted in him owning a third of Wales's highest summit. The farmer is recorded as saying the decision to sell caused him 'much heartache', but if that was the case, did he really need to sell 'his' land, 'his' mountain? He said he was selling the land because he didn't have time to farm *all* his estates, so why couldn't this wealthy individual show the same philanthropic spirit as Sir Anthony Hopkins and give it away, or at least lease/sell it for a peppercorn figure?

It's all water under the bridge now, I suppose, and thanks to people like Sir Anthony Hopkins and the late Chris Brasher, Wales managed to hang onto its highest peak. Despite winning this time, however, I will never change my view that mountains like Snowdon and Cnicht should belong to everyone and not passed down through the generations to a privileged few.

I could have stood there and gazed up the valley for hours, but Capel Curig was beckoning below and we still had several hours walking ahead of us.

It's probably fair to say that Capel Curig is one of the prettiest villages in Snowdonia – it's also officially the wettest (although the weather station that records these things is actually located a couple of miles outside the village in Dyffyn Mymbyr). According to the *Guardian* newspaper, May 2014 was the wettest month in the UK for six years, with the highest rainfall in Capel Curig where 212 mm fell. I'm just relieved we decided to walk through Wales in June and not May!

From the outset, we'd been determined that this adventure should be enjoyable, so rather than push on with our day's hiking, we decided to be tourists for a while and linger around Capel Curig to buy Kendal mint cake (which I adore and Harri detests) and have a beer.

We headed for an ivy-covered stone cafe called Bryn Glo which was strewn with handwritten signage – my favourite was a notice on the door stating 'Please note: NO purchase, NO pee! Thanks!' Bryn Glo is the quirky kind of place that we occasionally stumble upon and instantly adore.

We sat outside with two cans of lager and tried to ignore the delectable smell of pizza baking a few yards away. It's hard to get going again after a pint and a packet of crisps; if we'd succumbed to temptation and ordered (and eaten) a whole pizza, we'd undoubtedly have spent the rest of the afternoon supping ale and falling off benches in Capel Curig. As it was, the only thing that kept falling off was our empty beer cans, much to the chagrin of a terrier which was tied to a fence post and dozing contentedly while its owner was eating inside. The poor creature nearly jumped out of its skin when a sudden gust of wind lifted an empty can off our table and hurled it at him. This happened several times much to the dog's consternation and our hilarity. I think the poor mutt was quite relieved when its owner finally emerged to rescue it from our scary flying beer cans (none of which actually struck the dog, I should stress).

When we were last here, a local walking guide highly recommended the nearby Moel Siabod cafe. Unfortunately, we were pushed for time, having two AA walks to complete before nightfall. On this occasion, we weren't so rushed but we'd emerged too far down the valley to pay the cafe a visit. Apparently, the coffee and food are excellent and the cafe website is really funky (with an up-to-date blog). We're determined to check it out ourselves on our next visit to Capel Curig!

It's always hard to get going again when you've indulged in a pub stop and today was no different. Worse, it was a pub stop in a valley which was *not* the valley we were hoping to reach today. That could mean only one thing... more climbing.

We headed back to the bridge above the Pont Cyfyng waterfall. This time round we weren't climbing Moel Siabod so took the lower path, which climbs steeply at first before levelling out. By now the wind was really picking up and the track, though very pretty, provided little shelter from the gusts. We perched on a grassy bank and stopped for the briefest of lunches before heading off again.

We emerged from woodland to be greeted by amazing views over the incredibly pretty Lledr valley, where the little village of Dolwyddelan lies (the village name means 'Gwyddelan's meadow'). The tranquillity of this lovely valley came as a surprise after touristy Capel Curig, and I found it hard to believe that Wales's main road from south to north – the 186-mile A470 – runs right through the middle. (Wikipedia usefully informs us that it's also known as the Cardiff to Glan Conwy Trunk Road. Maybe by northerners, but it's not a term I've ever heard!),

Perhaps the road's busier on weekdays, or at rush hour, but as we walked into Dolwyddelan there was very little to suggest Wales's main thoroughfare was alongside us.

What struck us about Dolwyddelan was that it possessed all the natural attributes of its neighbours, Capel Curig and Beddgelert, yet seemed to attract none of the tourists. Maybe the mountains were a little less rugged – probably better to describe them as hills rather than full-blown mountains – but the valley had a lovely feel about it and its scenery was breathtaking. So where was everyone? If the village hadn't been marked on the OS map, we might have started thinking we'd stumbled upon a Welsh Brigadoon, appearing to visitors only one day every hundred years.

Dolwyddelan has one major claim to fame. Its original wooden castle on a rocky knoll known as Tomen Castell is believed to have been the birthplace of Llywelyn the Great (c.1172). The stone castle which perches dramatically on a precipice above the A470 was probably built soon after 1200.

The present-day castle owes its condition to a renewed interest in Welsh nationalism – and in Llywelyn himself – in the middle of the nineteenth century during which time the castle underwent a dramatic restoration. For history enthusiasts, there's detailed information about the structure at www.dolwyddelan.org and in Adrian Pettifer's excellent book *Welsh Castles*.

After last night's lack of sleep, we were feeling decidedly weary by the time we walked into the village and, with our resistance low, we found ourselves disappearing into the first pub we spotted, the four-hundred-year-old Y Gwydyr. The pub is directly opposite the church of Sant Gwyddelan, where an old Celtic bell, said to date back to the sixth century, hangs. Originally called Y Gwydyr Arms Hotel, Dolwyddelan's sole inn was once one of three in the village and was established just before the Conwy Valley Railway Line was extended from Betws-y-Coed (the line remains open today with trains running from Llandudno to Blaenau Ffestiniog, stopping at Dolwyddelan).

We planned to have a quick pint before heading to a campsite in the valley, but as the weather outside deteriorated, our good intentions turned to fantasies involving warm beds and hot showers. There was a good atmosphere in the bar, the locals were friendly. We suspected that most were Welsh-speaking, but they immediately started chatting to us in English which was nice (no one ever realises that Harri is a fluent Welsh speaker).

The temptation to ask about bed and breakfast was proving irresistible. The landlord wasn't around, but the barmaid made a quick phone call and, hey presto, we had a room for the night.

That night was to mark the beginning of a slippery slope. Until now, we'd tried to convince ourselves that we were willing to wild camp if necessary, but our Carneddau experience had put an end to the pretence. Our expedition wasn't headed up by Sir Ranulph Fiennes and we weren't tough military types. From now on, it was going to be proper campsites all the way ... or cosy pubs offering bed and breakfast like Y Gwydyr.

The locals were enjoying *Britain's Got Talent* so we settled down to watch the final countdown when the winners would be announced. We don't have a television at home so this being the first time we'd ever seen the show, we had to rely on our new friends to tell us a little about each performer and whether they deserved to win. In the event, the overall winners were the operatic boy band Collabro.

(See how you get drawn into these things? We've survived perfectly well without a television and the myriad of talent and reality shows which bombard the country's viewers for seven years. Ten minutes in a pub, and we're both staring inanely at the flat screen and actually taking an *interest* in this over-hyped Saturday night show.)

We didn't linger long in the bar, though we really appreciated the friendliness of the locals and the trouble they'd taken to involve us in conversation. We were tired and just wanted to plonk in a comfortable hotel room. Our accommodation at Y Gwydyr was absolutely lovely, with a very modern, spacious bathroom and lots of thoughtful little touches like a shower cap, cotton wool and a sewing kit.

Outside, the weather was doing its worst and we thanked our lucky stars that we were spending the night under Welsh slate and not canvas.

For photographs visit <u>uk.pinterest.com/thewalkerswife</u>

JUNE 9: DOLWYDDELAN TO BEDDGELERT

A week before my twentieth birthday, I chucked my steady job with a large furniture and carpet retailer and jumped onto a train heading to Cornwall. My journey didn't end at Penzance; an hour or two later, I was peering down at the grey waves of the Atlantic Ocean from a British Airways Sikorsky helicopter.

My sister had inadvertently got herself a waitressing job on the Isles of Scilly a few months earlier. We'd grown so used to Jobcentre misspellings (remember those hand-written cards on the walls?), for a week or two we thought she'd be heading off to Italian waters. Fortunately, her error became apparent before she set off; even more fortunately, upon arrival at St Mary's she found the tiny Cornish island quite idyllic with not a hint of Mafioso activity at the Smuggler's Ride guesthouse.

Over the following decades, hampered by a somewhat 'interesting' CV (their words not mine), I often wished I'd resisted the youthful urge to keep moving from one bottom-tier job to the next. One thing I have never regretted, however, is those two summer seasons I spent working on the Isles of Scilly.

They were halcyon days, where the focus was entirely on enjoying ourselves. Life revolved around the beach, cheap (and more often free) boat trips to the numerous offshore islands, and the legendary Scillonian partying. Work was undemanding and the hours unbelievably short. As a chambermaid at the Atlantic Hotel in 1981, I worked roughly three hours each morning, with another hour in the evening to 'turn the beds down' (a completely pointless exercise if ever there was). Few people actually wanted this service so we were usually finished in half an hour.

When I returned to Scilly in 1983, it was to work as a silver service waitress at Tregarthen's Hotel where I waited on German holidaymakers, French sailors and English millionaires alike. On several occasions I served Sunday lunch to former Prime Minister Harold Wilson (who I recall as being one of our more taciturn customers) and his wife Mary (they owned a holiday home on St Mary's). Again, our leisure time far outweighed the hours spent working, although I clearly remember the strange practice of serving large pieces of plaice on two fish knives and inadvertently laying tables with lobster picks when it was snails on the menu (this last misdemeanour resulted in me getting a good telling off from the head chef, Ron).

The seasonal workers tended to stick together, which is not to say the local youngsters weren't friendly but with 'proper' jobs, they generally had less free time than we emmets.

We walked, swam, sunbathed, shopped, ate, drank, danced, and did a whole lot of other things that young people do when their parents are hundreds of miles away. There was a disco at the end of the old stone quay, which thirty years on seems like the maddest, most 'accident-likely-to-happen' bit of town planning ever but there you go. There's a rumour that an ever-so-slightly-tipsy Welsh girl once tried to demonstrate a 'tishy-over' to interested islanders and instantly disappeared off the edge of the quay. The tide was out as onlookers rushed to the wet sand below, only to find her wedged between the quay wall and a beached yacht. It's only hearsay, of course, but I heard she was found without a scratch on her and suffers no ill effects to this day.

If I'd ever been asked to describe paradise, the Scilly of the early 1980s would have been it.

For decades the memories of those long-ago friends remained just that – memories. Then Friends Reunited arrived on the scene, encouraging middle-aged people who should have known better to look up old acquaintances, workmates and in some cases, that never-forgotten lover (sometimes with dire consequences). You remember what it was like: the excitement that you were back in touch with someone you worked with in 1979. You didn't like them then, but time is a great healer. Some tentative exchanges about family and careers would follow before the enthusiasm dimmed – on both sides – and messages abruptly stopped.

It wasn't until Facebook that we *properly* started linking up with one another again, those twenty-something seasonal workers now in our fifties. Again, we politely asked about each other's lives, reminded each other of incidents from the past, and shared old photographs (how few we took compared to young people of today), but this time it was different. We didn't need to have that awkward one-to-one conversation, we didn't even have to be spoken to in the first place but could just jump into a conversation mid-way or easiest of all, 'Like' someone's status. It felt more natural, more like real life; now we could comment at will and reminisce about the past in groups, withdraw for a while, then start all over again.

Shane was a kitchen porter at the centuries-old Star Castle Hotel when we met in 1981. In fact, I might not have got to know him at all had my room-mate Sheila not already forged a friendship with him in part due to the fact they had the same day off each week. Later, my sister began a long-term relationship with one of Shane's close friends so our paths coincided more frequently. In the winter of 1983, when I was back in Newport, he visited and I showed him what my hometown had to offer in terms of nightlife. He was a nice bloke from Norfolk; our lives moved on and we lost touch ... until Facebook.

We hadn't seen each other in person for thirty years, but we now intended to remedy that. Shane, who had trained as a chef not long after we lost touch, was working in Beddgelert; Harri and I were meeting up with him this evening.

I was really looking forward to seeing my old mate again, albeit slightly concerned that we'd not yet been able to make definite arrangements. Originally, we'd not been absolutely certain of our arrival day (let alone time) in Beddgelert, and now the lack of both mobile phone signal *and* internet access (for Shane and us) meant that we'd not yet alerted him to the fact we were going to be passing through later that day. It would be ironic if the modern technology that enabled us to be in touch again failed us at the eleventh hour.

The weather hadn't improved overnight. Worse, the clothes we'd washed and hung on cold radiators before we went to sleep didn't feel much drier than when we'd put them there. Harri's new bamboo tee-shirts were proving a disaster too; they were just impossible to get dry without heating. There's nothing worse than wriggling into damp clothes (wet pants are the worst!), though judging from the persistent rain outside, it wouldn't make much difference if our clothes were wet or dry when we set off. We were certain to be soaked before we had left Dolwyddelan we'd be soaked again.

We didn't get to meet the landlord last night but the barmaid had asked if we would mind having breakfast early because he'd be cooking our breakfast and he had to be somewhere else at 10 a.m. It transpired that as well as running Y Gwydyr, this man also worked as a guide at a nearby tourist attraction *and* found time to take his children to school. His mornings involved more juggling than a circus act, but he was very amiable and determined we were going to eat before he left the premises ... and eat extremely well.

Enormous plates of cooked breakfast were placed in front us, each one brimming with three sausages, two eggs, bacon, tomatoes, mushrooms, and beans; there were also several rounds of toast *each*. There was sufficient food on the table to feed a family of four with leftovers for the dog. We made a gallant effort to do this early morning feast justice, but even though I managed to eat two sausages for the first time in years, I couldn't face the fried eggs and even a hungry Harri wasn't up to four!

While we tucked in, our hard-working host excused himself to do the school run. Afterwards, he explained apologetically, he'd have to leave for work; he emphasised that there really wasn't any rush for us to leave our room and we were welcome to remain upstairs as long as we liked (while we needed to get going anyway, we really appreciated his kind gesture). If you find yourself in Dolwyddelan anytime soon, we can't recommend the friendly Y Gwydyr highly enough; and if you skip dinner the night before you might just manage to do that huge breakfast justice.

On days like this when the Welsh weather is doing its worst, it would be easy to find reasons to postpone the moment of departure. Our room might not have been overly warm, but it was dry with a television and tea-making facilities. It would have been easy to idle away a few hours inside while the rain lashed against the windows.

In the past week, we'd come to the realisation that neither of us enjoys roughing it. We're happy to walk from dawn to dusk as long as we've got our home comforts to look forward to each evening. In our first week on the road, we'd slept in bed and breakfast establishments four times and our tent three times – not quite the four nights camping/one night bed and breakfast ratio we'd intended.

We wondered now if booking luxurious accommodation for our first two nights had been a mistake. We had set the bar high and we were now loathe to start slumming it, especially now we were in Snowdonia where the weather was not conducive to sleeping under canvas.

At Penmon, we'd set up camp very early on a gloriously warm and sunny evening, which left us with plenty of daylight hours to eat, write up notes and generally get ourselves organised (had I not spent most of the evening dozing in the tent). Memories of the early morning light on Trwyn Du lighthouse and Puffin Island would remain with us for a long time.

Our night on the Carneddau was also memorable, but for all the wrong reasons. We'd made basic mistakes which an experienced long-distance walker would have avoided. First, we should have stopped much earlier, and not waited until we were physically and mentally exhausted before we looked for somewhere to camp. Another big mistake was continuing to climb when it was clear the wind was picking up and the clouds gathering overhead.

'We'll learn from the experience and choose our next wild camping spot more carefully,' Harri told me.

'Definitely,' I said, crossing my fingers behind my back. I had no intention of wild camping again … *ever*.

We left Dolwyddelan in our damp underwear and followed a low-level route along the hillside. The enchanting valley views of the previous day had all but vanished under a veil of fog, which was especially frustrating to me, the expedition photographer, because I'd wanted a decent photograph of the castle.

It was a shame to find ourselves passing through this stunning – and hitherto unvisited – landscape in such bleak weather. Every now and then it stopped raining and the sun would attempt to break through the clouds. Our spirits would soar briefly, only to be cruelly dashed when the heavens opened again.

As we climbed and the rain showed no sign of relenting, the stony tracks became brooks and it was pointless even trying to keep my feet dry. As I've mentioned, I couldn't risk wearing the trail shoes that had given me so much grief in Somerset but neither did I want to commit myself to a month of heavy walking boots. After much deliberation and handwringing, I'd chosen to wear running shoes and to stash my seven-year-old Brasher sandals in my rucksack. Comfortable as they were, my lightweight Brooks weren't designed to be watertight. The merest hint of water – morning dew, light rainfall, a puddle – and my feet were wet. On the bright side, when the dew evaporated or the rain stopped, running shoes dried much faster than heavy boots.

While I knew I'd made the right call with my footwear, there were still moments – generally when I was squelching through bogs with rainwater trickling down my nose and ground water rising *up* my trouser legs – when I start to fantasise about roomy, rubbery, knee-height wellingtons. Actually, forget the wellingtons; make it a pair of those thigh-waders so beloved of all coarse anglers.

The weather was starting to improve slightly as we came over the mountain and started heading steeply downhill towards Llyn Gwynant in the stunningly beautiful valley of Nantgwynant.

There's a 14-acre campsite on the edge of the lake and I was flabbergasted to learn Llyn Gwynant remains open until early December (and will even open in February for what it terms 'large events'). I can't imagine anyone willingly choosing to willing to sleep under canvas in sub-zero temperatures ... except maybe the wildling from Game of Thrones.

According to its website, Llyn Gwynant campsite's stunning lakeside location has made it popular with film-makers (usually during the quieter autumn months) and it has featured on the silver screen in various guises over the years.

Llyn Gwynant was the main Welsh location in *Lara Croft Tomb Raider: The Cradle of Life* (2003), when it was transformed into the Chinese village where Lara battled with her adversary Chen Lo. Chinese extras were drafted in from Carnarfon and a local farmer supplied chickens, geese and a mule.

A few years prior to that, scenes for the feature film *Merlin* (starring the wonderful actresses Helena Bonham Carter and Miranda Richardson) were shot at Llyn Gwynant. Apparently, the mound behind the campsite's toilet block featured as Camelot, which just goes to show how creative production designers have to be! The mini-series *Merlin of the Crystal Cave* also set its Camelot alongside Llyn Gwynant.

We weren't stopping here, however, but carrying on to Beddgelert. Harri's planned route meant crossing the valley slightly above the campsite before following an elevated path along the lake's edge. It promised to be scenic, but first we had to reach the lake.

While we'd been meandering around the Anglesey Coast Path in glorious sunshine, Snowdonia's mountains had attracted the worst of the rain. And the heavy rain had continued overnight and into this morning. The clouds were now lifting with the promise of late afternoon sunshine but there seemed little likelihood of the boggy ground drying out anytime soon.

We'd had a brief reprieve as we descended into the valley on a steep, rocky footpath. Slow-going and tough on the knees, it at least provided a welcome change from the endless sloshing through mud. At last, the footpath joined a tarmac lane and I finally allowed myself to relax, confident it would be easier underfoot from this point onwards. But Harri had other ideas. To my astonishment, he strode straight across the lane to join more watery terrain on the far side.

I was starting to wonder if I'd stumbled into a long-forgotten set of *Waterworld*. At this rate, my feet would have rotted long before we reached the Brecon Beacons. We'd been wading through ground water for hours. Enough was enough.

Harri turned and saw I hadn't moved.

'I'm not walking through there,' I announced.

Ignoring me, he pointed to a square of green squiggles on his OS map. 'There's a footpath will take us down the valley. It's here, see, on the map. We've just have to find it on the ground.'

I looked at the 'path' ahead; not that there was any sign of an actual path, just a field full of those distinctive bog-loving grasses which sway menacingly in the breeze.

'I'm not walking through there,' I repeated, then watched open-mouthed as Harri strode off purposefully in the direction of a wire fence running through the middle of a pond. He looked back, expecting me to follow as I generally do. I didn't budge.

For hour after hour, I'd had no choice but to traipse across waterlogged hills in torrential rain. I was soaked from the top down and the bottom up. My pants were damp when I put them on and saturated now. My feet were certain to be wrinkled and prune-like, but what terrified me most was the likelihood of blisters - blisters of the magnitude of the agonising 'Somerset blisters'. Blisters would almost certainly mean an end to our hike.

'What you waiting for?' Harri called over his shoulder.

'I am *not* walking through there,' I told him for the third and final time.

I'm afraid at this point we had a minor altercation (Harri prefers the term 'hissy fit'), and I made a great display of marching back to the track. In my defence, it was obvious the route was going to be impassable in all but the driest conditions, therefore it seemed pointless following it if we weren't going to be able to use it as part of our recommended route.

Harri is a pretty even-tempered human being, but even he can get a little hot under the collar when his orientation skills are called into question. And to be fair, we had spent every hour of the day together for over a week now. The occasional bickering was to be expected.

I marched off up the track with as much dignity as it's possible to muster when you resemble something from the deep.

On top of everything else, I was getting a little worried about our (lack of) arrangements with Shane; I'd been really looking forward to our social evening but the lack of any mobile signal was putting our plans in jeopardy.

I hadn't progressed far along the track when Harri caught up with me. Fortunately, he was in a conciliatory mood; he still thought people might prefer to walk around the perimeter of Llyn Gwynant, but could see my point and had decided he was going to instruct people to follow the lane rather than lead them along a water-logged footpath.

As we neared Beddgelert, he suggested a change of plan. Instead of traipsing into the village with our rucksacks, why not pitch our tent at Cae Du Campsite, freshen up and *then* go in search of Shane? This made sense; now we were walking along the valley floor with towering mountains either side there was zilch chance that I'd get a mobile signal.

After the horrors of the morning, the weather had taken an unexpected turn for the better. Snowdon, that iconic peak so frequently obscured by cloud, was suddenly there behind us, rising magnificently against a clear blue sky. It was such a shock to see the summit that I kept turning around to make sure it wasn't a mirage.

There's a second, much smaller lake in the Nant Gwynant valley, Llyn Dinas. At around 60 acres, Llyn Dinas is less than half the size of its neighbour, but the scenery from the lakeside paths is glorious. The lake gets its name from the nearby hill fort of Dinas Emrys, but just looked like a small wooded hill from our perspective. The fort is said to have provided shelter for King Vortigern, who escaped into Wales from the invading Anglo-Saxons. After his death, Dinas Emrys passed into the ownership of the Romano-British war leader Aurelius Ambrosius, from whom the hill fort derives its name (Ambrosius was also known as Emrys Wledig).

Llyn Dinas is not without its own glamorous associations. Scenes in the popular film *Inn of the Sixth Happiness*, starring Ingrid Bergman as the missionary Gladys Aylward, were shot on the lake. Legend also identifies Llyn Dinas as the site of a battle between Owein, one of Arthur's greatest warriors, and a giant. There were a lot of giants in Wales at one time!

It's amazing how rapidly my mood improves when the sun is shining. Our disagreement forgotten, Harri quickly erected our tent while I did the laundry. With all thoughts of rain and wet weather fading, we pegged out our washing and changed into clean clothes for our evening out. We still hadn't made contact with Shane but Beddgelert isn't Cardiff, and I was confident that the first person we asked would know exactly where we could find him.

Actually, I wasn't far wrong on that count because when we went into the local post office/grocery/off licence, the lady behind the counter did know Shane and she told us he'd called in several times that day. There was just one snag – she had no idea where he might be right now or even where he worked. Fortunately for us, the Beddgelert postmistress is one determined lady. Several phone calls later she'd established where Shane worked – the National Trust property Craflwyn Hall on the edge of Beddgelert – and the fact that he wasn't actually there right now.

As our manhunt continued, we took comfort from the fact that Beddgelert is not a big place and all the local gathering places are within a stone's throw from one another. With just 455 people living in Beddgelert (Census, 2011), how long could it be before we ran into my long-lost friend? Especially as he would also be looking for us.

Beddgelert is one of those picture-postcard pretty villages which attract zillions of tourists during the summer months. Its proximity to Snowdon means it's become a popular base for serious climbers, hill-walkers, and even sedentary types who are content to gaze up at Moel Hebog and Cerrig Llan from the valley below.

For a long time, the village's name was linked to a 'legend' involving a devoted canine and his hot-headed owner (who just happened to be Llywelyn the Great); even now, there remains a 'grave' alongside the river, which is dedicated to the animal.

The inscription on the grave tells the tragic story of Gelert, the dog who saved his infant charge from a wolf only to be mistaken for the child's attacker. The English wording reads as follows:

> In the 13th century, Llywelyn, Prince of North Wales, had a palace at Beddgelert. One day he went hunting without Gelert 'the faithful hound' who was unaccountably absent. On Llywelyn's return, the truant, stained and smeared with blood, joyfully sprang to meet his master. The Prince, alarmed, hastened to find his son, and saw the infant's cot empty, the bedclothes and floor covered with blood. The frantic father plunged the sword into the hound's side thinking it had killed his heir. The dog's dying yell [sic] was answered by a child's cry. Llywelyn searched and discovered his boy unharmed but nearby lay the body of a mighty wolf which Gelert had slain. The Prince, filled with remorse, is said never to have smiled again. He buried Gelert here. The spot is called Beddgelert.

In Wild Wales, George Borrow embellishes the legend further. Faithful to the end, Gelert dies 'in the act of licking his master's hand', after which, 'Llywelyn mourned over him as over a brother, buried him with funeral honours in the valley, and erected a tomb over him as over a hero'.

It's enough to make the hairs on your neck tingle, but sadly the story is not true. In the late eighteenth century, David Pritchard, landlord of the Goat Hotel, was keen to promote tourism in the village and so publically connected the familiar faithful dog legend to Beddgelert. Disingenuous or ingenious?

There is no evidence that Gelert ever existed, but what is said to be his tomb lies under a willow tree in a meadow; a bronze statue of Llywelyn's best friend stands alongside it.

Meanwhile, the truth is pretty humdrum; it's now generally conceded that Beddgelert got its name from an eighth-century Christian missionary called Celert or Cilert.

In the early hours of September 21, 1949, something *did* occur in Beddgelert that was far from humdrum and this time there was evidence to prove it had happened. After a series of what were described as 'dull explosions', a meteorite weighing 794 g smashed through the roof and an upstairs ceiling of the Prince Llewelyn Hotel. And had a local miner not recognised it the uncommon black chrondite for what it was then it might have been tossed onto someone's fireplace.

Shane or no Shane, it was good to be back. We were last here in March 2014 when Harri was working on a new version of the AA guidebook *50 Walks in Snowdonia and North Wales*. On that occasion, we stayed at nearby Porthmadog; however, in April 2012 we rented a cottage in Beddgelert for a week and hiked up Snowdon via the tough Watkin Path (parking is at Bethania on the A498 Beddgelert to Capel Curig road).

Anticipating freezing temperatures on the summit, I had piled on the layers – and stripped everything off again as we followed the path through woodland and emerged under the sun's warm rays. As we climbed, the wind picked up and the temperature plummeted; the various items of clothing I'd stuffed into my rucksack or tied around my waist quickly found their way back onto my body. I was glad I'd listened to Harri that day; it's so easy to get caught out in the mountains. Warm clothes can be lifesavers when mountain conditions suddenly change for the worse.

Harri had chosen one of the toughest routes to the summit. The eight-mile Watkin trail ascends 3,400 feet from just above sea level, representing the biggest climb of any of the routes. Depending on which way you look at it, this could be considered a bonus (it means you're likely to get the mountains to yourself for most of the route), or a negative (there's less likely to be anyone around if you do find you need assistance, e.g. with navigation).

The path was named after the Liberal MP and railway owner Sir Edward Watkin, who had a summer home in Cwm Llan, the ruins of which the path passes. A track leading to the (by that time closed) South Snowdon Slate Quarry already existed so Sir Edward went about extending this to Snowdon's summit. The Watkin Path thus became the first designated footpath in Britain and was such a significant step in opening up the countryside to walkers that it was officially opened in

1892 by none other than the prime minister of the day, William Gladstone. The 83-year-old addressed a crowd of over 2,000 from a rock near Plas Cwmllan, his theme being 'Justice for Wales'. Gladstone Rock, as it is now called, bears a memorial plaque, which helpfully informs passers-by how Gladstone's audience responded by singing 'Cymric hymns and "The land of my fathers".'

And another interesting snippet: scenes from the 1968 comedy *Carry On ... Up the Khyber* (the sixteenth film in the popular series) were filmed on the lower part of the Watkin Path in 1968. In 2005, a plaque at the precise location was unveiled by actress Angela Douglas, who played the Khasi's daughter Princess Jelhi (and incidentally was married to the English actor Kenneth More until his death in 1982).

The Watkin Path starts off easily enough, but gradually becomes steeper and rockier underfoot, until you're almost scrambling up the final section to the top (by which time all five layers were firmly wrapped around my shivering body!). When we finally reached the Snowdon Summit Visitor Centre, Harri surprised me by choosing a warming cup of tea over an alcoholic beverage, testimony to the dramatic drop in temperature as we climbed ever higher.

Prince Charles famously described the previous, very ugly 1930s summit cafe as 'a carbuncle'; however, if you can accept the concept that facilities/refreshments are needed on Wales's highest mountain (and many can't), the current glass-fronted granite building with its Welsh oak-lined walls and lines of poetry (from former National Poet of Wales, Gwyn Thomas) is probably as good as it's going to get.

The £8.3m Hafod Eyri (meaning 'summer residence in Snowdonia') opened in 2009 and was designed by architect Ray Hole to withstand extreme weather conditions, i.e. winds over 150 mph (twice hurricane force), over five metres of rain (have I mentioned Wales is wet?), and temperatures as low as -20°C excluding wind chill. Rain water is used to flush the toilets; alas, the extreme weather (and potential vandalism) ruled out running facilities with solar and wind energy.

During the centre's construction, many workdays were lost due to high winds, and when gusts hit 42 mph, the builders were forced to disembark from the train at Clogwyn and walk the remainder of the way. Building continued through two of the wettest summers on record and in snow; it sounds tough, but I suspect if the construction team worked only when weather conditions were ideal, we'd be waiting until the *next* millennium for the project to be finished.

Snowdon's visitor centre – it goes without saying that it's the highest building in Wales – also acts as a terminus for the Snowdon Mountain Railway, which operates from Llanberis (and incidentally transported all the building materials to the summit). The railway dates back to 1896 when passengers were greeted by a cluster of wooden huts around the summit cairn.

You detect a sort of 'them' and 'us' feeling when you reach the summit. Many of those lining up for photographs next to the cairn have handed over up to £35 (Heritage Steam Experience) for the two-and-a-half-hour round trip and are enjoying their thirty-minute stop with a coffee or a pint (let's face it, a train journey can be thirsty work).

Those of us who have legged our way up thousands of feet of rugged rock face are immediately recognisable. We're the ones huddled on the benches, frozen fingers wrapped around a mug of something hot. We've taken all the photographs we'll ever need on the long, slow ascent and now we're just trying to thaw out before we set off again on the long, slow descent. Moreover, we have utter disdain for those who have opted for an easy ride to the summit.

On a clear day, the views from Snowdon are incredible and apparently extend as far as Ireland, England, Scotland, and the Isle of Man. We weren't so fortunate but still enjoyed the magnificent vista across Snowdonia's mountains, with Anglesey's green fields laid out below like a patchwork of tiny squares.

Despite the allure of Snowdon, Harri decided not to take the main 'O Fôn i Fynwy' route to the summit because he believes weather conditions (and not an arbitrary and inflexible route) should determine whether an ascent to the summit is feasible (and safe) or otherwise. Instead, he outlines an optional detour, which we both feel is sensible given the landscape and its propensity for extreme weather.

But while we didn't have a mountain to climb on this occasion, we did have a long-lost friend to locate and, believe me, even in a place as small and friendly as Beddgelert, finding Shane was not to prove easy. Despite help from the postmistress, we still hadn't managed to track him down. We called in several hotels but it seemed no one had heard of a newcomer called Shane.

Harri thought it best to retire for a pint and consider our options so, after checking the name of its chef at reception, we settled down in the window seat of the Tanronnen Inn (from where I figured we could keep an eye on village activity).

Then, as we sat there supping our drinks, a miracle happened. There was still no mobile signal; however, a Facebook message had arrived. It was from Shane, sent an hour and a half earlier. 'Had to go back home,' he wrote. 'I'll be back in the village about 6.30 p.m. for some fish and chips.'

It was now just after half six so, fearing we might miss him again, I sprang from my seat and charged across the bridge (there's not a huge amount of traffic in Beddgelert) towards the chip shop.

There were no customers inside so I explained my predicament to the friendly lads behind the counter. They pointed to a lone man occupying a nearby bench seat. Maybe that was my long lost friend, they wondered?

I craned my neck. The man certainly looked like he was waiting for someone. He didn't look like the Shane I remembered but it had been three decades. Until that moment, it hadn't occurred to me that I might not recognise him, might walk past my old friend without even realising. I studied the stranger again. He was certainly the right age; however, even allowing for the passing of time, he didn't look remotely familiar. 'He's from Holland,' one of the lads chipped in helpfully. So not Shane then.

I dashed back to the Tanronnen Inn and Harri, ignoring the curious glances from people sitting outside. When you're part of the running community, it feels perfectly natural to inject a little bit of speed into everyday life.

I quickly messaged Shane our destination and we settled down to wait. Of course, I recognised him the moment I saw him striding across the bridge.

Reunions with long-lost friends can go one way or the other, so I was relieved when, after the first few minutes of polite questioning about what we'd each done with our lives, we fell into an easy rapport.

Shane insisted on treating us to a meal at Hebog, a cafe by day and a candlelit bistro by night. The premises aren't too grand but manage to achieve the feel of a small, intimate restaurant. The food was delicious. I've long learned to expect disappointment where my favourite chicken caesar salad is concerned (a Wetherspoon pub once served it without any dressing at all, let alone the Parmesan cheese) but on this occasion the chef delivered a perfect meal. Harri and Shane also enjoyed their curry and lasagne respectively.

After we'd eaten, we wandered a little way along the river before settling outside the Prince Llewellyn Hotel where we were quickly driven inside by the relentless midges. Needless to say, we all drank more alcohol than is good for us though not quite enough to lose track of the time.

We walked along the now deserted main road with Shane and past the terraced stone cottage which we'd briefly called home back in 2012. At the turning to the campsite, we said our farewells and hoped our paths would meet again, though if we wait another thirty years, I doubt it'll be while I'm undertaking a long-distance hike.

As we tipsily approached our tent, the final glimmers of light were disappearing behind the mountains; above us, the stars were out in force. Out of season, the campsite was quiet and peaceful. On nights like tonight, I can almost convince myself I like camping, but of course, the advent of bad weather changes everything and tomorrow morning was to bring some of the most torrential rainfall of our entire trip.

For photographs visit uk.pinterest.com/thewalkerswife

JUNE 10: BEDDGELERT TO PENRHYNDEUDRAETH

After a remarkably good night's sleep – no doubt aided by copious amounts of cider – we awoke to the pitter-patter of raindrops and the gusting of wind. My heart sank. Not more rain. Under the stars last night, I'd convinced myself that the worst of the weather was over. It was supposed to be summer, after all.

If the return of foul weather wasn't bad enough, my waking face was aflame with angry lumps. The midges that had driven us crazy last night had feasted on me just as enthusiastically as I'd tucked into my chicken caesar salad. From my hairline to my chin, there wasn't an inch that wasn't itching like crazy. I distracted myself with morning chores, like taking in last night's washing, now wetter than when we had hung it out.

The toilet/shower block is one of the nicest we've encountered. Each spacious cubicle boasts a good-sized shelf set right back from the shower where you can place your towel, clothes and other essentials. This seems such a practical solution to the age-old problem of keeping one's smalls dry that it's amazing so few campsite showers have shelving.

There's a shop onsite and I was amused to note they were selling Avon's Skin So Soft; many (though not Avon itself) claim this body lotion/spray to be a panacea for avoiding insect bites. Others don't believe a word of it and stick to applications containing Deet, like Jungle Formula. I guess the jury's still out on this one, but setting off across Wales without either was probably not one of my better ideas.

Great facilities aside, there's a wonderful sense of peace and tranquillity at Cae Du, despite its proximity to Beddgelert along a riverside path. The site is bound to be busier on fine weekends and in the school holidays, but on this weekday in early June there were very few people around and we had the toilets and showers pretty much to ourselves.

We needed to stock up on supplies so we headed back to Beddgelert Post Office where we were able to update the postmistress on the previous evening's happenings *and* stock up on nibbles (including the ever-so-naughty Kendal mint cake for me).

We finally left Beddgelert around ten, and had made little progress along the pretty Fisherman's Path when the heavens emptied. What is it about us and Beddgelert? The weather was dire last time we'd followed the River Glaslyn through the Aberglaslyn Pass and now history seemed intent on repeating itself.

It's not only that I hate getting wet – which I do – but there's also the danger factor. The large flat slabs that form the popular path get really slippery when they're wet. And there are the jutting boulders to consider – and circumnavigate. Several hand-holds have been secured into the rock face at the most perilous and narrow points; however, ducking and diving with a large rucksack on your back is a skill I've yet to acquire. Consequently, my balance was all over the place and Harri walked with his heart in his mouth, expecting me to topple into the gorge at any minute.

Just before the gorge narrows, we'd passed across a footbridge beside a railway bridge. The bridge is part of the narrow gauge Welsh Highland Railway, which first opened in 1923 but closed in 1937 when the slate industry – and demand for the railway – declined.

The railway runs 25 miles from Caernarfon to Porthmadog and has a station at Beddgelert (it was reopened in 2009 after being closed for 73 years); there is actually a level crossing on the riverside path. The endless popularity of steam railways in Wales makes it hard to believe that there was actually some local opposition to the plans to reopen the station at Beddgelert. Fears that it would increase traffic in the village were taken so seriously by WHR that there is no car park and no direct road access to the station (access is via public footpaths).

After the terrifying experience in the gorge, I'd have been perfectly happy to stick to road and solid ground for the rest of the day. As it was, we were soon leaving the perfectly pleasant tarmac lane and joining a water-logged mountain track.

The amount of lane walking 'allowed' on a route is something we argue about all the time. Unfortunately, pavements and roads are anathema to Harri so whenever we do veer onto tarmac, I can be pretty certain we'll be hopping over a stile to rejoin a footpath or track at the first opportunity. Me, I'd prefer to walk on man-made surfaces when the alternative is a boggy mountain or field of bullocks ... like today.

In good weather, the views from this area near Nantmor must be stunning. Even today, when the cloud was low and the rain unrelenting, there was plenty to admire, not least the spectacular views of the long tidal estuary of the Dwyryd marking the beginning of the magnificent Llŷn Peninsula. At low tide, the sand seemed to stretch for miles.

From here, the nearest mountain is the superbly-named Cnicht (pronounced with a hard 'c' if you're wondering). Like Ceredigion's wonderful coastal bus service, the Cardi Bach (which sadly is no more – another casualty of local government cuts), Cnicht is a name I find myself wanting to repeat ... *repeatedly*.

Harri tells me the name originates from the English word 'knight' (because the mountain is supposed to look like a knight's helm). In Middle English, the 'k' in knight was pronounced (think Monty Python) and this has been retained in the Welsh word. Cnicht. I just love it.

Those wishing to climb Cnicht frequently do so from the village of Croesor. At the far end of the village there's a gate across the main track, presumably to keep out sheep, but giving a whole new meaning to the phrase gated community.

Again we left a solid surface to plough across more waterlogged moorland. It's one thing being aware of Snowdonia's geology and its propensity for soddenness, another to squelch across it for mile after mile.

Whether I'm hiking or running, I dread climbing hills and generally approach any downhill section with gusto so it's rare to be faced with a descent that's so steep you almost wish you were walking up it. Still, at least the surface underfoot was hard and, for once, dry.

For reasons known only to me, I'd decided today was a good day to start wearing shorts (Harri's legs were beginning to take on a lovely sun-kissed glow while mine were still horribly pale). Of course, it was a big mistake to think I could dress for summer in the second week of June and I was chilled to the bone by the time we began our descent into Penrhyndeudraeth. I reassured myself with the knowledge that once we'd set up our lovely, warm, spacious tent (!!!) on this gloriously sunny late afternoon (!!!!) I could abandon the madness that made me think of shorts and Snowdonia in the same breath and wriggle back into full-length, if rather grubby, trousers.

Not that the prospect of spending a second night under canvas filled either of us with enthusiasm (more like dread). As we'd discovered in Moelfre, there's nothing more miserable than lying in your sleeping bag when it's still light outside, listening to the wind gusting and raindrops splashing onto your tent.

We braced ourselves for a long evening and headed for Penrhyn's sole campsite (locals don't bother with the full four syllables), where we were immediately struck by the lack of tents. Caravans, yes. Big posh recreational vehicles, yes. But tents? Not one. Anywhere. Hope was gurgling up inside me. Maybe this campsite didn't take tents. And with it being the only campsite within miles that could only mean one thing: we wouldn't be able to camp tonight *no matter how much we wanted to*. I suppressed a whoop of happiness as we wandered around the deserted campsite. No tents. We looked at the slate-grey sky, then at each other, and shook our heads firmly. Not a tent in sight. It would have to be bed and breakfast then.

Have I mentioned that I've never been a fan of camping? I put it down to the fact that I never went camping as a child. If my mam thought spending a week in my Auntie Min's four-berth caravan was slumming it (every trip she would devote her first day's holiday to scrubbing it from top to bottom), then she absolutely drew the line at sleeping under canvas.

After my miserable pre-pubescence camping experience, I wisely abandoned tents (and Girl Guides) for many years. I might never have stepped foot in a tent again had my first husband's best man not started selling the damn things on commission. Before you could say Jack Robinson we were the proud owners of a three-bedroom luxury model costing over £300.

Two more camping holidays – in north Wales and Cornwall – did nothing to change my view that camping is for masochists. After our divorce, I subsequently led a blissful and tent-free life for many years.

Then I met Harri and discovered that long-distance hiking is nigh impossible unless you have a tent or happen to be a millionaire. We're not wealthy so a tent it was. First, a family-sized one with three bedrooms, which took an age to erect and was not exactly practicable for most purposes and then a two-person Vango. It's just about long enough for me to curl up in a sleeping bag with my rucksack at my feet but there's so little headroom that Harri can't sit up inside without hitting his head on the 'roof'. The lightweight Vango has enabled us to walk continually for days – and I loathe every khaki-green inch of it!

Our romantic notions of wild camping in picturesque countryside alongside the cascading waters of a mountain stream weren't quite turning into reality. True, the night near Penmon hadn't been too bad, but our Carneddau experience had put us both off wild camping for a while.

Penrhyndeudraeth dates back to the second half of the nineteenth century when the land it's built on was reclaimed by the drainage of stagnant marshes. Today's High Street is actually the site of a former lake and the street names reflect this, e.g. Glanllyn (lakeside) and Penllyn (the furthest side of the lake).

It's another of those places which, while located within a stone's throw of some of Snowdonia's most beautiful scenery, has been overlooked by tourism. We struggled to find accommodation and wandered up and down the main street several times before we eventually found somewhere to stay.

The Croeso/Welcome to Penrhyndeudraeth sign intriguingly adds the line 'First Networked Village in Wales' underneath. At the time of walking we had no idea what this meant, but a little research revealed that the title dates back to 2002 when internet-ready PCs were being rolled out to households and online training and support was being provided to proactively encourage communities to get online. Thirteen years later, a pre-internet world is hard to imagine and the sign seems as antiquated and irrelevant as those sad claims that this or that community won a Best Kept Village award back in the 1980s (justifiably provoking the question 'And never since?').

As we quickly discovered, this Welsh-speaking village just two miles from the ever-popular Portmeirion has little to get excited about, just a supermarket and a few takeaways. It ended up in the news in June 2011, however, when the new landlord of the Royal Oak pub was charged with pulling an air rifle on customers who continued to order drinks in Welsh after his partner banned them from doing so. He was eventually handed a 32-week suspended jail sentence in September 2012 for the lesser charge of possessing a firearm in a public place.

Penrhyn stands on one side of the Afon Dwyryd and tomorrow we needed to reach Llandecwyn on the other side where we would be joining the 24-mile Ardudwy Way, which would take us all the way to Barmouth.

There was a slight problem. The official Wales Coast Path currently diverted walkers inland and work was underway on a new road and railway bridge, complete with footpath. The plan was that the Grade II listed 154-year-old wooden Pont Briwet Bridge would remain open throughout construction work; however, it was closed permanently in January 2014 amidst safety fears. We had no desire to waste a day walking a route that would be history by the time 'O Fôn i Fynwy' was published so Harri decided the best option would be to catch the replacement bus to Llandecwyn (trains stopped running when Pont Briwet Bridge closed).

Pont Briwet Bridge is actually a great example of a tautological place name, in this instance repeating the meaning of the place name not twice but three times, the words 'pont' and 'briwet' both meaning 'bridge'.

Despite an unpromising start, our night in Penrhyn turned out to be quite pleasant. We found a room at the comfortable Cae Gwyn Bed and Breakfast where we turned the heating up and sizzled contently as the skies grew ever blacker outside. At some point, I toddled off to a Chinese takeaway and bought a bottle of cider to drink with our meal, but other than that, we were happy to mindlessly watch television and sit out the weather. It was all a far cry from the wild camping we'd envisaged.

A BBC weatherwoman promised the weather was about to change for the better and (I swear) even used the word 'stable' – a brave promise indeed when you're talking about the UK in general and north Wales in particular. We allowed ourselves to hope.

Perhaps it was the wind howling outside, but sleep was slow in coming tonight despite our warm bed and cosy surroundings. My body itched like crazy and I kept succumbing to mad bouts of scratching.

Believe me, the delights of the great outdoors are greatly exaggerated!

For photographs visit uk.pinterest.com/thewalkerswife

JUNE 11: PENRHYNDEUDRAETH TO BARMOUTH

With memories of our gruelling walk along the west of England coast between Chepstow and Watchet still fresh in our minds, we set off from Holyhead determined to stick to sensible daily distances. No point pushing ourselves to the point of exhaustion, we agreed; we had a whole month to do this.

The problem is that like most people, we're incapable of sticking to our self-imposed rules as today's epic hike was to attest. Not that we set out this morning with the intention of walking all three sections of the Ardudwy Way.

We woke to more of the same in terms of weather. While we looked out onto a grey, cold and blustery morning, the London-centric BBC forecasters waxed lyrically about the wonderful weather the UK was experiencing. Harri has a keen, some would say obsessive, interest in all things weather related, and he was confident things would improve very soon. I wish I had as much confidence, but it's very difficult to think sunny thoughts when the evidence outside your window tell a very different story.

The Ardudwy Way was devised in 2010 and officially launched during the Barmouth Walking Festival in September 2011. The official guide describes it in the opposite direction to the way we'd be tackling it, i.e. Barmouth to Llandecwyn, and splits it into three sections:

> Southern: Barmouth to Tal-y-bont, 8 miles
> Central: Tal-y-bont to Harlech, 13 miles
> Northern: Harlech to Llandecwyn, 12 miles

(The extra miles take into account walkers leaving and re-joining the Ardudwy Way each day.)

Most notably, this mid-level route runs parallel to the Rhinogs, with the high peaks on one side (our left) and the (mostly not visible) sea on the other. There are no villages or facilities en route.

Knowing this, but not wishing to leave the route overnight and add extra miles, our plan was to stop at a campsite at Dinas roughly halfway along the route. Twelve miles seemed a sensible distance to aim for on a day when we were being forced to start later than usual due to circumstances beyond our control.

We thought it best to be at Penrhyndeudraeth railway station in plenty of time, just in case. There was no indication that those of us who needed to cross the estuary should wait in any particular place so we just 'stationed' ourselves at the roadside and hoped for the best.

We needn't have worried because within minutes a minibus appeared to take us on our eight-mile journey through Maentwrog; better still, there was no charge. Our female driver was a jolly individual who regaled us with banter about this and that, before remarking on a very recent announcement that the new railway crossing would open on 19 July. Our fellow passengers – all locals – viewed this news with outright scepticism. (And they were right to be sceptical. While the new railway crossing opened that autumn, the road crossing and cycle path are not now expected to be ready for use until the end of June 2015.)

My ears pricked up when our driver started talking about a race that had taken place the previous weekend and the traffic chaos that had ensued as queues of vehicles waited for runners to pass through. I realised she must be talking about the Welsh Castles Relay, a popular annual race organised by the Cardiff running club, Les Croupiers. The race is a two-day, 20-stage, 211-mile, staggered relay race (each runner starts at a set time and doesn't need to wait until his/her teammate finishes the previous stage). The route starts at Caernarfon Castle in the north and finishes at Cardiff Castle.

In 2014, an amazing 65 teams entered the relay, including my own club Lliswerry Runners. I wasn't free this year, but I don't think I'd be tempted by the Castles Relay anyway; the terrain is hilly and the sections long so it's not really a race for less-than-brilliant athletes (which counts me out).

The bus driver told us she'd got so fed up of queuing that she offered the female runner at the back a lift (it was refused of course!). Her comments raised a laugh and I suppose I do understand how difficult it can be when you're stuck in traffic and you have a timetable you must adhere to, but it was clear our driver just didn't 'get' the spirit of athletic events. The last runner might have been bringing up the rear, but she was still putting in a tremendous performance and giving an incredibly tough race 100%. She deserved support and admiration, not derision from impatient drivers.

Within months of its launch, the Ardudwy Way won the *Lonely Planet* award for the 'best reason to buy a pair of hiking boots'. I'm guessing they mean proper, ankle-high, waterproof boots and not my own lightweight variety which, though comfortable, were probably not the ideal footwear for the boggy foothills of the Rhinogs.

The track was solid enough as we began the initial ascent from Llandecwyn. Before long we reached St Tecwyn's Church, one of many isolated Welsh churches in picture-perfect locations. I wondered how many would-be preachers had been lured to the ministry by the prospect of spending one's working life looking down on the panoramic estuary views across Portmeirion and the Llŷn Peninsula. Unfortunately, low-lying cloud and sea fog combined to obscure those views today, leaving us to imagine how beautiful the landscape might look in clearer weather.

The current church is relatively modern, dating from 1879, but there was once a much older church on the site, the remains of which are evident in a small stone basin on the south wall and an eleventh-century memorial to Tecwyn, who founded the first mission church here in the sixth century.

St Tecwyn's was the inspiration for the Small Pilgrim Places Network, set up by the late Reverend Jim Cotter, a writer and theologian. Reverend Cotter first went inside the little church in September 1997 and afterwards described it in his journal as, 'Benign, a little forlorn, the life of the spirit latent but not far away. Needs loving into life.'

And that's what he did: breathed life into the rarely open church by offering it as a place for quiet prayer, reflection and thoughtful conversation to passing 'pilgrims' of all faiths. He sensed people sometimes sought a place 'where they could breathe free' and, for him, St Tecwyn's was that place. Over time, Reverend Cotter assumed the role of 'hospitaller' and inspired others to volunteer and make tea or coffee for visitors and engage them in 'thoughtful conversation'.

This inspirational human being was also a great lover of the outdoors, a visionary who likened the miles walked to the passing decades of someone's life. His final post was as vicar of St Hywyn's at

Aberdaron (the church where R. S. Thomas was vicar from 1967 to 1978) from where he would walk the eight miles to the tip of the Llyn peninsula 'imagining that each mile represents ten years of my life'.

Reverend Cotter urged people to walk with others from each of the eight decades, to share memories and hopes for the future. 'It's a very pilgrim kind of way of spending a day out,' he concluded.

Reverend Jim Cotter died of leukaemia in April 2014, barely two months before we arrived at St Tecwyn's. I often think how sad it is when we learn of a kindred spirit's existence too late.

On a warm, clear day we might have lingered longer in this peaceful spot, perhaps savouring the views as we ate our elevenses, but it was cold up here and there was still no sign of a break in the weather and so, with heavy hearts, we headed inland.

The Ardudwy Way itself is named after a historic commote (an administrative area in the Middle Ages) between the Dwyryd and Mawddach rivers, and we should have had views of the medieval Harlech Castle, perched atop its rocky spur. Though it wasn't our intention to leave the route and head towards Harlech, it was disappointing to see nothing of the castle that UNESCO considers to be one of 'the finest examples of late 13th century and early 14th century military architecture in Europe'.

An hour or two later, we spied an even older relic: the burial site at Bryn Cader Faner, whose thin stone slabs leaning outwards from the circle have been said to resemble a 'crown of thorns'. Around 30 feet in diameter, it was 600 feet off the main route but the brief detour was well worth it. This impressive prehistoric monument comprises a series of slabs leaning at angles from a blanket of large rocks. There were once more slabs – perhaps as many as 30 – but, incredibly, the army used them as targets for gunnery practice before the Second World War.

From this point, the Ardudwy Way follows a Bronze Age trackway and passes several ancient burial, ceremonial and settlement sites, some from the later Iron Age. Interesting as all these ancient mounds and stones were, I was getting a little preoccupied with my feet. For hours now, we'd been walking across saturated moorland, and if I didn't end up with blisters then I was becoming a likely candidate for foot rot.

We splashed along the track, catching the occasional glimpse of the higher peaks. I wasn't sure I cared for the Rhinogs. Bleak moorlands have a certain appeal in the sunshine, but on an overcast and miserable day like today, when the views were limited and the ground underfoot sodden, I think I'd have preferred to have tackled the ironing.

While we were walking the Cambrian Way a few years ago, Harri tackled the Rhinogs alone and in dreadful weather (it would have been impossible to rely on public transport so it seemed sensible for me to act as chauffeur and pick him up at the end of the day). The Rhinogs aren't the easiest of walking terrains in perfect weather – there is a lot of bare rock, rough boulders, and few obvious footpaths – but they become treacherous in bad conditions.

In his guidebook to the Cambrian Way, Tony Drake acknowledged the tyranny of these rocky mountains, writing: 'The Rhinogs section of the Cambrian Way is at the same time the most demanding, the most rewarding, the most controversial part of the whole route and the one part where there is no accommodation.'

At the outset, his vision had been to create an official promoted route; however, establishing consensus on where that route should go, or indeed whether it should exist at all, proved so controversial – both Brecon Beacons and Snowdonia National Parks opposed the idea as did Dyfed, Gwynedd and Powys county councils – that the project was originally abandoned.

The British Mountaineering Council North Wales Committee's main opposition to the project was including the Rhinogs. Their members were concerned about safety and the belief that national trail designation would 'encourage peak baggers and merit badge enthusiasts into difficult and remote areas'.

Tony Drake eventually decided to go ahead with his unofficial route – and to ignore advice and include the Rhinogs. Whether you agree with him or not depends on how much risk you are prepared to take when out hiking.

Harri's own experience of the Rhinogs had only confirmed his own concerns that these were not mountains to be tackling in poor visibility, heavy rain or high winds. Having risked life and limb traversing these mountains in the middle of summer, he refused to put others at risk. He understood that long-distance hikers are generally unwilling or unable to hang around waiting for the weather to improve. Most people walking the Cambrian Way would be on a tight schedule and would decide to tackle the Rhinogs when they reached that stage of the route, regardless of conditions. Harri believed it would be irresponsible to lure walkers into potentially dangerous situations and I wholeheartedly agreed.

Unlike the Cambrian Way, the Ardudwy Way is a mid-level route and, despite several steep climbs, the terrain is generally not too arduous for a hiker of average fitness. For me, the downside was that despite the route being so close to my beloved coast we walked for hours with no sea views.

There was a really tough section when the path all but disappeared and we seemed to be clambering up and down fern-covered boulders. This was one of my favourite sections of the route; lush and green and dotted with stone farmhouses and outbuildings.

At some point during its midsection, the trail follows a steep section of old drovers' track; this not only provided easy access to grazing on the mountains above but also allowed the sheep and cattle to be driven from local farms to markets beyond Offa's Dyke. Back in the 1990s, the BBC produced a drama series called *Drovers' Gold* which told the story of the Welsh cattle drivers and their running feud with the landowner of their tenanted farms. The drama was set in 1843 and followed the drovers' journey to London and their adventures *en route*. I'm sorry to admit that I missed it, particularly as one of my nicest university mates, Keith Dixie Dixon, appeared in it. Sorry, Dixie.

If there are any advantages to experiencing bad weather in the mountains, it must be that it encourages you to walk faster. With low-lying clouds obscuring mountain summits and distant views, I had scant inclination to photograph the bleak landscape, or even to stop and eat. Thus, we found ourselves marching along the Ardudwy Way, until very slowly the clouds lifted and the promised sunshine finally made its appearance.

By the time we reached the midway point of the route, the miserable, grey morning had transformed itself into a warm, sunny afternoon. In fact, Dinas Farm looked so enticing in its idyllic lakeside setting we almost regretted our mid-morning decision to push ahead to Barmouth. It would mean walking the entire Ardudwy Way in one day but, as we were more than capable of covering 24 miles, we weren't unduly concerned.

Famous last words. No sooner had we passed the only place where we could have stopped, than the reasonably flat terrain decided suddenly to get hillier. And hillier. As the hours ticked by, I grew wearier and wearier, until by six o'clock I felt like I was losing the plot. Who in their right mind would tackle this monster of a walk in one day, I raved at Harri. It wasn't as though we'd set off early; the closure of Bridge-Bridge-Bridge had made sure of that.

We spent an inordinate amount of time skirting around the base of Moelfre, one of the outlying peaks of the Rhinogs, before heading for a high mountain pass called Bwlch y Rhiwgyr (Pass of the Drovers). This pass has been used as a route to and from the Ardudwy coast since people first settled in the area and was, until the eighteenth century, on the main route between Harlech and London.

Incidentally, Ardudwy apparently features prominently in Welsh mythology, but as the closest I've ever got to the Mabinogion is watching my older daughters perform in a musical, Welsh-language, primary school performance of the story of Blodeuwedd (in which, bizarrely now I think of it, the school caretaker had a starring role) then I'm perhaps not the best person to go into detail.

Across the valley the pass looked depressingly high; on the bright side, it looked relatively close. When, oh when, will I learn? You'd think I'd done enough hiking to realise that because something *looks* relatively close, it doesn't necessarily mean it *is* close. Not in terms of getting there on foot anyway. Having taken an age skirting around Moelfre's entire base, we were now found ourselves heading up a valley *away from the pass.*

At times like this, I start asking rhetorical questions. *If Barmouth's on the coast, how come we're heading inland? Who in their right mind thought it was a good idea to walk the entire Ardudwy Way in one day?* The answer to that one, of course, is me! When I really hit rock bottom, the questions get really desperate. *Why did we leave our mindless, boring jobs in local government to fulfil our dream? Whose stupid idea was it to walk the length of Wales? What is the point of this existence?* Etcetera, etcetera.

Thankfully, Harri does what any rational, level-headed person would do: he ignores me. Fortunately after eight years of walking together, he understands I have a tendency to become mildly unhinged when I'm physically exhausted; he also knows I'll retract every word I've uttered once I'm sitting in a pub with a half of cider in my hand!

The one – the only – highlight of the whole valley detour was a gorgeous little stone bridge we crossed. Pont Scethin now appears completely isolated but this route once bustled with activity; as well as being used by drovers, the track and bridge are claimed to be part of an old coach road (though how the coach wheels didn't get stuck in the wet ground is beyond me). We hadn't passed a single person since we set off from Llandecwyn, yet once upon a time hordes of people and livestock passed over the Afon Ysgethin on their way between Harlech and Dolgellau. I think I'd have liked to live in a time when the pace of life was so much slower, when walking was the only way for most people to get anywhere.

At some point during the unrelenting circumnavigation of Moelfre, it dawned on Harri that this very long day's hiking was not likely to be ending anytime soon and it might be best to phone ahead and book some accommodation in Barmouth. His mother, back home in Henllys (and frequently catapulted into a tourist information role during our various hiking expeditions) supplied us with telephone numbers for several guest houses. We were fortunate that the first Harri contacted – Crystal House – had a double room available. I was pretty sure this was the friendly establishment where we'd stayed for three nights in August 2011 but Harri couldn't remember. We'd have to wait and see.

The descent from the Rhinogs to Barmouth provided some of the most spectacular views of our Welsh journey so far. From the moment you emerge through the pass, the landscape opens up dramatically to reveal the dramatic peaks of the Cadair Idris mountain range on the far side of the Mawddach estuary. This is the scenery that pulls visitors to Snowdonia time and time again; you don't need to be a long-distance hiker to appreciate the stark beauty of those majestic peaks, finally freed from the clouds and bathed with late evening sunshine.

Barmouth is one of my favourite Welsh seaside resorts and it was down there, far below; we couldn't see it yet but it was definitely there, tucked around the corner. As we'd climbed the steep and rocky track to Bwlch y Rhiwgyr I'd consoled myself that that would be the last hard *uphill* slog of the day. After all, when you're standing over 1,600 feet above sea level and your destination is down there on the coast, it's not unreasonable to assume the remaining few miles will all be downhill.

But we were in Wales, a country famed for its mountains. My sigh of relief had been premature.

The final descent into Barmouth was incredibly steep. It was nearing nine o'clock and our legs, our feet, and our backs were aching. In the foreground, sheep grazed between rocky outcrops before the land appeared to drop abruptly onto the rooftops of tall Victorian terraces basking in the warm glow of a fast-sinking sun. At high tide, the Mawddach estuary with its mountainous backdrop was picture-postcard perfect.

At that moment, all I wanted to do was abandon our hike, hang up the boots and spend the rest of June in Barmouth. The long-promised summer had finally arrived, we were back at the coast, and I was in no rush to leave paradise.

(When he'd finished plotting today's route on mapping software, Harri was surprised to learn that during the course of today's 25 mile section, we'd done roughly 4,593 feet of climbing. To put it into perspective, remember the summit of Snowdon stands at 3,560 feet above sea level. It's no wonder we could barely put one foot in front of the other by the time we reached Barmouth.)

For photographs visit uk.pinterest.com/thewalkerswife

JUNE 12: BARMOUTH TO ABERGYNOLWYN

I was right about Crystal House; it *was* the same guest house we'd stayed last time we visited Barmouth. Back then, I'd just taken redundancy from my local government job, and I was still in that honeymoon phase when I thought the world was my oyster and an amazing opportunity would soon fall in my lap (sadly, it didn't).

With the exception of our first day, the weather wasn't great (and was mostly dreadful); while Harri tackled various nearby sections of the Cambrian Way, I ran, hiked, browsed shops, read and devised the plot for a Mills & Boon novel about a Welsh vet that I've never got round to writing.

It's probably fair to say that Crystal House isn't one of the more luxurious places we've stayed; however, its young owners, Steve and Katie, were so friendly and accommodating on our first visit that I was delighted we'd inadvertently arrived there again. The establishment is in a great location, right on Barmouth's promenade but at the far end, past all the fast-food outlets and amusement arcades. From the dining room window, you look out onto grass, sand and sea.

Katie, bless her, didn't bat an eyelid when we finally rolled in around 9.20 p.m. the previous night, assuring us that with Steve out fishing, she'd have been staying up late anyway. A warm welcome like hers makes all the difference … and is far more important to us than luxurious furnishings (which we're usually far too tired to appreciate anyway).

We had a good cooked breakfast and a chat with Steve about this and that: his fishing trip, the Barmouth lifeboat, the future of the ill-fated community of Fairbourne just across the estuary (the village is expected to enter into managed retreat from the sea in 2025 with more than 400 homes likely to be abandoned by 2055) and the pros and cons of running a B & B.

One of the best things about long-distance hiking is getting the chance to chat to people from all walks of life. I enjoy this social element of our trips so much I often get carried away and forget the *real* purpose of our being wherever we are: to get those daily miles walked. For Harri, my well-honed conversational skills are a mixed blessing. He admits that he'd probably not talk to anywhere near as many fascinating people if he was travelling and walking alone, but he does get frustrated when these conversations slow us down (particularly the breakfast conversations as he's always itching to get going).

We finally said our farewells to Katie and Steve and headed back up the promenade. What a difference a day makes. Yesterday, we'd left Penrhyndeudraeth in cold drizzle under grey skies; twenty-four hours later, the skies were clear and we could already feel the warmth of the sun on our skin. A good night's sleep had done wonders for our energy levels too. Where last night we were limping into Barmouth, this morning we were positively bouncing along.

Barmouth's palm-tree lined promenade looked splendid and positively balmy; the wide expanse of white sandy beach with waves lapping gently along its shore was more reminiscent of a southern California resort than north Wales. A deckchair attendant was lining up old-fashioned stripy deck chairs in readiness for a busy day, while three donkeys waited patiently for the first riders of the day.

Barmouth was one of many UK resorts that took a battering at the beginning of 2014, when waves crashed over the sea defences. Back in 2011, Harri and I sat *inside* the wonderfully atmospheric fifteenth-century Last Inn supping a pint or two alongside a mountain spring and freshwater pond (the mountain itself forms part of the pub wall). Unfortunately, the Last Inn was just that little bit too close to the sea to escape flooding.

It wasn't only the historic pub that was damaged by the ferocity of the elements; the road into Barmouth was badly flooded, a café owner had to be rescued by boat, and residents at the local caravan park were forced to leave their homes. Altogether, fifteen properties were evacuated and the railway was littered with rocks tossed over the sea wall by waves. On a still, hot summer's day six months later, it was difficult for us to visualise the terrifying scenes back then.

Barmouth was set to be our final encounter with the Welsh coastline. From today, we'd be veering inland to walk through mid Wales before eventually turning eastwards proper at Llandovery. After yesterday's miserable experience in the saturated, unpopulated foothills of the Rhinogs, I wasn't ready to leave this wondrous place of sun, sea, sand, pavements and proper shops.

'Does 'O Fôn i Fynwy' really have to finish in Chepstow?' I asked.

Knowing where this conversation was going, Harri looked at me pityingly. 'We couldn't call it 'O Fôn i Fynwy' if it didn't finish in Monmouthshire, could we?'

I looked at the sparkling sea, the boats bobbing in the bay.

'Well, it's not as though anyone knows where it's supposed to end,' I persisted. 'It's a new route, and I don't see why it couldn't finish here in Barmouth.'

Harri's face said it all. When he's committed to a project, he is 100% committed. No ifs, no buts, he will see it through to the end. No amount of wheedling or pleading from me was going to change our plans. Today we would be walking to Abergynolwyn as planned and that was that.

And so it was with a heavy heart that I waved Barmouth goodbye, though not before we'd popped into Iceland and stocked up with supplies for tonight's dinner and tomorrow's lunch.

Meal planning on this trip has been difficult. We agreed not to carry a camping stove because even the smallest gas canisters are heavy, but as chief cook and bottle opener I was struggling to feed us without cooking facilities. Factor in the lack of refrigeration and the lack of durability and availability of fresh foods in small village shops and you'll begin to understand what I was up against. And no, we weren't exactly walking in the wilderness, but you'd be surprised how difficult it is to feed two people without the facilities we all take for granted. It meant we were eating far more processed foods than usual and an awful lot of Pringles!

What with one thing and another, it was after 11 a.m. when we finally left Barmouth. Not that I minded, but with a reasonably long day's walking ahead of us and a steep climb over Cadair Idris to boot, it was time to get going.

Three years ago, I crossed the 136-year-old wooden railway viaduct over the Mawddach estuary to meet Harri as he walked the final stretch of a section of the Cambrian Way, and I was immediately bowled over by the spectacular views both up the estuary and along the coast.

The original bridge was built by the Aberystwyth and Welsh Coast Railway in 1867 and was constructed entirely of wood. Thirty-odd years later, the drawbridge section was replaced by a swing bridge with two steel spans. A pedestrian pathway – now part of the Wales Coast Path – runs parallel to the single-track railway line.

Back in 2011, a 90p toll was charged between Easter and September; however, in June 2013 the couple who collected the toll left their posts and it is currently free to cross the 764 yards.

A word of warning here … well, two actually. First, this wonderfully scenic walking route has been part of the National Cycle Network since 1996 and is also open to motorcyclists. So, while it might be wonderful to stand awhile gazing up the Mawddach estuary or back towards Barmouth, it's a good idea to keep your wits about you.

My next warning comes as a direct result of a mishap that happened right in front of us. We were midway across the bridge when an older lady hurried past carrying a shopping bag. Suddenly, the heel of her sandal got stuck between the wooden slats and she went flying. The contents of her bag scattered and, unfortunately, the most important item she'd bought – a card for a friend who was celebrating her 100th birthday – slipped between the slats and tumbled into the water far below. We rushed to her aid, but she insisted she was fine and was more concerned about losing the card. Nothing I said would convince her that life would go on without that birthday card and despite telling me the accident had happened because she was late and rushing, she immediately turned round and rushed back to Barmouth.

The moral here is to wear sensible shoes when you're crossing Barmouth Bridge. Crucially, don't drop anything that's less than two inches wide!

At the far side of the bridge, we joined the Mawddach Trail and followed it along the southern edge of the estuary. This cycle path follows a section of the disused railway line which once ran from Ruabon to Barmouth (the line was another casualty of the Beeching cuts in the 1960s). While the path wasn't entirely new territory for us, we hadn't walked the entire stretch before.

I must admit to having mixed feelings about these so-called rail trails. While they are undeniably popular with cyclists, families and dog walkers (and many runners I know), they tend to be rather dull in terms of scenic variety. Many are lined with such dense woodland that all you have to focus on is the unending track ahead. There's nothing to dislike, but not a huge amount to get enthusiastic about either (though I have to admit that when walking in Wales the occasional flat terrain can be very welcome).

We left the trail at Arthog, a small village with just 1,000 residents. This sleepy little backwater might be a very different place today had nineteenth century entrepreneur Solomon Andrews realised his vision for a purpose-built quality holiday resort in the area.

In 1894, Andrews, who hailed from Cardiff, purchased several farms in the area and began building the first of what he hoped would be many terraces of holiday homes. Only three were actually completed – Mawddach Crescent, St Mary's Terrace and Arthog Terrace – because the surrounding marshy land proved spectacularly unsuitable for building (in fact, the end house of Mawddach Crescent and two in St Mary's Terrace collapsed soon after completion due to subsidence!). Not surprisingly, the project never quite reached its grand conclusion and was eventually abandoned.

We left the trail and crossed the road next to St Catherine's Church. The present building dates from 1914 when it replaced a former chapel of ease built in 1808. Nowadays, it would seem this lonely centenarian is convenient for no one; in 2012, the weekly Sunday service was cut to once a month and a Facebook page, last updated in May 2012, attracted just 16 likes. Though I'm not a churchgoer myself, I do have a certain fondness for the little churches and chapels we pass on our travels; there's a certain pathos in seeing buildings that were once the focal point of a community falling into disuse and disrepair.

From the village, we headed up a steep wooded gorge to Arthog Waterfalls. When we last were here in March, I spotted a £1 coin lying on the path so I kept my eyes firmly peeled just in case. Despite my heavy rucksack, I found the ascent up the meandering wooded footpath much easier than last time – which I embraced as a sign of my improving fitness.

Arthog Falls are certainly impressive; however, it's the natural beauty of the open mountainside directly above the gorge that always takes my breath away. There are times when mere words will not suffice, when the devastating beauty of a landscape cannot be evoked with a few well-chosen adjectives. The landscape above Arthog Falls is one such place. I'm not certain I could even pinpoint what it is about this place that renders it so special: the nearby mountains, particularly Cadair Idris, the large boulders strewn across the landscape, the beautiful stone clapper bridge over the stream? The landscape is all these things yet somehow it's much *more* than the sum of its parts. My only plea to anyone planning to visit Snowdonia is to take a few hours to explore this delightful place; no, it's not as awe-inspiring as Snowdon itself, or as bustling as at Capel Curig and Beddgelert, but it's equally wonderful in its own special way … and you'll often have it all to yourself.

This perfect spot was the perfect place to stop for our one o'clock elevenses (does time really matter when you're in the wilderness? Does it ever *really* matter?).

We'd passed a couple of hikers minutes earlier and, though I'm usually more than happy to chat to fellow walkers, I suddenly found myself really, *really* hoping they wouldn't decide to join us in our special place. My wish was granted as they veered off in a completely different direction and we settled down to quietly wash socks (Harri) and eat more Pringles (me).

Later, as we walked, I thought how different the landscape looks at different times of the year. Back in March, the endless lines of drystone wall blended in with the general greyness of the day, but today, they stood out from the green landscape, proud and timeless.

In the spring, we'd been impressed by an uninhabited stone cottage we passed. It was tiny – just one room – but the stonework was remarkably intact, with exposed beams and wooden struts supporting the roof. In the warm June sunshine, I could imagine someone living there, perhaps pursuing an eco-friendly lifestyle. It certainly didn't look any worse than many of the cheap European properties for sale on the internet, and there was a nice walled garden thrown in too. It's places like this that Harri and I envisaged stumbling upon when we needed to wild camp … though when we peeped inside, we were disappointed to discover our rural idyll reeked from years of livestock use.

We paused to look down on the Mawddach estuary, where at low tide Barmouth Bridge now presided over a narrow water channel and expansive sand banks. From this height, the resort was dwarfed by the towering craggy foothills of the Rhinogs behind and the sparkling ocean beyond. Man makes but a fleeting impression on the world, I thought. Two hundred years ago, none of those Victorian terraces existed; with predicted rising sea levels who knows what the Barmouth of 2215 would look like? One thing was certain, whatever damage human beings inflicted on the planet in the next two hundred years, Rhinog Fawr and Rhinog Fach weren't going anywhere in a hurry.

Our next stop was definitely on the tourist trail. Cregennen Lakes are frequently described as the most photographed expanse of water in Wales – and given the number of lakes and reservoirs in our small country, that's a pretty substantial claim. The name always seemed something of a misnomer as on our various visits, we could only ever see one lake.

Contrary to what most hikers see, there are, in fact, two lakes. The larger lake covers 27 acres and has a small island; it is this lake that everyone photographs. The smaller lake, at 13 acres, is less than half the size and is hidden from view on the main walking route.

At the lake's edge, we waited briefly while a couple heaved their eleven-year-old Labrador across the stile; it was clearly a practice they'd got down to a fine art, and the poor creature just lay there inert, long having accepting the indignity of being manhandled over an obstacle he would once have vaulted effortlessly.

We stopped for a chat with them, talking dogs, hiking and Wales. Like many of the people we meet on our travels, they love our country and visit regularly. One of their favourite destinations is the Llŷn Peninsula, a stunning landscape which didn't really fit into this specific long-distance route but a place that's close to our hearts and one we hope to revisit before too long.

While it now pains me to admit it, I didn't properly 'discover' Wales until I met Harri. I'd visited various towns and cities over the years: Cardiff (a mere 12 miles from home), Swansea (where my dad once lived), Wrexham (Urdd Eisteddfod), Aberystwyth (middle daughter, university), and most of the seaside resorts along the south Wales coastline; however, as a monoglot English speaker there were certain parts of my own country which felt alien. Vast swathes of inland Wales were unknown to me, most of Snowdonia was unvisited, and I'm ashamed to admit I had no inclination to visit anywhere north of Llandrindod Wells.

Like those people who embark on 'once-in-a-lifetime' trips to tour Australia and New Zealand yet have no interest in exploring their local beauty spots, I perhaps thought other nations had more to offer than Wales in terms of landscape, beauty and culture. How wrong I was and how relieved I am that I have had the opportunity to 'discover' Wales with a man who has such passion for this 'land of my fathers'.

As is frequently the case, once the visible 'half' of the Cregennen Lakes faded from view, we again found ourselves alone. The familiar mountain landscape was now dominated by Cadair Idris. In March, we'd been following a circular route back to the Mawddach estuary; today we were going up and over the big one. And it was getting hot.

We were soon passing the late Gwynfor Evans's summer home Ty'n Llidiart. The double-fronted stone house stands alone in a wonderfully isolated spot, the perfect place to escape the madness of politics.

The Welsh politician was president of Plaid Cymru for 36 years and became Plaid's first Member of Parliament when he won the 1966 Carmarthen by-election.

A committed Christian and pacifist, Dr Evans belongs to an exclusive club of people who managed to get the better of Margaret Thatcher. Furious that she had reneged on a Government commitment to set up a Welsh-medium television channel (S4C), he threatened to starve himself. His actions provoked one of the few U-turns from the woman who once publically declared 'This lady's not for turning'.

A little further along the footpath, we came across the dilapidated Rehoboth Chapel. While the chapel itself has fallen victim to the elements (and vandals?), the small sloping graveyard behind is well-maintained. Among the weathered stone gravestones stand several newer marble memorials, including one (in Welsh) dedicated to Gwynfor Evans and his wife, who was always known as Nannon (her birth name was Rhiannon).

Their names circle a simple cross and wording in an outer circle: '∘ In tender remembrance of ∘ Rhiannon Prys 1919–2006 ∘ Gwynfor Evans 1912–2005 ∘' with their various homes listed.

Underneath is poem in Welsh from their children, which roughly translates: '*On the marble are the names of parents who contributed their utmost*

to the continuation of the land of our fathers. United are the two in their diligence.'
Then, on its own line: *'Love never dies.'*

It was time to get going. We headed downhill through some lovely woods and past the wonderfully located Kings Youth Hostel. The scenery was absolutely gorgeous so I couldn't believe it when we followed a footpath through a farm. Despite being lucky enough to live in one of the prettiest parts of Snowdonia, the farm owners clearly had no qualms about using the land as their own private rubbish tip. It was an absolute dump and their complete disregard for the environment upset and angered me.

Harri grew up on a small dairy farm and, attempting to pacify me, he explained that farmers tend to hang onto things pretty much forever. My views on land ownership aside, I still think people have a responsibility to maintain the land they buy or inherit to a reasonable standard. On occasion, we've followed footpaths through farms where the stench was so bad (and not from livestock) that I had to hold my breath until we reached the other side. There is generally an uproar from neighbours when a town dweller uses their garden as a rubbish dump (and quite rightly); however, farmers living in some of the most unspoilt parts of Wales can seemingly show complete contempt for the environment without any fear of comeback. Grrrrr ... it makes me so mad.

By now it was getting really hot and, after several hours of climbing, we were tiring; it was time for lunch.

We'd just settled ourselves down at the top of a grassy slope and were absorbed in our own thoughts, when the tranquillity of the moment was shattered by men's voices – and they were using some very choice vocabulary. All became clear a few moments later when five mountain bikers emerged over the crest of the hill pulling bicycle trailers. Someone clearly hadn't done their research because they'd just cycled and pushed their way up a rocky lane with a hideously steep gradient. Of course, being perfect gentlemen, they stopped swearing the minute they realised a lady was within earshot.

We've walked up Cadair Idris once before (on a clear October day), on that occasion following the Minffordd Path on the southern side. The route had involved some tough scrambling over rocks as we neared the summit and I remember being surprised that although we'd seen hardly anyone during our ascent, there were lots of people enjoying the views from the top. Harri explained it was because most of those autumn mountain-baggers had chosen to scale Cader Idris via the more popular Pony Path, at around 3.1 miles the longest but easiest of the three main trails.

Earlier in the day, I'd voiced some concern about whether I'd be able to climb Cadair Idris in hot sunshine. I needn't have worried because it was 4.30 p.m. by the time we reached the busy car park at Tŷ Nant.

It's great that Snowdonia attracts so many visitors from all over the world – they certainly help the Welsh economy – but with so many mountains to go round, I wonder why everyone has to flock to the same few eroding summits. Cadair Idris itself is a huge magnet, presumably because it's so close to the coastal resorts. A 2013 report from Snowdonia National Park revealed that 49,240 people visited the mountain that year, slightly fewer than in 2012.

Perhaps there were fewer people on Cadair Idris in 2013 because they were all busy summiting the big one. 2013 was the busiest year on Snowdon since records began – an incredible 449,327 walkers and climbers used the mountain's main routes (up from 365,943 visitors in 2012). I suppose it's natural to want to climb Wales's highest mountain but *there are other peaks.*

Most visits to Wales's mountain tops take place in August or on Saturdays – and (I'm making a supposition here as no statistics exist) the majority of hikers will choose to start their ascent before noon – so this being tea-time on a Thursday in June, we would probably be safe from the madding crowds.

The Pony Path is so-called because it was originally used by local people who used ponies to transport foodstuffs like flour and butter over the mountain to the market at Dolgellau. Later, in Georgian times, it was used by ponies carrying wealthy, and dare I say it, extremely lazy people who demanded the visual rewards of the summit (on a fine day, the views are magnificent) but were loath to put in any physical effort themselves. How those poor little ponies must have struggled up the steep rocky terrain; thankfully, nowadays there's no way to reach the top of Cadair Idris but to walk, which is how it should be.

According to Welsh legend, the mountain was named after a giant, Idris, who would sit above his kingdom on the rocky crag of Cwm Cau studying the stars, composing poetry and philosophising. It is said that anyone brave enough to sleep on Idris's bed will awaken as a poet or a madman.

The popularity of the relatively easy (and safe) Pony Path has inevitably resulted in erosion and much of the path has now been restored using large slabs of stone. The clearly defined path means it's practically impossible to get lost. That is, unless you're a young person participating in the Duke of Edinburgh Award.

These youthful outdoorsy types (or not!) have provided us with much hilarity over the years. From Easter until June, we see them dotted all over the Welsh landscape, generally huddled in groups and poring over their (brand new) OS maps. When they do get going they're generally quite energetic, despite the enormous packs the poor things are made to carry, but from what we've seen, they don't *keep* going for long.

I don't know a whole lot about the DoE award, but presumably the sole purpose of the whole 'stagger around the Welsh mountains with the equivalent of a large sheep strapped to your back' is to engender some sort of team spirit, so you've got some real concrete evidence to back up those essential words 'team player' on your Personal Statement and your Curriculum Vitae (though what benefit is gained by being a team player in the modern dog-eat-dog workplace is questionable but that debate is for another time). And herein lies the problem – too many cooks. When destined-for-leadership William studies the map and instructs everyone to head in a sort of southerly-easterly direction, the diplomatic James shakes his head and quietly insists it should be southerly-westerly. Meanwhile, entrepreneurial Duncan has spotted a short cut: they can 'do' the whole walk and have time left for the pub if they cut across that ridge over there.

We see it time and time again. Boys are the worst because they won't admit to being lost and so don't ask for directions (though we have, on occasion, noticed how a huddled group has watched us pass and then waited a suitable amount of time before trailing after us). Girls, on the whole, are far more willing to ask for help, frequently waving a map under Harri's nose and demanding 'where are we?' I really shouldn't mock as my own map-reading skills haven't really improved since O-level Geography (which I failed) but sometimes we do despair.

On this occasion, we were halfway up the Pony Path when we heard a commotion coming from the vicinity of two large pillow lavas outlined against the skyline. It's incredible when you think that these rocks, near the top of one of Snowdonia's highest peaks, were actually formed underwater about 460 million years ago – sort of makes geology really exciting (which it is, of course!).

Back to the present-day and a group of young people had emerged from behind the pillow lavas. Harri and I saw the bulging rucksacks and nodded at one another knowingly – DoE participants. Surprisingly (because most young people in Wales are quite friendly and amicable no matter what you've heard) only one of the group even acknowledged our presence as they bounded downhill past us. Minutes later and – you've guessed it – they were in a huddle around a map and there they remained for an age. A fit-looking outdoors type passed us on his descent and we half expected the young people to accost him as he neared but they didn't even look up.

From our now much higher point on the mountain, Harri deduced they must be looking for a footpath they'd already passed. They were probably lost but we weren't too concerned; it wasn't yet 6 p.m. and, this being the second week in June, there were hours of daylight remaining. We suspected their teachers wouldn't start looking for them for another hour or so … most likely on a different mountain altogether, the one they were supposed to be climbing!

As we were ambling up the lower section of the path, a lady of around my age stopped us and said she'd just commented to her companions that she didn't know how we could walk up the track carrying such enormous rucksacks. After all the doubts I'd harboured at the outset about being too old for backpacking, her words struck a chord. In that instant, I realised that my fears had been unfounded. This was my eleventh consecutive day of walking with a heavy rucksack and I was heading up one of Wales's highest mountains in warm sunshine without too much difficulty. I could do it! The funny thing is, compared to the humungous backpacks the DoE guys and gals were carrying, our own no longer seemed so bad.

The plan wasn't to climb all the way to the summit of Cadair Idris; while it's certainly a fantastic summit and features as an 'optional extra' in Harri's guidebook, we've done it before. Besides, the clock was ticking and we still had miles (and miles) to walk.

Our descent was via a grassy track and, although the higher summits were now behind us, Snowdonia's scenery was still dramatic with lots of drystone walls and long-abandoned farmhouses peppering the steep, grass-covered slopes (it seems no-one wants a house without vehicle access anymore).

It was hot and airless lower down the valley so when we came across a mountain spring, Harri did the only thing a man can do – he leapt in fully clothed. I think he'd have liked slightly deeper water (it barely covered him even when he lay down) but he insisted it was refreshing and that I should join him. I felt like a real spoilsport but I've been so paranoid about getting blistered feet that I didn't want to risk getting them wet with so many miles left to walk.

On evenings like this, it's impossible to imagine wanting to be anywhere other than high in the Welsh mountains. Everything is so green, so lush … undulating and gorgeous. I think perhaps the sun was getting to me a bit by this point because I kept hanging behind taking photographs.

Two magnificent black horses spotted me and came galloping over to the gate to say hello (another photograph). I hate seeing horses in fields alone but these two had one another for company and a very large field to cavort in. They seemed very content with their lot and indeed, who wouldn't be, living in a landscape like this?

At some point in the valley, we passed a ruined homestead (Ty'n-y-ddôl). Within what little remained of the stonewalls, was a monument to Mary Jones, 'who in the year 1800, at the age of 16 walked from here to Bala to procure from the Revd Thomas Charles, B.A. a copy of the Welsh Bible, this incident was the occasion of the formation of the British and Foreign Bible Society'. Phew (the punctuation is theirs by the way)!

Mary had become a Christian at the tender age of eight, but her parents were poor and couldn't afford to buy her the Bible she longed for. The determined child saved for six long years and, when she had enough money, she undertook the 25-mile journey to Bala, barefoot as always. In Bala, she was heartbroken to learn that there were no copies available; however, the Reverend was deeply touched by her despair and he sold her a copy already promised to another.

In fact, Mary's visit had such a profound effect on the Reverend Charles that he instigated the formation of the British and Foreign

Bible Society (now the Bible Society) four years later. When his calls for support from the richer echelons of society failed, the Reverend turned to the lower classes of England and Wales to fund the mass production of the Christian Bible. When they suspected people were giving more than they could realistically afford, the kind Reverend and his supporters would only accept a small donation.

Mary's Bible now resides in the archives of Cambridge University Library. The Mary Jones Heritage Centre opened in October 2014.

Two hundred years later and I wonder how many young people would walk 30 miles for a new Harry Potter novel let alone a Bible. And Mary herself must have had a keenly-developed sense of direction, for we've already seen what happens when many of today's young people are let loose in the wilds of Wales.

A little further down the valley and we passed another ruin linked to a determined and long-remembered individual. Castell y Bere was built by Llywelyn the Great (Llywelyn ab Iorwerth) and its site on top of a steep flat-topped rock would have provided an incredible vantage point over which the great man could survey the valley below. In fact (again according to the interpretation board), such was the importance of the site that Llywelyn took it from his own son Gruffudd in 1221 so he could build a castle there to defend his borders (one of the first sophisticated stone castles in Wales).

More than forty years after Llywellyn's death in 1240, Castell y Bere was taken again, this time by the English King Edward I who made alterations in the hope an English frontier town would grow around it. It never happened and the English finally abandoned Castell y Bere in 1294, just eleven years after they'd seized it.

While the scenery was faultless and the terrain perfect for tired feet (we were walking on secluded country lanes by now), we were now tiring rapidly. And with another night under canvas ahead of us, we needed to abandon our escapades into history and step up the pace. Craig yr Aderyn (Bird's Rock in English) rises 820 feet and is an important nesting place for many bird species, including 60 pairs of cormorants and the increasingly rare chough.

As we approached we could see someone up there on the Rock; a person silhouetted against the skyline and performing slow martial arts movements. Despite our fatigue, it was so tempting to climb this rocky outcrop and enjoy the last remnants of the evening light gazing down at the Dysynni valley.

But we didn't wish to intrude upon someone's meditation and Harri thought we should prioritise sorting out our camping arrangements before dark. Despite being sorely tempted, we agreed this climb was one best left for another time.

Though we'd speeded up over the last few miles, it was after 8.30 p.m. when we reached Llanllwyda Farm. There was no one around so we had little choice but to set up camp and leave the matter of payment until the morning.

I loved the campsite immediately. The surrounding crags and scenery was quite stunning, but it was the quaintness of the farm campsite itself that captivated me, the little personal touches. Like the stone slabs that made it possible to cross a small stream that flowed directly past the toilet block or the little kitchen complete with kettle, fridge and washing machine. The farmer's wife, who I suspected was a lady of more mature years, had posted numerous handwritten notes, all politely signed 'Mrs E. Williams'. There was a 50p charge for the showers, but once the coin was inserted, the hot water just lasted and lasted. Shower gel and soap was provided free of charge (it's these small touches that make all the difference, especially when you're carrying all your worldly possessions on your back). Even the midges weren't as bad as at Beddgelert – and with that happy thought in mind, I fell asleep.

For photographs visit uk.pinterest.com/thewalkerswife

JUNE 13: ABERGYNOLWYN TO MACHYNLLETH

Llanllwyda Farm looked just as pretty in the morning sunshine as it had done at dusk. The sounds of nature, too, were all around us: sheep in the field to our left, cows on a nearby slope, birds trilling away in the trees that dotted the campsite.

My midge bites had stopped itching quite as much and, as a result, I'd managed a half-decent night's sleep. Hallelujah. There's nothing worse than waking up feeling like you need a good night's sleep!

One of the hardest things about this trip has been the need to keep moving; sometimes it would have been nice just to stick around and have a mosey. Today, for instance, I'd have liked to have climbed Craig yr Aderyn before setting off. It probably wouldn't have taken long, being a mere minnow of a mountain by Welsh standards.

However, miles don't walk themselves and Harri was keen to push on, particularly as we'd strayed one mile off route to reach the campsite and now we needed to veer inland again towards Abergynolwyn.

But first, we needed to settle up with Mrs E. Williams at the farmhouse. We'd been right in supposing she was an older lady and she was a real dear; while chickens pecked around our feet, she deliberated about how much she should charge us before eventually deciding on a figure much lower than we'd expected. We got the feeling that she runs the campsite simply because she enjoys doing it, rather than any great desire to make money. One of our fellow campers, a man I'd guess to be in his early sixties, told Harri he's been coming to Llanllwyda Farm for holidays since he was a child, which is about the best recommendation any campsite can receive.

Tent packed away and breakfast eaten, we set off back along the pretty lane we'd walked the previous evening. Before long, we passed the early childhood home of Dr William Owen Pughe (1759–1835), author of the *Welsh and English Dictionary*, published in 1803, and other grammar books.

After two long, tough days, Harri decreed that we were walking just twelve miles today. When we reached Machynlleth we would stop, no matter how early in the day it was or how many miles we had left in our feet. It sounded like a plan. Twelve miles should take us up to mid-afternoon, meaning we could enjoy a leisurely browse around Machynlleth. We might not be able to purchase much (due to weight restrictions), but it didn't mean we couldn't go window shopping.

I celebrated my 50th birthday just outside Machynlleth. We stayed at the sixteenth-century Felin Crewi Water Mill which had been restored back in the 1980s and later converted to offer self-catering and bed & breakfast accommodation. We had a lovely few nights there, though I did manage to knock my head on one of the original low beams (and at five foot four inches that's quite a feat).

Interestingly, Machynlleth is the only point where the Wales Coast Path enters the vast and landlocked county of Powys. Mind you, you're not there for long. Just a few miles after crossing the Gwynedd/Powys border into Machynlleth, you're leaving again, this time to enter Ceredigion to the south. Blink and you could miss Powys altogether.

But first things first. Feeling well-rested and cheerful, we retraced last night's final mile along the lane and were soon heading towards Abergynolwyn on a grassy bridle track snaking along the slope of a steep, narrow valley above the Afon Dysynni.

We'd walked this pretty, meandering section in the opposite direction when Harri was commissioned to check out some routes for AA Publishing's book *50 Walks in Snowdonia*, and we liked the area so much we even recommended it to the Wales and dog-loving couple we talked to at Cregennen Lakes yesterday.

As we neared Abergynolwyn, we passed a rocky outcrop with a small iron ring embedded into the rock. We'd been intrigued by this on our last visit, but now knew it would have been used historically by local women to tether their cows on the lush valley slopes.

Abergynolwyn itself is a rather delicious little village located on the confluence of the Nant Gwernol and the Afon Dysynni (its Welsh name translates roughly as 'mouth of the river with a whirlpool').

The distinctive terraces of stone quarrymen houses alongside the stream were built in the 1860s to house workers from the nearby Bryn Eglwys slate quarry, where production was increasing thanks to the recently improved transportation links, i.e. the Tal-y-llyn Railway. The quarry's fortunes soared – at its peak in the 1870s it employed nearly 300 people and produced 300,000 tons of slate and slabs – and waned several times before it finally closed at the end of 1946.

These days, Abergynolwyn feels like a sleepy backwater, albeit an incredibly beautiful one and the villagers earn their living from farming, forestry and tourism. The old-fashioned signposts and lack of any discernible traffic only add to the impression that you've stepped back in time. We were impressed with a wooden sculpture outside the modern community centre. Sculptor Nanal Hemming created the two river nymphs from Welsh oak, referencing a legend where the Gwernol and Dysynni rivers merge in a whirlpool.

The climb out of the valley led us past grander terraces, presumably the residences of those who managed the quarries, and past Abergynolwyn station. Yes, despite the demise of the slate industry here, the Talyllyn Railway continues to thrive thanks to enthusiastic volunteers who put in hours of tireless work and the stream of passengers, both testimony to people's boundless love for steam trains.

The line opened in 1865 and runs for seven and a quarter miles through the Fathew valley from Tywyn (on the Cardigan Bay coast) to Nant Gwernol. The line beyond Abergynolwyn was originally used only by freight trains. The defunct railway might have been scrapped in the 1950s had it not been for the foresight of a group of enthusiasts who determined to save it (and the generosity of the owner's widow who allowed them to take over the running of the deteriorating line).

Fast forward sixty years, and the Talyllyn Railway now enthrals thousands of passengers every years as it makes its unhurried journey through the beautiful local scenery. Steam-railway loving romantics can even get married in the tea room at Abergynolwyn Station and can hire a steam-hauled train to carry them and their guests there. What a lovely idea.

Talyllyn also featured in the 1953 film *Railway with a Heart of Gold* by US film producer Carson Davidson, who described it as 'a relic, this railway, a bit of ornamental scrollwork lifted from the pattern of yesterday and kept, as a memento …'

Sadly, our early start meant we passed through Abergynolwyn long before the first train of the day arrived... maybe next time?

From the station, we climbed through the lush, sun-speckled woodland of the Nant Gwernol valley Again, the ravine wasn't virgin territory for us, though last time we were walking down the ravine and this time we were heading uphill. We passed a group of young people wearing buoyancy aids and hard hats, who were leaping into one of the natural pools formed as the river cascades down the ravine. Harri watched with a slightly envious look on his face, while I stepped surreptitiously back from the water's edge just in case … water sports have never really been my thing and plunging into an ice-cold pool in a Welsh ravine isn't high up there on my bucket list.

We were nearing the top of the ravine when we encountered a sign with those dreaded words plastered across it: 'Footpath Temporarily Closed'. And just to emphasise they meant business, someone had strung that familiar striped tape across the route.

I probably shouldn't admit this, but Harri and I generally ignore these bureaucratic dictates. Experience has shown that in almost every instance the path is in fact completely passable and has been closed presumably because over-zealous officials have identified that terrifying possibility – a risk. A few years back, a section of the Monmouthshire and Brecon Canal was once closed to walkers for months; it seemed not to matter one iota that you'd have needed to be blindfolded and three sheets to the wind to topple off the towpath into the (drained) canal. On the Usk Valley Walk, the identification of an 'unstable' wall sent officials into such a panic that they deemed it less dangerous to direct hikers onto a busy stretch of road.

Confronted with this unexpected footpath closure, we weighed up our options. Neither of us had any desire to retrace our steps *downhill* to Abergynolwyn and follow the road back *uphill* to reach a spot not very far from where we were now standing (when devising O Fôn i Fynwy, we've tried to avoid as much road walking as possible); however, if we crossed the river as the sign directed it was possible we'd end up heading in entirely the wrong direction.

We decided we'd follow our tried-and-tested approach: ignore the sign and push ahead. And wouldn't you just know it … this time, the footpath actually *was* impassable. Several trees had been uprooted and had slipped down the ravine's steep rocky side, tearing up the footpath as they tumbled. If we hadn't been carrying heavy rucksacks, it might *just* have been possible to scramble up the slope and around the missing footpath but the vegetation was thick and the slope just too steep. Besides, we certainly couldn't direct other walkers along such a precarious route. We had to admit defeat: it was road or bridge.

After much deliberation, we choose the latter and were pleasantly surprised by the high standard of the undulating paths and the ease with which we reached the top of the ravine. As we stood in the warm sunshine, congratulating ourselves on making the right choice, we had no idea everything was about to go badly wrong.

I used to think that when you chose to follow a published walk and it stated the route to be, say, eight miles, that the author had actually walked eight miles and no more. Ha! Since Harri has been writing walking books, I've realised that the distance the outdoor author covers in their determination to share the best possible walk with his/her readers tends to be more than the quoted ones – and sometimes an *awful* lot more (as our England Coast Path: Chepstow to Minehead experiences prove).

From the moment we spotted that first closed sign, we should have guessed today was going to be one of those days. Over the next few hours, we were confronted with confusing footpaths (in and around the quarry), footpaths that started well enough then mysteriously disappeared, footpaths that are there, bold as brass, on your OS map but have left no trace on the ground, etc.

In terms of terrain, tiredness and morale, today was undoubtedly our worst yet. The much-heralded summer had finally arrived but the unfamiliar heat sapped our energy levels and made the frequent climbing hard work. I had the benefit of a new and rather fetching khaki-coloured sunhat (purchased for £3 from a Cardiff charity shop) but Harri had to put up with the punishing rays of the sun bearing down on his head and neck (he'd left his own hat at home).

On the bright side, the hot sun was an excuse to plaster ourselves with Hawaiian Tropic; just a sniff of that stuff sends me straight back to the Isles of Scilly of the early 1980s. The horrors of sunburn hadn't been so well-documented thirty years ago and I remember how the 20-year-old me wilfully abandoned my mother's favourite Ambre Solaire cream factor 220 (far better suited for my fair skin) for what I considered to be the far more sophisticated and delectable-smelling Hawaiian Tropic. My liberal applications of the suntan *oil* ruined rather a lot of my beachwear, I recall, but hey, at least I smelt nice - and had a great tan.

After the lush vegetation and natural beauty of the ravine, the quarried landscape at Bryn Eglwys presented itself as a hideous blot on the landscape. I realise the quarrying industry brought much-needed work to rural areas like Abergynolwyn but is it possible for anything to devastate a landscape so completely and utterly as large-scale quarrying ? In fact, so ravaged was the landscape that I couldn't bring myself to take even one photograph.

Harri assured me that the scenery would soon improve, but emphasised that there was no other way of reaching Machynlleth except to follow this route up the ravine, past the quarry and up and over the mountain pass. At least we'd reach our destination mid-afternoon for a change.

So, in the muddle of abandoned quarry, meandering access roads and felled mountain slopes, we starting hunting for those elusive footpaths. This was Natural Resources Wales land and many footpaths, we feared, had been eradicated (or at least hidden) during the mass tree felling. It's a problem we've encountered across Wales and something which makes me livid, especially as Natural Resources of Wales states prominently on its website: 'Our purpose is to ensure that the natural resources of Wales are sustainably maintained, enhanced and used, now and in the future.' Presumably, walkers are not included in those groups they hope will use Wales's natural resources.

My next challenge was to cross an area of marshy ground without grumbling about wet feet. I failed... miserably ... because wet feet make me *really* miserable. Yet again, a promoted walk (Natural Resources Wales being the promoter on this occasion so I was wrong, they *must* want walkers to use the land) had been left to maintain itself. Just a few boardwalks here and there would have made such a difference ... in keeping my feet dry and my mood cheerful.

Knowing how much I hate wading through these marshy upland areas, Harri kept parking me in places with the two rucksacks (he can be gallant on occasions), while he checked out the various options. After several false starts, including an extremely steep scramble up a hill of slate (which thankfully was NOT the correct way), we finally got going again, crossed the beautiful old packhorse bridge of Pont Llaeron and headed towards a forestry plantation.

It was hot and sticky as we skirted the summit of Tarren y Gesail but at least the ground was firmer and the views were lovely. We were feeling far more cheerful as we began our descent and looking forward to wandering around Machynlleth, perhaps browse in some of the town's independent shops.

It was clearly going to be one of those days, however, because a few miles short of Machynlleth it all started going horribly wrong again.

We'd been forced to retrace our tracks several times because, despite very prominent footpath signposts, there didn't actually seem to be any sign of one on the ground, but by the time we were walking up a wide vehicle track we were feeling confident we were finally heading towards Machynlleth. Then I made a chance remark about how much taller the conifers seemed when your eyes followed them from ground level.

Hearing my words, Harri immediately pulled out his map. It transpired we were all back to front or at least the slopes either side of us were. The uphill slope on our right was meant to be running downhill and that descending land to our left … well, that was supposed to be heading uphill. We might be heading somewhere, but it certainly wasn't Machynlleth.

Grumbling about the misfortune of choosing a steep track in error on such a hot afternoon, we turned and made our way back to the wide area at the top of the track. Harri studied the map again, slightly bewildered by the configuration of turnings; the various tracks and footpaths we could see around us didn't seem to coincide with anything on the OS map.

We walked along a level road for a few hundred metres. While we continued deliberating about which route we should take, a car approached. The young male driver knew the forestry well and explained that we needed to follow a bridle track which started close to the track and went directly to Mack (he really did call it Mack, the only time we've heard anyone do that). He said local drivers occasionally used it as a shortcut, despite its narrowness.

We thanked him and returned to the 'crossroads'. If we ruled out our original path, the track we'd climbed in error and the level road, there was only one possibility left: a narrowish footpath. Somehow, I very much doubted this was the bridle track; it looked too overgrown to be used by anyone other than hikers (and clearly not very

128

frequently), but there seemed to be no other option so I trailed after Harri. You've guessed it. After about ten minutes of walking over more boggy *downhill* ground, Harri became convinced that we were once again heading in the wrong direction.

The trouble with walking through forestry land is that, unless a great swathe of woodland has been recently felled, it's practically impossible to see anything other than trees. There are trees to your left and trees to your right. There are trees in front of you, and if you turn around … even more trees. Consequently, Harri's growing conviction that we were NOT heading towards Mack (so much quicker to type) wasn't based on what he could see in front of us, but once again, on the discrepancy between the contours on his map and the slope of the land immediately around us.

Oh no, not again. The heat and endless backtracking was starting to get to us. Mack was down there somewhere, even if we couldn't see it. We just needed to work out how to reach it.

Energised by frustration, Harri sprinted back up the hill, instructing me to follow slowly so that if he determined we were on the right track after all, I wouldn't have trekked back to the top in vain. By the time I reached him, he had managed to work out where we'd gone wrong. The friendly local hadn't deliberately misled us, but knowing the area well, he'd failed to explain that the bridleway we were looking for was just beyond the rest of the tracks and paths. Had we walked another ten metres we'd have spotted it immediately. Hindsight is a wonderful thing!

As we descended, relieved to be finally walking on the right track, I was surprised to see signposts for the Wales Coast Path. Harri explained that the section of coast path between Aberdyfi and Machynlleth was routed across the hills above the estuary before dropping to the pavementless A493 road, which joins the busy A487 over the River Dyfi bridge crossing and into Machynlleth.

The general condition of the historic bridge (it was built in 1805 when traffic was considerably lighter) and its lack of a pavement have been a cause for concern for years. That it's prone to regular flooding and, as a result, frequent closure is also frustrating to local people who are forced to do a long inland detour at such times. Wales Coast Path and 'O Fôn i Fynwy' walkers will be pleased to hear the Welsh Government has announced a new bridge is to be constructed upstream, presumably to take vehicles from the current bridge. Sadly, this second crossing is not due for completion until 2018 so walkers have a few more years of traffic-dodging ahead of them yet.

It was late afternoon when we finally limped into Machynlleth. What should have been a short day's walking (nine miles) had ended up feeling like a marathon distance. My plans for some window-shopping thwarted, we decided to head straight for a pub to down a few much-needed pints at the Skinners Arms.

Despite the glorious weather, we'd already decided it was going to be bed and breakfast again tonight (dear me, we're not proving to be very hardy on this expedition). Fortunately, friendly landlord not only recommended a nearby B&B 'just around the corner' but even offered to ring them on our behalf.

We meandered past the town clock, one of the most instantly recognisable landmarks in Machynlleth. The clock, now demoted to the role of traffic island, was built by the town's residents to celebrate the coming of age of the eldest son of the Fifth Marquess of Londonderry, who lived at Y Plas. Charles Stewart Vane-Tempest, who was Viscount Castlereagh, turned 21 on 16 July 1873, but family bereavement put paid to the planned celebrations and the foundation stone wasn't laid until a year later on 15 July 1874.

In the twenty-first century it seems strange that the man on the street would be so keen to contribute towards a rather big present for the son of the local landowner, but I suppose things were done differently back then … and the ornate stone clock tower is rather a nice addition to the high street.

Machynlleth is a pretty enough market town but its real claim to fame – the reason most tourists visit – is its association with Owain Glyndŵr. Not that Glyndŵr was born in the town – neither did he die here. Machynlleth happens to be the location of his famous parliament of 1404 when he was crowned Prince of Wales (the Owain Glyndŵr Centre was built on the site). It was here that the charismatic Glyndŵr declared his vision of an independent Welsh state with a parliament, two universities and a separate Welsh church. Like the tenth-century Welsh king Hywel Dda (Hywel the Good), Owain Glyndŵr wanted a legal system that was just and good, where compassion was an important as punishment and where common sense prevailed. When you consider he also wanted women's rights recognised in law, you start to realise what a visionary this man was (remember this was 600 years ago) and why he was able to command so much loyal support in his long-running (but ultimately unsuccessful) revolt against the English rule of Wales.

A political visionary delivering a rousing oratory is a revolutionary idea in itself in this age of bland politicians trotting out their constant on-message sound bites pandering to the most recent public opinion.

Suffice to say, Machynlleth has embraced its Welsh prince in the way Bath has adopted Jane Austen and the Lake District Beatrix Potter. Let's face it, having Wales's greatest hero deliver his most famous speech on a street near you must be a gift from marketing heaven. So next time you find yourself strolling along Machynlleth's main street, be sure to keep your eyes peeled for all those references to the mighty one.

Our 'just round the corner' accommodation turned out to be nearly half a mile's walk away but maybe it doesn't seem so far when you haven't been hiking all day.

Once we'd settled into our room at the very nice Maenllwyd, I left Harri writing up notes and popped out to get food from the nearest chippy. Having intended to be out and back in ten minutes tops, I was a little bit taken aback to see the long queue on the pavement outside Hennighans Top Shop.

'Surely all these people aren't waiting for fish and chips?' I'd obviously voiced my incredulity because the man at the back of the queue turned.

'Best chip shop in Machynlleth,' he said, nodding at the overhead sign. 'Best in Wales, in fact.'

I was ever-so-tempted to ignore him and head back up the high street where I knew there was at least one other takeaway, but sensing my plans, the man shook his head knowingly. 'You'll regret it,' he said with some authority. 'These are chips worth waiting for.'

I rarely eat chips of the fried and wrapped-in-newspaper variety, not because I'm overly diet-conscious but because I find the British favourite quite dull in culinary terms. Who in their right mind would settle for fried slices of potato when there's even the possibility of something delicious involving tomatoes, garlic, herbs, cheese and olive oil? But now a stranger was promising me gastronomic ecstasy if only I could muster the patience to hang around on the pavement for half an hour.

I craned my neck. How far down the high street was that other takeaway? I was growing wearier by the second.

'You won't regret it,' my new friend repeated seductively in my ear.

Oh, what the ... and so it came to pass that I joined the longest chip shop queue *ever* for what promised to be the most delicious *pommes frites* in Wales. I was too tired to protest further. As it turned out, the fish and chips were very nice if you like that sort of thing, but I'm afraid deep-fried food will never be my meal of choice and I assure you that's the first and last time you'll find me lingering for 40 minutes outside a chip shop, only to be asked when I finally reached the counter, 'Have you pre-ordered?'. Of course, I hadn't. Nobody pre-orders chips!!

But far more interesting than chipped and fried potatoes was the story of Colm Farrell, recounted to me by my queuing companion.

In July 2013, Irish barman Colm set off to walk 5,000 miles through 86 counties in Scotland, England, and Wales. He walked 15–20 miles a day and used social media to find a free bed and food for the night. The Hazzard – as he was known to friends – planned to raise thousands of pounds for Ireland's anti-suicide charity Console without incurring any accommodation expenses.

The long-distance walk was Colm's third and on only one occasion had he failed to find a bed for the night. He'd passed through Wales way ahead of us, but it transpired that the warmth of the Welsh people had come to the fore and he'd had a hero's welcome in Machynlleth. The Hazzard finished his walk in Cornwall at the end of June 2014 and raised an amazing £100,000 for Console. What an amazing guy, eh?

I was intrigued by Colm's story, particularly because Harri and I are occasionally asked if we're doing whatever long-distance walk we're currently tackling for charity. The answer is always 'no', not because we're politically opposed to charity-fundraising (though there is an argument that certain services provided by charities should, in fact, be publicly funded) but because we'd feel disingenuous feigning altruistic reasons for doing something we enjoy so much. I'm much more inclined to donate to an unpleasant charitable feat, e.g. sitting in a bath of baked beans all day (now that's so disgusting that it deserves sponsorship!) than to part-finance even a tiny proportion of somebody's trip to the Great Wall of China.

Having successfully purchased one large cod and chips without pre-ordering, I was heading back to the Maenllwyd when Machynlleth delivered its final slice of excitement – a low-flying fixed wing aircraft flew right over my head. *Right* over.

If you spend any time in mid Wales, you get used to low-flying jets roaring past overhead; it's so common an occasion that even sheep, renowned for their timidity, rarely raise their heads at the thunderous noise.

The so-called Mach Loop where Royal Air Force jet pilots train is a system of valleys which stretch from Dolgellau in the north to Machynlleth in the south; flying can be as low as 250 feet. To the south of here, is a Tactical Training Area where, at specified times, the aircraft are permitted to fly as low as 100 feet.

This aircraft was flying so low you had to marvel at the pilot's skill in avoiding typical Welsh obstructions, like mountains and castles (fortunately there isn't one in Machynlleth). It was both thrilling and a little nerve-wrecking to be able to see the underside of a plane quite so clearly.

For some reason I couldn't put my finger on, I felt a bit glum this evening, a little homesick perhaps. With Anglesey and Snowdonia behind us, the Brecon Beacons still several days ahead and no more of Wales's stunning coastline to enjoy, I found it hard to summon up much enthusiasm for the next stage of our journey through mid Wales.

I was flagging, there was no doubt about it. Twelve days into our hike and I was once again wondering if I was ever-so-slightly old to be doing this. Walking through Wales with a heavy rucksack on my back? Who was I fooling? I might be physically fit, but why would I want to take myself away from everything familiar for no reason other than to walk?

Hiking would always be one of my passions, but perhaps I should knock long-distance backpacking on the head. I'd tell Harri tomorrow. Then I'd head home. Alone, if need be.

My decision made, I promptly fell asleep.

For photographs visit uk.pinterest.com/thewalkerswife

JUNE 14: MACHYNLLETH TO DYLIFE

I woke feeling energetic, adventurous and very, very fortunate. How many women of my age had the opportunity to walk the full length of their country with a handsome younger man, *their* younger man, I wondered?

Just over three years ago, I'd have been waking to face another soul-destroying day in the office, sending emails that frequently remained unanswered and attending too many meetings where my invitation was an afterthought. After more than a decade of tedium in a profession I'd never embraced, I saw my opportunity to escape and applied for voluntary redundancy. My only regret is I didn't do it sooner.

Like an animal that's been caged for years, I'd embraced my freedom enthusiastically, signing up for various courses, writing scripts and starting a novel, and, most significantly, embarking on our ebook publishing venture.

Now, after years of dreaming and planning, we were fulfilling Harri's lifelong ambition and walking across Wales. And despite being a grandmother of two, I was fit enough to walk marathon-length days over tough terrain. What on earth did I have to complain about?

The idea that age and fitness levels are not intrinsically linked resurfaced again over breakfast when we got chatting to an all-male group of cyclists who were completing a loop from Chepstow to Machynlleth via Brecon and Hay-on-Wye. They differed greatly in age and it seemed that the fitter members of the group – those who were having fewer problems with the daily distances – were the older ones. Of course, it could simply be that older people have more spare time than those with full-time careers and young families. In my running club, several of the men who do consistently amazing marathon times are in their sixties. Perhaps it's because we older outdoors types no longer take our general fitness for granted that we commit to feats that result in our fitness levels and stamina soaring?

Spending so much time in rural surroundings has made me realise what a townie I am deep down. I absolutely adore vast landscapes like Snowdonia and the Brecon Beacons; however, these past two weeks have forced me to realise how much I hate being deprived of my everyday 'essentials'... like internet access and *supermarkets*. I'm almost embarrassed to admit how much I'm missing supermarkets. The prospect of visiting a proper supermarket this morning had me almost giddy with excitement. Harri had to remind me – several times – that anything that went in the shopping trolley would ultimately have to be carried until it was eaten.

We were leaving Machynlleth along Glyndŵr's Way, which loops around Powys for 135 miles, starting at Knighton and ending in Welshpool. Unlike the waymarked paths we've followed so far, Glyndŵr's Way is a designated National Trail.

Never underestimate the importance of this status. Being a National Trail means a route is managed and maintained by Natural Resources Wales and not one of Wales's 22 local councils, whose various internal politics and changing priorities frequently result in the general neglect of footpaths.

Coveted National Trail status comes complete with a designated trail officer, someone who is charged with maintaining, adequately signposting and promoting the route. As a result, walking on a National Trail is usually a far more enjoyable experience than trying to follow local footpaths or councils' own promoted routes.

All National Trails display a distinctive acorn symbol on stiles, gates and signposts but Glyndŵr's Way also has its own logo, a dragon. According to the very informative National Trails website it usually takes around nine days to complete the trail and no one has yet attempted to set a record! I'm pretty certain Harri and I could cover more than 15 miles a day if we set our minds to it so maybe we should have a bash at it ourselves one day.

It still amazes us that the ambitious Wales Coast Path is not currently a designated National Trail, particularly as the England Coast Path (due for completion in 2020) is. However, we're hoping it's just a matter of time.

Another interesting snippet about Glyndwr's Way is that it joined the International Appalachian Trail in 2014. Using the memorable strapline 'Reuniting what oceans are dividing', the IAT aims to establish a long-distance walking trail across all the geographic regions once connected by the Appalachian-Caledonian orogen (a belt of the earth's crust involved in the creation of mountains) which was formed over 250 million years ago on the super-continent Pangaea.

Those behind the International Appalachian Trail hope it will connect people in different countries and cultures. As well as 'connecting people and places, the goal is to promote natural and cultural heritage, health and fitness, environmental stewardship, fellowship and understanding, cross-border cooperation, and rural economic development through eco and geo tourism.'

That's a pretty ambitious mission and one not likely to be achieved overnight. Each country that joins the IAT is known as a 'chapter' and Wales became a chapter in October 2010 along with England and Ireland (Scotland had been welcomed aboard four months earlier).

Glyndwr's Way was actually the third National Trail in Wales to join after Pembrokeshire Coast Path (October 2010) and Offa's Dyke Path (February 2013); the Wales Coast Path joined in December 2012. Perhaps, one day 'O Fôn i Fynwy' will be invited to join their illustrious ranks … but I'm getting ahead of myself now!

Anyway, after yesterday's bogs and disappearing footpaths, it was good to know we'd be on solid ground again today.

We left Machynlleth through the lovely grounds of Plas Machynlleth which, according to the slate plaque on a wall, 'were built and laid out in their present form by Sir John Edwards Bart (1770–1850) and were presented to the District Council of Machynlleth in 1947 by his great-grandson, the 7th Marquess of Londonderry … for their perpetual use and enjoyment by the inhabitants of this town and district'. Not for tourists or visiting walkers then?

Still, we were certain the Marquess wouldn't deny us our ten minutes of pleasure so in we trotted. Plas Machynlleth itself dates from the mid-nineteenth century (although a house existed on the site by 1673), and this striking mansion once played host to the Prince of Wales, later King Edward VII.

A less salubrious episode was the decade in which Plas Machynlleth masqueraded as a Celtic-themed attraction called Celtica. Thankfully, in 2008 the house was acquired by Machynlleth Town Council, which still holds meetings there. It also boasts an art gallery, shop and cafe, plus office and conference facilities and a 250-seat community hall.

As we wandered through these popular grounds, we couldn't miss the imposing slate monument erected by the Owain Glyndŵr Society in 2000. Wales celebrates its national hero on September 16 – the anniversary of Glyndŵr being named the Prince of Wales in 1400 (the last native Welshman to hold the title).

We left this pretty market town on the Machynlleth Town Trail (which forms part of Glyndŵr's Way). My heart sank when I saw the signage: Roman Steps. Fortunately, despite being very steep, there weren't too many steps – and neither did they look old enough to be Roman. While Romans did settle in the area, building a small fort at nearby Pennal, it's generally believed that the steps in Machynlleth are not their work.

The views from the grassy, well-marked track were faultless: gorgeous vistas back towards Machynlleth for the first few miles, followed by wonderful, undulating high moorland. We looked at the wooded slopes across the valley and tried to work out where we'd gone so wrong yesterday, but the thick forestry made it an impossible task.

For miles we walked on, enjoying the landscape and passing not another soul, walker or local. Harri was clearly in a generous mood (either that or his legs were as tired as mine) because at a point where there was an optional shortcut to avoid a steep climb, he uncharacteristically chose the lower level route. Later, on a winding country lane, he again chose the flatter option over a twisting and hillier detour. (The lack of a sunhat was clearly getting to him!)

Unfortunately, there was one monster of a climb that we couldn't avoid: the endless ascent to Glaslyn Lake. The lower section was really pretty and we were surprised to see rabbits bounding along the path a safe distance in front of us, disappearing into the bracken again as we came close.

Gradually – as we neared the top – the track became stonier and much steeper. Harri is much stronger on hills and stormed ahead, much to the consternation of some sheep peering over the crest of the hill. I lagged behind, wondering why hill-walking never gets any easier despite the years of practice (and all my running).

On our left, a ravine was becoming visible, though a perimeter fence kept me well away from the edge. These are the steep slopes

George Monbiot describes as looking 'like the hills of Afghanistan', a 'monotonous, impoverished moonscape' in his book *Feral* (2013). Peering down at the erosion gullies and lack of vegetation below, it's hard to disagree with him. The Cambrian Mountains are not one of Wales's most lush landscapes and, as Monbiot persistently argues, years of over-grazing by subsidy-pulling sheep has had a devastating effect on many hilltop habitats. If you need convincing, just take a moment to peer down at these barren slopes.

As we approached Glaslyn Lake, we spotted our first walkers of the day (the old car park rule never fails). A large teenage boy strode ahead purposefully, aided by poles, while his mother trailed so far behind her map-reading husband I feared she'd lose her family by the time they'd been walking ten minutes. After the horrors of the steep climb, I felt quite smug – fitness is relative, after all.

The 540-acre Glaslyn reserve is managed by the Montgomeryshire Wildlife Trust, which claims it is their 'wildest and most regionally important site'.

The usual interpretation boards were displayed prominently alongside the lake and we laughed as we read the wording. Far from claiming that this was some oasis of wildlife, the Trust seemed all too ready to admit there's not really much going on at Glaslyn. Under the heading, 'Why is it so important?' there follows the admission, 'the lake does not attract a lot of wildlife … one plant that survives in the lake is quillwort'.

We'd been undecided about what to do about tonight's accommodation but, as we'd probably camp at Devil's Bridge tomorrow night, Harri thought it might be an idea to stop at a B&B again tonight. The problem is the Cambrian Mountains are not exactly littered with such establishments; in fact, there's a real paucity of any kind of accommodation, even basic campsites. Ever the planner, he'd saved telephone numbers for two potential overnight stops on his mobile.

The Star Inn at Dylife was in the process of being refurbished and a nearby farm which offered accommodation was full. It was late afternoon and though we could have kept going for a few hours longer, the distance we'd be able to cover wouldn't be enough to reach anywhere likely to have accommodation.

It's at times like this that I despair of Wales. What was the Star Inn doing closed in the middle of June? Its remote hilltop location pretty much rules out any winter trade; it *needs* to be open when people are walking Glyndŵr's Way, the Cambrian Way, etc. Still, it's not for me to tell people how to run their business.

A few years back, we were walking the Pembrokeshire Coast Path on a baking August Bank Holiday when we reached a pretty little cove. There was a large pub/hotel right there on the beach so we decided to stop for a quick half before our picnic lunch. Imagine our shock when we discovered it was closed. There were tourists everywhere. What a missed opportunity for a great day's trading!

On another occasion, also on the Pembrokeshire Coast Path, I remember about twelve of us queuing outside the local pub in the early evening waiting for it to open so we could enjoy a pint and an evening meal. Somehow I can't imagine this kind of thing happening in a Mediterranean resort, or in London. I'm not naming names, but there are pubs in the Brecon Beacons which have such restrictive opening hours that it's a miracle anyone ever manages to order a pint in the time between the doors opening and them calling last orders.

I'm not decrying the hard work and dedication that many accommodation providers and publicans put in (running a pub is an awful lot tougher than sitting in an office nine to five), but if you have chosen to go into that line of work surely it makes sense to open when the punters are likely to show up?

It's hard to believe Dylife was once a thriving community with over 1,000 residents, three inns, a school, shops, four places of worship and a monthly fair. It's fair to say that you'd need a vivid imagination to picture this abandoned place in its heyday. Yet this remote location used to bustle with industrial and agricultural activity. In the nineteenth century, lead, copper, zinc and silver was mined here and huge waterwheels were part of the landscape. One of these – Rhod Goch (Red Wheel) – is believed to have been second largest in Britain with a 63-foot diameter. The excellent Abandoned Communities website has lots of information about Dylife's history.

Anyway, it seemed we were facing a problem. We either wild camped or we … wild camped. The idea of pitching our tent in this bleak landscape didn't exactly appeal; however, our predicament was exactly the reason Harri had carried a tent on his back since Holyhead.

We were still trying to talk ourselves round to wild camping (I personally favoured walking through the night; anything was better than a repeat of our Carneddau experience), when Harri spotted a sign pinned to a farm gate. It read: Bron y Llys B&B.

Deciding to investigate was probably one of the best decisions we've made on this journey. We assumed this hitherto unheard-of and unmapped accommodation must be located in what remains of Dylife proper, i.e. a few houses along the road and were heading in their direction when Harri realised that we'd arrived. Bron y Llys was right there on our left.

We pushed open the gate and ventured inside. In the large courtyard, three people were sitting at a garden table chatting animatedly, and making us wonder if we'd inadvertently strolled onto the wrong premises. Then one of the woman rose to her feet and greeted us warmly (we later learned this was the owner, Maya). Harri explained our predicament and asked if there was a double room available. We were told 'yes' and asked if we wanted to join the other guests for dinner that evening. We did have some supplies with us but the opportunity of a proper hot meal was too enticing to turn down so, once having established we weren't putting Maya out, we accepted her kind offer gracefully.

Maya must have sensed our weariness because she immediately invited us to sit down in the courtyard and enjoy tea and cakes with everyone. B&B owners take note: this is the kind of welcome we hungry hikers adore!

It transpired that the people she'd been talking to were Rachael and Steve, two paying guests who originally hailed from Bristol but had recently moved to Draethen, which is a stone's throw away from where we live in Rhiwderin. It is indeed a small world.

We were shown to a room called Hafan, which was located in a modern annexe to one side of the main house. The soft furnishings were absolutely fabulous and an opulent oriental throw covered the huge king-size bed. The room boasted windows on two sides and there was a proper writing desk underneath one (the presence of that simple piece of furniture impressed me so much, quite probably because it's so rare to stay anywhere where there's somewhere comfortable for me to write my notes). The bathroom was small but beautifully decorated and the white towels were definitely the thickest we've ever had.

On the tea-making side of things, there were proper mugs with saucers and lots of interesting tea-bags, including one to induce sleep (though after a day's hiking, I don't usually have any problems dozing off; to the contrary, I generally struggle to keep my eyes open after 9 p.m.).

When we were alone, Harri admitted he was concerned about the cost of all this luxury. We hadn't anticipated such luxury when we took the room and had felt too embarrassed to ask while Maya was showing us around. We looked through the information in our room. It said: 'Hafan is the Welsh for haven, refuge, sanctuary and that is what we hope this room and Bron y Llys will be for you. A warm, comfortable, peaceful oasis where you can find rest and relaxation.' Lovely words for a perfect place; however, we knew words like 'haven' and 'oasis' tend to be associated with high prices. On the other hand, we reasoned, Dylife was in the middle of nowhere and was more likely to attract passing hikers like us than those seeking luxury.

I reassured Harri that I'd contribute towards the cost, which we now suspected would be over £100. It turned out to be £105, which was actually quite reasonable when you consider the incredibly high standard of accommodation and our delicious two-course meal with coffee/chocolate served on the terrace afterwards. We just can't afford to do it every night.

I realised when I was halfway through this account of our travels, that I've rarely mentioned food – unlike travel writer Bill Bryson who generally recounts each meal with such gusto that you're either drooling or screwing up your face in disgust by the end. It wasn't a conscious decision to leave out meals, but what we've eaten on this trip generally doesn't make very interesting reading: lots of bread, crisps, cooked breakfasts and chips.

Our dinner at Bron y Llys was the culinary highlight of our journey across Wales, and for that reason alone (and no attempt to ape Mr Bryson's writing style), I'm going to describe exactly what we ate. Harri choose lamb and I opted for salmon (two pieces and seconds were offered) and these were served with a delicious Mediterranean-style mixed salad (olives, sundried tomatoes, etc) and new potatoes.

Dessert was summer fruit pudding with a choice of cream or yoghurt; I'd never tasted it before but can report it was absolutely delicious. After dinner (which was served in the large conservatory), we retired to the garden terrace where we were served coffee (tea for me) and chocolates. The service, the food, the attention to detail, the setting … everything was perfect. Around 9 p.m., the midges became too much of a nuisance so the four of us transferred to the sitting room/library where Maya joined us and we all chatted for an hour or so.

Maya is a wonderful host who makes you feel very welcome and takes a genuine interest in her guests' reasons for being in the area. We were surprised to learn that she and husband John had lived in Bristol until a few years ago and it was a happy accident that they stumbled upon Bron y Llys at all as they'd been heading farther north to view another property.

Something we loved about Bron y Llys was the number of book shelves lining the walls; visitors are encouraged to read whatever they like. This place isn't just a B&B, it's a library and would make a perfect writer's retreat for someone who wished to remove themselves from the distractions of urban life temporarily, but who loves good food and conversation.

The whole evening was very different from our usual B&B experience, where we are holed up in one room for the night eating variations on couscous meals (all you need is a kettle) or, if we're in a town, sharing a takeaway or fish and chips.

We had strayed a long way from our original intention to camp three or four nights in a row and book into bed and breakfast accommodation only occasionally. Luxurious retreats with slap-up meals and socialising on the terrace certainly hadn't featured in our planning.

That said, we didn't regret a penny of the money we spent at Bron y Llys. We had a very special evening with friendly, interesting people. After so many long days of Spartan living, our night of luxury gave us the boost we needed (though I still chuckle when I recall a barefooted Harri carefully picking his way across the stony courtyard for dinner – he only had one pair of shoes with him … his wet hiking ones!).

For photographs visit uk.pinterest.com/thewalkerswife

JUNE 15: DYLIFE TO PONTERWYD

When I was making the all-important decisions about my expedition wardrobe, I was torn between two pairs of brown hiking shorts. Should I pack the looser ones (better fit at the outset) or my ever-so-slightly too tight ones (surely no one can walk the length of Wales and *not* lose at least a few pounds?)? In the end, I 'plumped' for the larger size, reckoning that if I hadn't lost weight by the time the sun decided to come out I'd be in trouble with the other ones.

So, safe in the knowledge that I had a couple of inches to spare around my waistband, I tucked into pancakes and maple syrup for breakfast, though not before I'd devoured a large dish of fruit salad with yummy organic yoghurt.

I was a little bit disappointed we didn't have longer to explore the lovely garden at Bron y Llys. Since their arrival in mid Wales, Maya and John have been lovingly transforming their grounds into a place of wildlife and tranquillity; there's a pretty sage-coloured wooden cabin at the end of a path should someone wish to sit alone and enjoy the peaceful surroundings. Guests are even encouraged to get involved in the gardening if they wish to. I'd have loved the opportunity to spend a few more hours in this gorgeous place; however, another day of hiking beckoned.

After lingering so long over breakfast, Harri was now keen to get started on our 20-mile day. We bade farewell to Rachel and Steve, who kindly extended an invitation for us to drop in at their home anytime we were passing (they're hoping to start a major renovation project this summer so will be kept busy).

From the outset, Harri and I had agreed that our approach to 'O Fôn i Fynwy' needed to be flexible, both in terms of route and our daily mileage. While Harri spent a lot of time planning the proposed route, it was never intended to be set in stone and we accepted that it was possible, even likely, that we'd need to return to some areas later in the summer to explore alternative routes.

Until today's walking, we'd been really happy with the way things had gone. We'd been enthralled and delighted with the landscapes we'd passed through and we were confident the few problems we had encountered – such as the wild camping on the Carneddau or getting lost on our descent into Machynlleth – would not affect future walkers of our route (who'd have our mistakes to learn from).

The next two days' walking would push us to our limits, mentally and physically. Despite our wonderfully uplifting night in Dylife, Harri was never entirely happy with this section of the route, and he eventually made the decision to change the route so it now passes on the other side of the mountain. (Sadly, it means Bron y Llys is no longer en route for those hiking the whole 'O Fôn i Fynwy' route – though, of course, there's nothing to stop you visiting anyway.)

Despite the distance involved, Harri was hoping we could push on to Devil's Bridge today to make up for yesterday's four-mile shortfall. There's a really nice campsite there (Woodlands Caravan Park) with a shop and tea room; we stayed there a few summers ago and really liked this large site with its animal sculptures. The weather that time had been unseasonably cold for August; it would be good to return in warm sunshine.

We walked back up the track to Glyndŵr's Way and followed it for about four miles. This part of Wales is very much about sheep farming. Not far from Dylife is the incredibly beautiful Dylife Gorge, carved out during the last Ice Age. We weren't walking along the road that passes the top of the spectacular gorge, but from our vantage point on Glyndŵr's Way it was both fascinating and terrifying to see how the green fields suddenly drop away into the V-shaped gorge. I just hope there's a fence to stop sheep veering too near the edge and toppling into the river far below.

A little further along, we stopped to talk to a bare-chested male hiker who was struggling to unlatch a farm gate (something that happens to me all the time). It transpired he was from Dusseldorf in Germany and he was wandering around the UK for six weeks before heading back to Liverpool. Today's destination was Machynlleth via the Wales Coast Path, and he was confident he'd find his way without an OS map (he had a small-scale map of the whole area).

While we'd been living it up in Dylife, this guy had behaved like a serious long-distance hiker and camped in the wild. It certainly looked like he was carrying enough equipment for a small army and it was all crammed into one of those horrendously heavy-looking khaki rucksacks. We've been using ultralight GoLite rucksacks for the past few years and we love them.

He was a nice young man, though I did have some motherly concerns about his inadequate clothing, his lack of a decent map, and the enormous weight he was carrying. Remembering our own recent struggle to find Machynlleth, albeit from the opposite direction, we wished him all the luck in the world. Still, he was in no real rush – he had several weeks before he needed to be in Liverpool (presumably for his flight home).

We were treated to unexpected alpine scenery for the next few miles and with a good solid track underfoot, there was plenty of opportunity to look around us and really enjoy the scenery of the Hafren Forest. At one point, my curiosity was aroused by a cluster of people (and parked cars) at the edge of the Clywedog Reservoir, several of whom were relaxing in those easy-to-fold camping chairs. There was no obvious scenery to attract them at this end; the reservoir snakes unimpressively around grass-covered slopes and the really impressive bit – the dam – is six miles away. Harri guessed they were birdwatchers (there have been occasional sightings of ospreys here), but I wasn't so certain.

But to return to that massive dam … at 236 feet high it's the tallest concrete dam in the UK, a fact seized upon by Land Rover when they featured a Defender 90 winching up the face of the dam under its own power in an advert.

Clywedog is another reservoir that was built to supply water to England, in this instance Birmingham and the Midlands. There was strong local opposition, but astonishingly English MPs had the power to ignore Welsh politicians' views and overwhelmingly vote in the necessary Acts of Parliament. Unsurprisingly, people were angry; 615 acres of farmland was lost when the Clywedog valley was drowned. Strength of feeling was running so high that a bomb was detonated to delay construction work, the suspected work of the Welsh nationalist organisation Mudiad Amddiffyn Cymru (Movement for the Defence of Wales), which had also employed bombing in its protests against the flooding of the doomed Tryweryn valley where homes and farms were destroyed to provide Liverpool with water.

The bomb might have delayed construction but it couldn't halt it for good. Clywedog opened in 1967 and has been in use ever since; forty-odd years on, this vast lake (the equivalent of 230 football pitches ... yikes!) has become a popular leisure area for sailing, water activities, walkers, anglers and families. It's not the widest reservoir in Wales – its maximum width is only 500 yards – or the deepest, but, when full to capacity, it holds around 50,000 million litres of water. That's an awful lot of baths.

Somewhere in the Hafren Forest, we passed a T-junction which confusingly signposted Llanidloes in opposing directions. You'd imagine that one option took a more convoluted route, but whichever direction you chose, Llanidloes was apparently nine miles away.

We soon reached Cwmbiga Farm where we'd hoped to stay last night and it did look very pretty, but I don't think it could have surpassed Bron y Llys in terms of accommodation, food or company (though if you spend two nights there to complete two stages of a walk, the owners will very kindly pick you up and drop you off both days for no extra charge). Interestingly, the farm's website states that it, too, is nine miles from Llanidloes!

Just after the farm, we joined the good quality path which would lead us to a very exciting natural landmark: the Source of the Severn. We were quite excited when we first visited this landmark on the Pumlumon massif a few years ago but, to be honest, it's just an inscribed wooden sign in the middle of a boggy mountain 2,000 feet above sea level. On a positive note, the popularity of the place has led to a decent stone footpath being created so no one actually has to get wet feet in their quest to visit the source of the UK's longest river.

The Roman name for the Severn was Sabrina and there's also a Celtic myth about a water nymph of the same name who is said to inhabit the waters of the Severn. A 25-mile circular trail – the Sarn Sabrina – has been created in her honour and is waymarked with distinctive blue and white circles depicting Sabrina rising from the waves at night.

If you're feeling energetic and have already walked O Fôn i Fynwy, you might like to tackle the substantially shorter Severn Way, a 210-mile waymarked trail which follows the river course from its source to its mouth at Bristol. We followed a small section of the trail when we were walking the England Coast Path from Chepstow.

146

Nothing you see on the open mountain suggests that this is the birthplace of the mighty Severn, a waterway which meanders 220 miles through Wales and England and passes through Newtown, Welshpool, Shrewsbury, Ironbridge, Worcester, Tewkesbury and Gloucester (to name but a few). Tributaries of the Severn include the River Stour, River Wye and River Avon. The point at which the River Severn becomes the Severn Estuary is not an absolute but is generally taken to be the site of the old Severn Bridge where the estuary is about two miles wide or the nearby Second Severn Crossing (which the M4 motorway now follows) where it's already widened to three miles.

The massive funnel-shaped estuary has the second highest tidal range in the world at around 50 feet (the Bay of Fundy in Canada has the largest at over 53 feet), which in turn causes the incoming tide up the River Severn to create a solitary wave known as the Severn Bore.

The bore, one of the biggest in the world, occurs all year round with spring tides; however, it is at its biggest and most visually impressive near an equinox (the highest daytime bores in 2014 were on 2 February and 3 March). The largest Severn Bore ever recorded was back in October 1966 when it reached a height of 9.25 feet at Stonebench.

Watching the bore travelling upstream has become such a spectator sport that this natural phenomenon actually has its own website providing lots of information including tide tables, best locations to view it, local accommodation and a useful FAQ section.

And in case you're wondering, the biggest bore in the world can be found on the Qiantang River in Hangzhou, China. This monster of a wave reaches heights of up to 30ft and travels at 13–15 knots (although even faster speeds have been recorded). As the bore advances, its roar can be allegedly be heard 14 miles away. The Qiantang's probably not a great place to sail your dinghy.

River sources, estuaries and tides – all fascinating stuff as the sudden presence of *people* around the wooden marker proved. We took the obligatory photographs and set off across Pumlumon (frequently spelt Plynlimon in English). At 2,467 feet, Pumlumon is the highest mountain in mid Wales and contains the largest watershed. As well as the Severn, it is also the source of the rivers Wye and Rheidol. The highest point in mid Wales, it dominates the northern side of Ceredigion.

In March, we approached this massif (the Welsh name means five peaks) from the other direction and when we reached the highest peak – Pumlumon Fawr – we were bowled over by the breathtaking scenery which surrounded us in every direction. In addition to far-reaching views across Cardigan Bay, we could also see Snowdonia in the north and the summits of Pen y Fan and Corn Du in the Brecon Beacons in the south.

Having tackled Pumlumon on several occasions, I was under no illusion that the climb was going to be tough, but I hadn't anticipated just how much longer we'd be walking without decent views on our approach from the north-east. For me, these long, uphill slogs are never particularly enjoyable so I need to motivate myself to keep going. Generally I know that as I climb the distant views will get better and better, but today's ascent wasn't offering any great views. High on the Pumlumon massif, the weather had once again taken a turn for the worse (frustratingly, it looked bright and sunny on the coast). All I could see ahead of me and either side was moorland and judging from the colour of the sky, a heavy downpour was imminent.

I also felt rather irritated by the new fencing which ran across the slopes in various directions and was restricting us from wandering in the direction we might otherwise have taken. We weren't sure if it was something to do with the Pumlumon Project, a brave attempt by Montgomeryshire Wildlife Trust to reverse decades of intensive use and overgrazing which, their website claims, has led to 'a significant loss of biodiversity, with many of the habitats being either lost or degraded to poor condition'.

Looking around at the desolate upland landscape, it was hard to disagree with this assessment. Of course, what is at risk is far more important than the aesthetically pleasing landscape which I, as a photographer, crave. As their natural habitats are gradually destroyed, many plants and animals are being eradicated. Flooding, too, has become a major problem in many areas of the UK and this is directly linked to what's happening upstream and uphill. As the Trust rightly points out, 'Unhealthy bogs are dry and cannot hold much water … a healthy bog can hold enormous quantities of water like a giant sponge.'

As someone whose spirits tend to plummet when confronted with a healthy bog, I admit to feeling a little guilty at reading this. It seems my dry feet high in the mountains come at the expense of someone else's misery down there on the flooded levels.

The Pumlumon 'problem' continued to bother us as we headed downhill. There's no denying the bleak massif offers little in the way of scenic variety, especially when visibility is poor.

'There is absolutely nothing to relieve the monotony of the landscape on this route,' wrote W. A. Poucher in his 1962 book *The Welsh Peaks*. 'No trees to break the skyline, no colourful flowers to carpet the wayside, no birds to charm both ear and eye, just the green and brown of grass and bog.'

In other words, Poucher found Pumlumon boring, and more than fifty years later little had changed. The monotony of the landscape was broken only by the rectangular standing stones we passed, each one carved with the same letters and date: W.W.W. 1865.

Harri, always a mine of useful information, explained that these were boundary stones, erected to mark the outer perimeter of the owner's land. There are seven of these markers on Pumlumon and they were erected by Sir Watkin Williams Wynn, 6th Baronet, a Denbighshire landowner and Welsh Conservative MP who sat in the House of Commons from 1841–85. Clearly a man who didn't like his borders tinkered with!

After several false starts caused by not being able to see the summit, we eventually managed to get back on track and climbed to the cairn. The huge grey storm cloud looming overhead was getting more menacing by the minute so we thought it better not to loiter. Fortunately, this time, the rain held off and we were able to get off the mountain without a soaking.

We passed a spot where Harri had braved the elements and stripped off for a swim back in March. On that spring day, the weather was absolutely glorious (much better than today); however, the water was icy, as one would expect so early in the year. We'd enjoyed elevenses close to the ruins of an old stone cottage and I remember saying it would be a perfect spot for wild camping if we ever walked the whole of Wales. Well, we were doing that now and I have to say, the location didn't look quite as alluring now pitching our tent was a real possibility. The ground was decidedly uneven and lumpy and the grass was too long; the ruined cottage that looked so enticing in the spring sunshine was now covered in vegetation and on closer inspection, the walls didn't look structurally sound (nothing like a few large stones falling on your head in the night!).

I had to agree with Harri when he said wild camping only sounds like a good idea early in the day when it's hypothetical and you're not faced with actually having to do it (I think that's the case with a lot of things in life like dieting, giving up alcohol, writing that novel …). When you've been walking all day and you're exhausted and hungry, the very last thing you want to do is set up camp on the side of a mountain and eat dry bread and cheese – or maybe that's just us?

Whatever. We didn't stop at our 'perfect spot' but carried on walking down a pretty lane towards Ponterwyd, still undecided on our destination. Now we were off the mountain, the sun felt really hot and we were growing weary. Harri had amended the route slightly so that it was shorter but the climb to Devil's Bridge was going to be tough in this heat, no doubt about it.

The landscape here was scattered with ruined and abandoned farmhouses. My friendly omniscient guide (Harri) informed me that the upland areas of Wales are emptier now – in terms of people – then they've been for a couple of centuries. And while former farms with vehicle access might be snatched up by those hoping to buy into the rural idyll, those without are deemed to be valueless and are left to the elements.

As we approached Ponterwyd, we passed a farmer riding a quad bike. I jokingly stuck my thumb out for a lift and he surprised us by stopping for a chat. We could have talked about our day's hiking, about Pumlumon and the dry bogs, but somehow we ended up talking about how sheep frequently get stuck on their backs and are unable to get up. This cheerful chap then recounted various incidents of sheep being eaten alive by crows as they lay there, four legs to the sky. It's during conversations like this that it hits me that most of us – me included – would prefer to remain blissfully unaware of the cruel realities of farming. I suppose it makes me a meat-eating hypocrite (though I do draw the line at eating lamb, veal and rabbits).

By now it was mid evening and we were longing for the day's walking to be over. In the distance, the final climb of the day was clearly visible and it looked like it was going to be a tough one – far too tough for two pairs of very tired legs. Harri tried to justified the cost of yet another night in a B&B by emphasising how rested we'd feel in the morning, how much farther we'd walk tomorrow if we just spent one more night in a comfortable bed. He stopped mid-sentence, realising that I didn't need any persuading.

There's only one place to head in Ponterwyd and that's the George Borrow Hotel. We were last here in March 2014 when we'd been allocated a spacious family room with great views. We were somewhat disappointed this time around then when we were allocated a standard double this time.

We're fast realising how limited the accommodation options are in mid Wales. There are no campsites for miles and just the one B&B in many areas (which may or may not have vacancies). It's a question of being thankful for whatever bed you can find, not quibbling about the quality of the accommodation or the room. Neither does the price charged reflect what you actually get; if you deduct the cost of last night's delicious dinner, Bron y Llys was actually the same price as the George Borrow Hotel.

The hotel has an air of dilapidated grandeur. Its namesake George Borrow was a nineteenth-century English author whose novels and travel writings were based on his own experiences. His account of living five years in Spain – *The Bible in Spain* – was published in 1843 and became a bestseller. It was Borrow's last major work in 1862 – *Wild Wales* – which forever linked the Victorian author with Wales. An accomplished linguist, Borrow had long been interested in the Welsh language and Welsh literature and enjoyed tracking down the places associated with his favourite Welsh medieval poets.

He was a long-distance hiker before it became commonplace, frequently tackling walks of hundreds of miles in Britain and the Isle of Man; however, *Wild Wales* is the only complete work to have resulted from his hiking exploits. The book was not an immediate success, and yet it has survived as what the George Borrow Society describes as 'a revealing and sympathetic account of the Welsh and their way of life at that period'.

We've had a copy on our bookshelf for years (shamefully I hadn't opened it until we embarked upon O Fôn i Fynwy) so I thought it would be interesting to find out what George had to say about our common accommodation at Ponterwyd.

He introduces the hotel thus: 'After passing by a few huts [we] came to a large house, which my guide told me was the inn of Pont

Erwyd.' Borrow did not get the welcome he expected; the landlord surveyed him 'with something of a supercilious air' and told him in no uncertain terms that while he sometimes welcomed guests into his home, he did not depend upon innkeeping for his livelihood.

Taken aback, Borrow suggested he might instead continue to Devil's Bridge, at which the landlord's antagonism thawed and he offered him a room and dinner. If Borrow's account of the encounter is to be believed, the landlord had a bit of a bee in his bonnet about the popularity of Devil's Bridge as a tourist attraction.

'We have a bridge here too quite as good as the Devil's Bridge; and as for the scenery, I'll back the scenery from this house against anything of the kind in the neighbourhood of the Devil's Bridge. Yet everybody goes to the Devil's Bridge and nobody comes here,' he apparently told his literary guest.

Nothing has changed in the intervening 150 years. Visitors still flock to nearby Devil's Bridge; anything Ponterwyd might once have offered free-spirited travellers in terms of rolling countryside and tranquillity has been wrecked by the constant roar of traffic hurtling through the village on the busy A44 linking the Midlands to Aberystwyth. Believe me, you need nerves of steel just to walk the short distance from the George Borrow Hotel to the village garage/shop.

The A44 has been named as one of the most dangerous roads in Wales; just three days before we arrived in Ponterwyd, there was a horrific accident nearby involving a fuel tanker and a car in which four members of the same family were killed (a toddler miraculously survived).

It wasn't until the following morning that Borrow had an opportunity to look properly at his surroundings. 'I found myself amongst wild, strange-looking hills,' he wrote. 'Not, however, of any particular height. The house, which seemed to front the east, stood on the side of a hill on a wide platform abutting on a deep and awful chasm, at the bottom of which chafed and foamed the Rheidol.'

In these safety-conscious times, hotel guests are protected from Borrow's 'awful chasm' by a wide, low-level wall and several warning signs. Nowadays, trees and vegetation completely obscure the Rheidol far below; however, you can enjoy panoramic views towards distant hills from the beer garden.

Like Abergynolwyn, Ponterwyd stands at the confluence of two rivers (the other being the Castell, and, like Devil's Bridge, the village has three bridges. Had they been built one above the other it's conceivable that Ponterwyd might now be drawing in as many tourists as its near neighbour, but unfortunately no-one was thinking that far ahead and the bridges were constructed to cross the two rivers in three separate locations.

It's unlikely Ponterwyd even existed until the first bridge was built over the Rheidol in the mid-eighteenth century. In the nineteenth century, the village population grew as local lead mines expanded; the drovers too would come here to buy cattle and sheep which they would then sell at markets in England.

Talking of sheep … I had no need to count them tonight. With no television to distract us (it wasn't working), we settled down for an early night and before very long, Harri and I were both dozing contentedly in the land of Nod.

For photographs visit uk.pinterest.com/thewalkerswife

JUNE 16: PONTERWYD TO PONTRHYDFENDIGAID

I get frustrated when Harri insists I've been somewhere, but I have absolutely no recollection of the occasion. In the case of Pontrhydfendigaid, I might struggle to pronounce the name of the village, but I remember our first visit all too well. Harri was trying to park our car as close to a stone wall as possible when he snagged one of the rear tyres on a jagged rock.

We'd have been less frustrated about hanging around for our breakdown company if there'd been the opportunity to enjoy a cold lager in a pub garden, but despite it being late afternoon on a glorious summer's day, the Red Lion Hotel was closed. Thus, we waited for almost an hour on the roadside, wondering yet again why Welsh publicans are so reluctant to open their doors.

This incident is the reason Pontrhydfendigaid (Bont to locals) has been filed away in my mind as the village of the jagged rock and closed pub. Today, the village was being given the opportunity to redeem itself, but first we had to get there.

Harri had hinted at a tough day's hiking over open moorland, so I tucked into a hearty breakfast of muesli, scrambled egg on toast, Harri's (stolen) tomatoes, baked beans and extra toast. My shorts, chosen for their dark colour, ease of washing and relative comfort, were already worryingly loose and we were only halfway to Chepstow. At this rate, I was in danger of losing them to gravity. And I hadn't brought a spare pair!

Over breakfast we mulled over other long-distance routes we might like to tackle in the future: an end to end through Madeira (an island that makes Wales look flat), the Galician coast path, perhaps a long-distance walk through Portugal. Relishing our vastly improved fitness levels and our new-found ability to swing our rucksacks onto our shoulders without even flinching, there was nowhere, no country or trail that was too daunting to tackle.

We'd discovered – somewhat to our mutual surprise – that we actually enjoyed being with each other twenty-four hours a day, that with domesticity and the workplace firmly out of the picture, we were more relaxed and less inclined to niggle at one another.

Harri has a doctorate (in Welsh writing in English) and is more academically-inclined than me. At home he spends much of his free time reading and, once a week, meets up with a group of long-time friends who have similar academic interests. When he's deeply engrossed in a book (fiction or non-fiction, he enjoys both), it's almost impossible to engage him in conversation. He might briefly raise his head and nod obligingly when I complain how carrots don't last as long these days, but I can always tell he's not really listening.

As for me, I love hiking and being outdoors but I also enjoy spending time with my family and friends. We frequently chat together about the things that bore Harri to death: parkrun PBs, *Corrie*'s latest cliff hanger or future birthday plans.

How then were Harri and I going to survive all these weeks in each other's company, with no one to talk to but the briefest of acquaintances? You know what? Each day brought with it so many new experiences that it was easy to talk non-stop all day without ever getting bored of one another (well, I never got bored of Harri, I can't speak for him). And there's nothing like escaping your life temporarily to get you wondering how you could do it permanently. If we could make walking across Wales a reality, what was to stop us making other things happen?

When walking these long-distance routes in other parts of the globe we'd sensibly schedule in a day of rest here and there … just to rest our weary feet and explore some of the local attractions. Neither of us has ever been drawn to the 'marching' mentality of some long-distance walkers.

I have long admired the determination, courage and honesty of Ffyona Campbell, a young woman who raised tens of thousands for charity in the 1980s and 1990s by walking across several continents, one at a time. As a young mum who frequently hankered after adventure, I kind of understood what it was that compelled Ffyona to lace her boots and get out there, all day every day, week after week, month after month. Reading her accounts of her frequently gruelling distances, what I found harder to understand was why her daily mileage had to be quite so enormous or why so many of her routes (in the States and Australia at least) followed major roads. I've read all Ms Campbell's books and her experiences as a teenager and young woman – yes, she was really that young when she undertook several of these epic hikes – make for fascinating reading; however, I always suspected that her experiences would have been far more enjoyable and memorable had she occasionally slowed down to savour her surroundings, to smell the roses and taste the wine.

Newport-born poet W. H. Davies voiced his fears that the hectic pace of modern life was having a harmful effect on people as long ago as 1911. In his poem 'Leisure', Davies posed the immortal question: 'What is this life if full of care / We have no time to stand and stare.'

Davies knew a lot about travel, having hitchhiked his way across North America and then documented his experiences in the 1908 memoir *Autobiography of a Super-Tramp*. He was an individual who loved nature and took the time to notice the changing seasons and the way the landscape varied dramatically depending on the time of year and time of day.

I'm convinced that had W. H. Davies met Ffyona Campbell (a theoretical impossibility because he died in 1940 and she was born in 1967), he'd have taken her aside and said, 'What's the rush, young lady? Slow down and enjoy the journey'. He would have been exasperated by the endless notching up of road miles for no fathomable reason other than to cover the distance between two distant points on a map.

'Leisure' concludes with the line, 'A poor life this if, full of care, / We have no time to stand and stare'. I couldn't agree more.

We were avoiding walking on or near busy roads wherever possible; we were also being sensible about the number of miles we hoped to complete each day. We hadn't factored in any rest days though; and if we considered them to be essential in foreign climes, why were we following such a punishing schedule here in Wales? Why not punctuate 'O Fôn i Fynwy' with the odd lazy day? Why not rest up today, for instance? Here in Ponterwyd.

We pondered the question over extra slices of toast. The answer was obvious. In sparsely populated mid Wales, there's nothing to do except hike. That's not strictly true, of course, but without transport and with limited funds, the only possible way of spending a rest day would be to go for a walk … or do absolutely nothing and find ourselves climbing not mountains but walls by midday.

It was easier to keep going each day, so that's what we were doing. That conundrum resolved to our satisfaction, we turned our attention to today's route. Unlike George Borrow, we weren't planning to go to Devil's Bridge. Though it's a lovely place and well worth a visit, the route Harri devised would instead cross the Rheidol and its deep gorge at Parson's Bridge.

Thankfully, the current bridge is somewhat more substantial than the one poor George encountered back in 1854. The original reputedly provided a shortcut for the parson walking from Llanbadarn Fawr to the church of Ysbyty Cynfyn. Borrow writes of it in *Wild Wales*, 'The bridge consisted of a couple of planks and a pole flung over a chasm about ten feet wide … without any trees or shrubs, by which those who used it might support themselves.' He was clearly unnerved by the prospective crossing and describes the channel below as 'tortuous' and 'like a cauldron'. 'The river was rushing and surging,' he elaborated. 'The pot was boiling and roaring, and everything looked wild and savage.'

If he wasn't exaggerating for dramatic effect, it's a wonder Borrow found the courage to cross – I'm not sure I'd have been willing – but despite fearing for his legs and his neck, Borrow walked those planks twice in quick succession.

Parson's Bridge remained a dangerous place to traverse the Rheidol until 1951; so dangerous, in fact, that the man responsible for maintaining the wood and chain structure was paid sixpence a day danger money.

I'm pleased to report you no longer have to take your life in your hands to cross Parson's Bridge. Despite its narrowness (75 cm), the current footbridge feels distinctively solid compared with its Victorian predecessor. Installing the new bridge in such an inaccessible location was not without its challenges; the 17.5-metre-long lightweight bridge (a glass-reinforced plastic construction weighing just one tonne) had to be lifted into place by a local helicopter.

It's a wonderful feat of modern engineering – although if you suffer from vertigo you should probably avoid looking down. I don't particularly like heights, but our hiking experiences in Madeira – where there are plenty of unprotected drops and dodgy-looking barriers –

have helped me overcome my vertigo to some extent. The result is that footpaths and routes which used to seem really scary no longer bother me quite as much.

This morning's walking started well enough and I was delighted to spot wild bilberries growing on the mountainside. I picked several and wandered along the undulating hillside path enjoying the sweet taste of my unexpected forage. My father loves reminding me how, on a childhood walk in the Brecon Beacons, I mistook sheep droppings for bilberries and 'picked' quite a pile of them before he realised my mistake. Fortunately, I was collecting my 'fruits' of the soil in a plastic container or goodness knows if I'd be here to tell the tale!

Harri's plan was to follow various sections of Ceredigion Council's promoted inland route – the Borth–Pontrhydfendigaid Linear Trail – which does what it says on the tin. Borth is a wonderfully quirky seaside resort six miles north of Aberystwyth; I'd happily while away several days there had it been en route. Pontrhydfendigaid, on the other hand, was the place we were heading.

The scenery was absolutely delightful as we joined the waymarked path alongside the Mynach (a small river which plunges into the Rheidol Valley below Devil's Bridge). The steep, wooded banks rose dramatically from the valley and the crystal-clear waters of the river were ever so tempting. Not that there was the slightest need to approach the river's edge to get wet; as we quickly discovered, the Mynach was happy to come to us. Almost the entire length of the riverside footpath was under water, which meant there was no alternative but to grit our teeth and wade through.

(It was with some regret that Harri decided not to include this section in the final version of 'O Fôn i Fynwy' because it is incredibly pretty, but it was just unacceptably waterlogged, even by Welsh standards.)

Ceredigion Council's website continues to ascribe Category 1 status to this promoted route in its 'prioritisation system', but if our experiences are typical we suspect that financial pressures and the need to prioritise statutory services have led to less-than-adequate maintenance of this waymarked route. Of course, if someone does find a pot of money to spend on footpaths, several hundred metres of boardwalks would be a valuable addition to the landscape.

After the joys of the waterlogged river path, we were immediately confronted with a section of woodland scrambling. As frequent runners and hikers, Harri and I like to think of ourselves as reasonably fit but, honestly, some sections of Ceredigion's promoted route were so ridiculously steep and slippery it was impossible to imagine the average walker managing to clamber to the top. At one point, I was hanging onto vegetation to avoid sliding back down the path. (Don't fret, faithful reader, this entire section has now been deleted from Harri's final route.)

Having risked life and limb in the pursuit of fame (no one writes hiking books for money), we soon arrived in Cwmystwyth. Despite its diminutive size, the village holds a very significant title; the Ordnance Survey has calculated it is the geographic centre point of Wales. While it might seem a little strange that the centre of the nation is someplace close to the coast, the calculations (which include Wales's islands) were made using the most preferred method and denote the point at which a cardboard cut-out of Wales could be perfectly balanced on the tip of a pencil.

I'm not certain there's any practical value in this discovery, but it's good to know I've stood in the middle of Wales at least once in my lifetime.

Despite its notable status, Cwmystwyth rather resembled a ghost town on this warm Sunday afternoon. Where were all the Centre-of-Wales hunters? People determined to have their photograph taken in the absolute middle of their country? It seems everyone was giving Cwmystwyth a miss today. There was no-one around … *anywhere*. It's sad to think how different things used to be in rural communities; back in the 1970s Cwmystwyth had its own bustling Post Office and village shop. (Interestingly, the English couple who took it over in 1978 now run the Old Post Office B&B from the same premises.)

All day I'd been desperate to get a mobile signal so I could ring my youngest daughter who was getting her art and design foundation course results this morning (a coveted merit grade was needed for her place at university). Wales has never been renowned for its great mobile coverage (all those mountains must get in the way) and, unfortunately, it doesn't look like things are going to change anytime soon – neither of us had had a signal all day.

It was now mid-afternoon and I'd yet to make my promised phone call home. Cwmystwyth might be lacking any obvious human beings, but it appeared to possess the one thing I needed – an old-fashioned red telephone box. It was years since I'd last squeezed into one and as I tugged open the heavy metal door I remembered why that was. There were cobwebs clinging to every surface; not the recently-spun ones that look rather pretty but massive clumps of dusty spider homes everywhere. I shuddered and picked up the receiver. I couldn't understand why I couldn't locate the 20p slot until I noticed the sign indicating current charges. Since I last braved a telephone box, BT had put up the minimum charge to £1.20. You can no longer use coins either; a debit or credit card is required.

It could have been worse. In January 2014, BT raised the minimum charge for those using credit or debit cards in public phone boxes to £6.50, but following concerns from Ofcom, the company reversed the price hike just a month later. And there was me thinking £1.20 was a rip-off. Oh, and in instances where the telephone box will accept coins, the minimum cost of making a call has risen to 60p.

I was surprised to learn that there are still 58,500 BT payphones operating across the UK; only 10,000 of these are traditional red phone boxes like the one in Cwmystwyth. I suppose you can understand why BT needs to charge so much for the service when you consider vandalism (all those panes of glass to replace) and theft costs the company almost £5.2 million a year.

Apparently, in more than 12,000 rural phone boxes fewer than one call a month is made; I suspect Cwmystwyth is one of them. Did I make my own? No. I daren't risk a large spider walking out from those cobwebs when I was midway through my conversation.

Historically, Cwmystwyth has been an important mining site since the Bronze Age, with silver, lead and zinc excavated at various times. The village itself probably grew up during the eighteenth and nineteenth centuries when metal mining was at its height; however, there has been no mining activity for the past century.

In 2002, a 4,000 year old gold ornament was discovered on the site of Roman and medieval lead-smelting hearths. The small funerary ornament known as the Banc Ty'nddôl sun-disc is the earliest gold artefact found in Wales.

Had we stuck to the waymarked linear trail, we'd have witnessed first-hand the ruinous effect centuries of mining workings have had on the natural landscape. The Spirit of the Miners' excellent website provides lots of information as well as a photo gallery.

As we came to the edge of this tiny village, we passed some delightful stone cottages. Two terraces face one another and there is a rough track running up the middle. There was no pavement, just a rough grass verge on either side. The houses wouldn't have looked out of place in St Fagan's National History Museum in Cardiff. Though the doors of the houses nearest to us looked modern and there were wheelie bins outside another home, there was no one around, which only strengthened our suspicion that no one actually lives in Cwmystwyth.

It wasn't long before we were back in woodland, this time following a footpath alongside the River Ystwyth and into the dilapidated but still rather magnificent Hafod estate.

It felt a little bit strange to encounter sweeping lawns and overgrown rhododendron bushes here in the wilderness of mid Wales, and yet Hafod is described as one of the finest example of a 'picturesque' landscape in Europe.

Thomas Johnes (1748–1816) inherited the vast Hafod estate from his father in 1780, having never before visited Wales. When he did arrive in Cardiganshire, the philanthropic Johnes fell instantly in love with the rugged scenery and set about transforming his rundown estate into a beautiful dramatic landscape resplendent with ravines, trees and artificial ruins.

The creation of 'picturesque' gardens had grown in popularity towards the end of the eighteenth century and was influenced by the larger Romantic movement. Wealthy landowners began to reject the perfectly ordered and manicured gardens of the past, seeking gardens which had a wilder, untamed quality. Paths, follies and bridges were frequently introduced to add interest for visiting guests.

After Johnes' death, the 'picturesque' elements of the Hafod estate were neglected and most eventually fell into disuse. It wasn't until 1990 that a private benefactor initiated a project through the Welsh Historic Gardens Trust to save and restore this unique landscape. The Hafod Trust – a charity formed in 1994 and funded from various sources –

has overseen and carried out the amazing restoration work that allows people like Harri and I access to the estate.

Harri couldn't remember whether Johnes' manor house was still standing, but we could see a railed viewpoint high above us on the opposite side of the river and figured any ruins must be close to it. Harri wasn't keen on going off exploring, so I left him sitting in the sunshine with the bags while I explored the immediate vicinity of the viewpoint. Sadly, and despite my best efforts, I was unable to find any trace of an actual building.

There was a wide driveway cut through rock but it didn't appear to go anywhere. A large sloping field was full of sheep, and its shape and the way the trees followed the outer perimeter of the land suggested that this was once the large sweeping lawn that the Johnes would have looked out upon.

I thought I could see the remains of a stone pillar on an overgrown rocky outcrop, but the climb would have been difficult so I abandoned my search and returned to Harri. We later learned the dilapidated manor was dynamited into oblivion in 1958, nearly a decade after fixtures and fittings including windows, stairs and floors (!) were sold off. The Forestry Commission apparently tried to find a use or buyer for the windowless, stairless and floorless property the following year, but, surprise, surprise, their mission proved unsuccessful.

We rejoined our riverside path leaving the woodland behind. Now the path was overgrown, hard to follow and very soggy underfoot. I was getting a little fed up of paddling today and we still had a long way to walk.

Realising I needed cheering up – and fast – Harri suggested we stop for a drink at the Miner's Arms in Pontrhyd-y-groes before the final leg of our journey. Like Cwmystwyth, the village was once dominated by mining, in this instance lead and zinc.

Once again, we were let down by the vagaries of the Welsh hospitality industry. The Miner's Arms, though happily still open for business, unhappily wasn't open for our business. It was just gone five and the pub didn't open until six. We could have waited an hour, but it would probably have meant walking into Pontrhydfendigaid by torchlight.

We headed towards the village shop, thinking that while a beer would have been nice, an ice cream or lolly would have to do instead.

You've guessed it. The shop closed at five. Between five and six Pontrhyd-y-groes seemingly enters a twilight zone when it's deemed to be too late for ice cream yet too early for alcohol. So if you have an inkling you might fancy an alcoholic beverage or just an ice lolly as you pass through this village, I suggest you schedule your arrival very, very carefully.

Despite the abysmal lack of facilities (the village toilets were also closed – permanently), Pontrhyd-y-groes is rather a prepossessing little place. The natural scenery is stunning and the houses are fashioned in such a higgledy-piggledy manner one can almost imagine them sprouting from a careless scattering of stones. Narrow lanes meandered intriguingly between the properties and we left the village on one of them.

There was still no mobile signal, something else that was really beginning to niggle me. Neither was there BT or (any) free Wi-Fi access so a quick conversation on Facebook was also out of the question. My poor daughter had now waited over four hours for my promised call and my guilt was mounting.

A number of years ago, the lack of mobile coverage in Wales was seen as advantageous. I remember a series of advertising posters which flouted that fact that holidaying here meant you were essentially incommunicado. Against a stunning mountain landscape, one boasted in large letters 'area of outstandingly bad mobile reception' which, a decade or so later, seems like an outstandingly bad marketing idea, even if it is still as true as ever.

I remember the baffled look a Madeiran waitress once gave me when I asked if the small village we were visiting had internet access; I guess it's only a Welsh tourist who would voice such a daft question.

It's safe to assume that I wasn't in the best of moods when we left Pontrhyd-y-groes. Denied a phone call home, a cider, even an ice lolly, I doubted my spirits could sink much lower and we still had about seven miles to walk.

We climbed steps to emerge onto a track. Here the houses were smaller but equally interesting and quirky; someone had set up a few garden chairs on a patch of overgrown grass which, even in my black mood, made me chuckle.

My mood lightened further when I was finally able to make contact with my youngest daughter. Though the signal still wasn't good enough for a long chat, I learned that she'd passed her art foundation course with flying colours and would be heading to university in September.

It's not unusual for footpaths to run through private gardens and it's very rare for us to encounter any problems. The majority of owners are quite accustomed to seeing hikers climbing over stiles and walking across their lawns, and they'll often give us a friendly wave or stop to ask us where we're heading. On more than one occasion, we've been very grateful for a bit of local knowledge.

We were still taken aback when, having just joined a grassy track, the lady living in the adjacent property called out to us to apologise for it being a little overgrown. She explained how she and her husband usually maintained and cleared the path but that in the past few weeks their time had been taken up with the newest members of the family … several goats.

We assured her it wasn't the worst footpath we'd encountered on our journey, or even that day. We were still following the Borth–Pontrhydfendigaid Linear Trail, one of Ceredigion Council's promoted routes. If anyone was responsible for the poor state of the footpath, it was the council and not a local resident.

What was more worrying right now was the mountain that had appeared on the horizon in front of me.

'We're not climbing another mountain, are we?' I demanded. I'd mentally prepared myself for the mileage but hadn't factored in any more steep climbs today.

'No,' Harri answered, continuing to head towards said mountain.

'You promised there'd be no more mountains today,' I growled.

'There aren't.' He didn't change direction. And there was definitely a mountain ahead.

Perhaps we're skirting around the edge, I thought, grasping at straws; although if our Moelfre experience in the Rhinogs was anything to go by it's probably quicker – much quicker – to walk up and over the wretched thing. Still, I wasn't letting Harri off the hook that easily.

'So, if there are no more mountains, why are we walking up one now?' By now, I was dragging my feet to show him I meant business. You can't say one thing and mean another.

'It's not a mountain, it's a hill.'

I stared at the rising ground ahead of me. Mountain or hill, it looked steep. Too steep to be climbing this late in the day when all I wanted to do was collapse. Not for the first time, I wondered about my sanity. Backpacking was something that young people did; people in their early fifties did city breaks and cruises. Moreover, backpacking was new to me; despite my professed wanderlust, I was never quite brave enough to take off on my own in my younger days.

In the early eighties, working-class girls like me tended to work in mundane jobs for a few years before settling down and having families. My friends weren't interested in travelling the world – unless it was for a week in Benidorm – but that didn't stop me yearning to see other countries, other cultures. By the time I was 22, I had saved sufficient money for a return airfare to Australia plus the requisite six months' spending money. So why didn't I board that plane and set about exploring Down Under? I guess I just lacked the courage. My longed-for adventure never quite got off the ground and I eventually used my savings as a deposit on my first house.

Maybe I'd been kidding myself all along? Trying to keep up with the super-fit Harri was lunacy. What my tired old legs considered to be a mountain probably *was* just a hill to his younger muscular ones.

True, we were remaining on home territory for this first expedition, but the principles were still the same: a rucksack, a tent and a lot of walking.

Thankfully, camping equipment has advanced dramatically in the past three decades; I doubt I'd have been able to lift one of those humungous metal-framed things off the ground let alone carry it around on my back all day. A running friend who enjoys long-distance hiking – and courageously undertakes epic hikes on her own – told me about her first ever solo walk. She'd borrowed her husband's 1950s framed rucksack, which weighed roughly the same as a St Bernard dog *before* she'd packed her smalls. A day into her journey she realised she couldn't possibly continue with such a massive load; her wonderful husband rode to north Wales on a motorbike to hand over a newly purchased and much lighter rucksack. We learn the hard way.

During the early stages of this journey, there wasn't a moment when Harri and I weren't acutely aware of the oppressive weight of our own rucksacks. Every time, we stopped to rest or eat and were temporarily relieved of our loads, we would dread the moment when we'd have to strap them on again. Two weeks into the hike and we were *almost* getting used to them (although each time we stocked up on supplies, we would again struggle until we'd got used to the extra weight).

And now, as we neared the end of another long day, all I wanted to do was hurl the damned thing onto the ground and curl up on a comfortable bed and sleep. Hurl and curl. A marketing strapline for camping hostels perhaps?

I was silently cursing Harri for devising such an undulating route, then as we came over the crest of the *hill* I realised he had taken the route this way because the industrial landscape, with its remnants of the lead- and zinc-mining industries, was unmissable. The abandoned mine workings and bleak landscape of Esgair Mwyn brought to mind a ghost town in California called Bodie, albeit minus the wooden houses.

This area has long been known for its rich deposits of ore and it's likely that mining here dates back to medieval times. When Esgair Mwyn was rediscovered again in 1746, a thousand tonnes of ore was raised in one year. The resumed mining activity wasn't without its problems though – a dispute between its 'discoverer' Lewis Morris (working the mine on behalf of the Crown) and local people (including two magistrates, the sheriff, his deputy and many miners) escalated to the point where bloodshed was only narrowly avoided and Morris ended up in Cardigan gaol. Ultimately, the king retained the land, but the ringleaders of the opposition were not prosecuted.

Over the next two centuries, Esgair Mwyn experienced mixed fortunes. New shafts were sunk and aqueducts and tramways added. When lead prices slumped in the 1890s, the mine was one of many forced to close, albeit temporarily. Before long, Thomas Ward had resumed operations, extracting ore from such depths that it took three-quarters of an hour to raise. Esgair Mwyn closed once more in 1927 but the mine's fate was not yet sealed. In 1947, a Gloucestershire company invested heavily in Esgair Mwyn and the mine enjoyed success until 1994 when it closed for the final time amid concerns over water pollution.

I'm mildly claustrophobic so I can't imagine anything more terrifying than spending your days working far below the earth's surface. Some of the workings at Esgair Mwyn were nearly a thousand feet down, the deepest in Cardiganshire.

How often must those miners have yearned for a different life? Yet, work was work and there was little alternative for most men than to work in blackness, hunched over for hours as they breathed in the poisonous lead fumes.

We were walking across this ravaged and desolate landscape by choice, not because of economic necessity. After my 'hissy fit' over the hill/mountain semantics, I'd resigned myself to several more hours' walking when a car suddenly pulled up alongside us. The Good Samaritan behind the wheel was a man in his sixties who, upon learning of our destination, immediately offered us a lift to Pontrhydfendigaid. Harri said afterwards that he half expected me to accept but I wasn't even tempted; I intend to walk every inch of the way from Holyhead to Monmouth and hitching a ride, even for a few miles, would have been cheating.

We were feeling more than a little weary when we walked through the little village of Ffair Rhos, so-called because it was once the location of the medieval wool fairs organised by the monks of nearby Strata Florida Abbey. In fact, wool from the area was being exported from Carmarthen to continental Europe as far back as the fourteenth century and the remains of the summer huts used by the abbey's shepherds can still be seen dotted across the landscape. Long after the abbey's demise, the drovers would come here with their animals.

The fair eventually moved to Pontrhydfendigaid, leaving Ffair Rhos to be settled by the miners who worked at Esgair Mwyn. The late Mary Thomas (1905–83) offers a disturbing explanation about why the fair was moved to Bont. Mrs Thomas claimed the 'Brwcsod' – descendants of a man from Cornwall – would go up the Nant y Bedde (the brook of the graves) between Pontrhydfendigaid and Rhaeadr and attack drovers as they returned from the fair. Not content with robbery, the cruel Brwcsod would murder their victims and bury them on the mountainside. Her full account can be read on the National Museum of Wales website.

As we approached, we couldn't see a pub sign on the Teifi Inn and assumed it was another casualty of the distressed brewery trade, but as we passed we could see people inside, sitting around tables and drinking. It was so tempting to stop and join them but I don't think we'd have found the mental strength to get going again. Determined not to find ourselves without accommodation again, Harri had rung ahead and booked a room at the Black Lion Hotel.

As we walked towards our much-needed bed, Harri pointed out a large swathe of unusually flat ground close to the coast.

'Two thousand acres of your favourite terrain,' he announced. 'Bog.'

It transpired we were looking down at Cors Caron National Nature Reserve, otherwise known as Tregaron Bog. Cors Caron is what's known as a raised bog, which means it developed from a lake or flat marshy area about 12,000 years ago. In 2003, a countryside warden found the remains of ancient oaks believed to be over 5,000 years old in the peat bog, evidence of a dense forest which receded when the climate became colder.

At last – after nineteen miles of walking – we reached Pontrhydfendigaid where our second priority was to check into the Black Lion and our first to get a drink at the bar. It wasn't long before we'd struck up conversation with a lone traveller.

This Englishman, who we guessed to be in his 70s, moved to Ruthin in North Wales as a boy. He was in Bont because 'I thought it was about time I explored mid Wales'. He was stopping for a meal so we joined him at his table, resisting the wonderful aromas wafting from the kitchen.

Our new friend (why do I never think to ask people their names?) was a fascinating character, an academic who'd studied Latin and Greek at Oxford and had maintained a strong interest in language and semantics. At 15, he'd determined to teach himself Welsh at the first opportunity; that proved to be while he was working in an administrative role in the RAF during his National Service. Our evening companion reminded me a lot of Harri, an intelligent individual who'd grown so disillusioned by the narrow confines of our overly-regulated education system that he'd made the brave decision to remain true to himself and leave academia. Interestingly, one of his peers at Oxford was Ned Thomas who founded the bi-monthly *Planet: the Welsh Internationalist* magazine in 1970.

As this fascinating man regaled us with stories past and present, one drink led to another and we grew hungrier and hungrier. His sausage and mash meal smelt wonderful but the pub had long since stopped serving food so we consoled ourselves with several packets of crisps.

It was well after ten when we finally reached our spacious room in a converted stable block behind the pub. Several drinks and the late hour contrived to make us so tired that it was an effort to eat more than a few mouthfuls of the bread rolls and cheese we'd carried around all day.

Just before we fell into bed, I glanced at my mobile phone; for the first time all day, I had a half-decent mobile signal.

For photographs visit uk.pinterest.com/thewalkerswife

JUNE 17: PONTRHYDFENDIGAID TO RHANDIRMWYN

Pontrhydfendigaid is one of those Welsh place names that no one seems able to pronounce. Alright, that's not strictly true, as I assume locals can recite their own address; however, it is sufficiently difficult to non-natives for the Black Lion's landlord to run a radio commercial featuring a lady visitor who is struggling to pronounce it.

'Locals call it Bont,' she is eventually told after failing to get her tongue around the five-syllable village name.

I have the same problem, so from this point on, Bont it will be. The village was once served by the Manchester–Milford railway line with the nearest station three miles from Bont at Strata Florida. I know that because while Harri and the academic were chatting together in Welsh last night – at my insistence – I crossed the bar and browsed through a book of old photographs I found on the windowsill. *From Mountain and Moor* by Lyn Ebenezer included several pictures of the station buildings as well as advertisements encouraging Victorian tourists to travel inland from Aberystwyth to visit Strata Florida. The station was awkwardly located between villages, meaning access in the pre-car era was always going to be difficult; moreover, the railway section north of Strata Florida (to Llanidloes) was never built, partly because the Manchester & Milford (M & M) Railway Company ran out of money and partly because extending the railway through the mountainous landscape beyond Strata Florida was certain to be an engineering nightmare.

Looking back, it is sad to consider how the hopes of local people were raised in 1864 only to be dashed a few years later when cold economics came into play.

Even in the halcyon days of railway expansion and travel, it seemed the topography of Wales was problematic. While the M & M Railway Company ostensibly offered tickets from Manchester to Milford (and *vice versa*), the lack of any direct trains meant at least eight changes and a three-day rail journey. It was thus far faster for people to travel to London and back out again. Time-consuming public transport in Wales? Easier to travel the length of the country by leaving it? No change there then.

We had another fabulous breakfast; the landlord is a trained chef and it shows. We laughed when he told us that our previous night's companion was so engaged in conversation with Harri he'd managed to leave the premises without settling his bill and hadn't realised his mistake until he was back at his B&B. As you'd expect, the poor man was mortified and had wanted to drive back across the mountain to settle up; our landlord wouldn't have any of it, and they'd agreed the bill would wait until this morning.

While Harri spent half an hour catching up with yesterday's notes (oh the follies of talking to strangers in Welsh bars), I toddled off to investigate Bont's sole grocery store. I was pleased to find it was reasonably well stocked and the prices weren't as exorbitant as in many tourist traps. I bought a few bits and bobs and headed back to the Black Lion where our companion of the previous evening was just parking up. I hesitated, wondering whether to start up a conversation again, but he hadn't spotted me so I decided against it on the grounds that he might be embarrassed if he realised we were aware of his oversight.

Modern-day Bont is a bustling village on the River Teifi which manages to support three pubs. It's the obvious stopping-off place for those wishing to visit the ruined Cisterian abbey of Strata Florida. The village likes its music and hosts an annual eisteddfod; there is also a Celtic Music Society which meets at the Black Lion.

In 1981, Bont found itself the centre of media attention when the 'beast of Bont' was blamed for the death of twelve sheep. The beast, believed to be a large cat, struck again in the mid-1990s when more sheep were killed by an animal 'more powerful than a fox or dog'. In 2012, a couple came across two large groups of slaughtered sheep about two miles apart, in the hills near Devil's Bridge.

'Beast of Bont returns' screamed *The Telegraph* headline, acknowledging the carnage had been continuing for decades but failing to point out that the 'beast' carrying out the killing spree would now be in his/her early thirties by now (at the very least). Other reports mention a possible puma or leopard on the loose but the lifespan of both species is too short for the attacks to be attributed to the same animal.

What also seems baffling (to me at least) is that so many animals were savagely attacked at the same time. Unlike humans, animals tend not to go around killing one another unless it's for reasons of self-preservation or because they intend to eat their prey. We're talking a big cat and sheep here, so self-preservation can be ruled out straightaway. Yet if the motivation for the killings was hunger, why did the 'beast' attack and kill so many animals on each occasion? Why didn't the sheep who weren't being attacked at that precise moment run away? Why were there no reported killings between 1981 and 1995, then no more until 2012?

Call me a cynic, but as with reported sightings of flying saucers, I take reports of big cats roaming the Welsh countryside with a pinch of salt.

George Monbiot writes about the big cat phenomenon in *Feral* (2013). In the wonderfully titled chapter 'The Never-spotted Leopard', he suggests that with the exception of the occasional escaped animal (most of which are quickly caught or killed), most sightings of big cats – the Pembrokeshire Panther is another – are actually imagined or, at the very least, the result of someone seeing something (a domestic cat perhaps) and the brain filling in the gaps to create a complete, if false, image.

After extensive research, Monbiot concludes: 'the hard evidence for an extant population of big cats in the UK is no stronger than the evidence for the Loch Ness monster'.

Bont's more tangible claim to fame is that it's the birthplace and childhood home of Caradog 'Crag' Jones, the first Welshman to reach the summit of Mount Everest on 23 May 1995 at the age of 33 – the same age Edmund Hillary became the first man to scale the world's highest mountain. Caradog has said he was inspired by the exploits of early Everest pioneers who trained in Snowdonia. Well, with a nickname like 'Crag' you couldn't really do anything but climb, could you?

We've walked in this area before, most recently earlier this year, so we were well aware that the pretty meadows and low moorland surrounding Strata Florida can become extremely waterlogged underfoot. After the past few days, the last thing we wanted to experience was more squelching feet so Harri called an emergency breakfast meeting and set out the options: a potentially soggy route across open moorland or a drier route along tracks through the vast Tywi Forest. No prizes for guessing which one I chose.

The only disadvantage of this new route was that our views might be obscured by forestry as we climbed, Harri warned me.

The entry fee for Strata Florida comes into force on April 1 (and remains until October 31) so it was quite fortuitous that our last visit was on March 31 when we could wander around the ruins of the former Cistercian abbey free of charge.

Strata Florida was founded in 1164 under the patronage of the Lord Rhys, a native prince of Deheubarth (the most southerly kingdom of Wales during the Norman period). The abbey was catapulted into significance in the twelfth century when St David's Abbey in Pembrokeshire was lost to the Normans. The Welsh princes of Deheubarth consequently transferred their patronage to the new abbey at Strata Florida, transforming it into their spiritual centre.

Over 800 years later and little of the abbey's towering structure remains except the impressive entrance archway to the abbey church. Some excellent interpretation boards help visitors to imagine what this place would have looked like in mediaeval times, but all that's really left today are its low-level walls. True, it's a beautiful setting, and it's easy to understand why it was chosen by the monks; however, Harri and I agree that the abbeys at Llanthony and Tintern (both en route) are far more impressive. There's certainly more of the original structure left to marvel at in the more southerly abbeys. Strata Florida undoubtedly paid the price for its support of Wales's native princes; it was badly damaged at the end of the thirteenth century and again during the Glyndŵr Rising of 1400–15.

Despite the paucity of intact arches, Strata Florida has to be admired for its recurring role in history. It was here that *Brut y Tywysogion* ('Chronicle of the Princes') was written, an important primary source for medieval Welsh history. Llywelyn ap Iorwerth – Llywelyn the Great – chose Strata Florida as the venue for his council of Welsh princes in 1238, encouraging them to accept his son Dafydd as their rightful leader. Even King Henry IV found a use for the abbey, commandeering it in the early 1400s as a military base during several campaigns again Owain Glyndŵr. Hell-bent on avenging the Crown, Henry expelled any monks who had supported the Welsh leader.

Strata Florida was finally dissolved in the 1540s; parts of the building were converted into a gentleman's house and the rest plundered for its stone by local people. It lay forgotten for centuries until the ambitions of the M & M Railway Company put it back on the map, for the first time becoming a tourist attraction.

In nearby Bont, the Black Lion Inn was so eager to attract passing trade that it enlarged its window openings and pretentiously added the word 'hotel' to its name.

An adjacent chapel was built around the same time as the abbey and was consecrated in 1201. St Mary's Church now stands on the site; the current church was built in 1814 and refurbished in 1875 and 1914. Dafydd ap Gwilym, one of Wales's greatest medieval poets, is said to be buried here and there is a memorial (in Welsh) to him under a yew tree. Whether the poet sleeps *ad infinitum* at Strata Florida or is in fact buried 30 miles away at Talley Abbey – or somewhere entirely different – remains contested, as do most aspects of the poet's life.

What is known is that Dafydd spent much of his life just a stone's throw away from where we live in south-east Wales. Though the age he arrived and the reasons for him coming to Gwern-y-cleppa, Bassaleg, are unclear, it *is* known that the bard enjoyed the hospitality and patronage of the man he named Ifor Hael (Ifor the Generous) for many years. Harri's friend, the historian Paul Busby, has written about their relationship on his blog (tredegarhouse.blogspot.co.uk).

Despite being born roughly 700 years ago, Dafydd's themes were surprisingly modern; he wrote frequently of retreating to the wildness of the forests to escape conventional society, waxing lyrically about birds and animals. Ironically, the luxurious (by medieval standards) court where Dafydd penned many of his poems has become something of a wilderness itself. The land upon which Ifor Hael's court stood is now privately-owned with access prohibited. Harri once went in search of the ruins but as he neared their known location, he deduced that any remaining stonework had long been subsumed by vegetation and trees. Dafydd ap Gwilym would undoubtedly have approved.

Dafydd's writings had a happier fate and 171 surviving poems are available online (www.dafyddapgwilym.net), in the original Welsh *cywydd* metre of seven-syllable lines in rhyming couplets and as English translations.

Near the north wall of St Mary's graveyard is a flat stone, which carries the rather poignant inscription dedicated to 'Unknown'. It begins: 'Died in a snowstorm by Teifi Pools Feb. 1929' and continues in verse:

> He died upon the hillside dreer
> Alone where snow was deep,
> By strangers to be carried here
> Where princes also sleep.

A scrap of paper was allegedly found in the deceased's pocket which suggested this unfortunate soul was a veteran of the Second Afghan War (1878–80). The tale is a sobering reminder of the age-old dangers of the mountains.

We needn't have worried about altering the route. The scenery and views were lovely throughout the Tywi Forest. We followed a stony and badly potholed track that climbed gradually and (mostly) ran parallel to the newer forestry track. In places, the track looked close to collapse, but the views it afforded were much better than we'd expected and we were pleased we'd decided to avoid the meadows and head uphill.

As we pushed ahead in the warm sunshine, we were a little taken aback to see a convoy of four-wheel-drive vehicles heading towards us. We stepped back and watched the passengers being tossed around inside like they were thrill seekers on some terrifying theme park ride. They were definitely having a very bumpy ride of it and, having already climbed the track, we knew their downhill journey promised even more thrills.

At last, we reached a point where the ground levelled off, and Harri announced we were about to cross a watershed, with streams and rivers on one side flowing west to the Ceredigion coast and on the other south to Carmarthen Bay. It's interesting that there can be a clear demarcation like that, but I guess where water's concerned it generally comes down to gravity.

Our huge breakfast kept us going until well after two o'clock when we settled down for a snack on a grassy outcrop overlooking the pretty (but smallish) waterfall at Nant-y-maen.

One of the most enjoyable things about this trip is how little clock-watching we've done – or needed to do. Apart from turning up for breakfast at a roughly agreed time when we've stayed at B & Bs, we've had no reason to be anywhere at any particular time. Freeing ourselves from Western culture's all-consuming obsession with time has been wonderful, and we're both relishing this simpler and healthier way of life which doesn't place unrealistic demands on our time and energy.

Why do humans obsess continually about time? Day after day, most of us charge around like headless chickens determined to complete an impossibly long list of tasks in an unfeasibly small amount of time. We allow ourselves to be persuaded that better 'time management' is all that's needed and wonder why we go to bed every night wondering why we achieved so little on our daily to-do list. I know this is true because it's exactly how I behave when I'm not walking through Wales.

In Stefan Klein's fascinating book, *Time: A User's Guide, Making Sense of Life's Scarcest Commodity*, the author talks about time perception and how we all try to control time by an over-reliance on clocks and calendars.

'The immediate future seems like a bulging suitcase into which there is far too much to stuff,' he writes. 'Most of us, it seems, are overly anxious about meeting deadlines, and women feel the time pressures of everyday life even more acutely than men.'

It's been wonderfully liberating just to go with the flow for a change. To wake up when my body decides it's had sufficient sleep, to eat when my stomach tells me it's hungry, to take a rest when my feet have had enough.

It might be difficult to imagine how society might function if we were all to abandon the ever-present timekeeper on our wrists, mobiles, laptops, ovens, central heating systems but that doesn't mean we can't all occasionally stick two fingers up at this thing we call time and relax a little.

We'd been walking for miles along forestry tracks without so much as a lone cyclist passing us; however, the moment we reached the junction of the most famously remote phone box in Wales there was a flurry of activity with vehicles whizzing around everywhere. First two huge juggernauts chugged up the hill in convoy, then several cars passed us, then a nifty sports car with the obligatory headscarf-clad female in the passenger seat, then more vehicles and so it went on. Where, we wondered, were all these drivers heading on this sunny Tuesday afternoon? Or maybe they were just enjoying the sudden arrival of summer and driving around pointlessly just for the sheer enjoyment of it?

This isolated and mainly unpopulated area was the inspiration for the late Harri Webb to produce a collection of poetry called *The Green Desert*.

Back in previously walked terrain, we enjoyed ticking off familiar landmarks – the small unnamed lake nestling alongside the track, the towering lines of conifers which seemed almost to spill onto the road below and eventually the isolated Soar y Mynydd Chapel, built in 1822 by Tregaron's minister Ebenezer Richard, when the road to Llandovery still ran past the spot.

There's nothing ornate or grand about Soar y Mynydd; we decided to pop in for old time's sake. In his 1884 manuscript *Welsh Calvinistic Methodism*, William Williams recalled his own visit to the chapel several years previously, writing 'the building was filled with attentive worshippers, and the adjoining yard was occupied by some fifty or sixty ponies, that had borne as many people to the place'.

Williams (not to be confused with Wales's great eighteenth-century hymn-writer William Williams of Pantycelyn) noted how: 'In the year 1779, a remarkable awakening began in this out-of-the-way place.'

Sadly, the whitewashed Soar y Mynydd no longer pulls in crowds of worshippers, but as the most remote place of worship in Wales it remains a popular stopping-off place for motorists, cyclists and hikers seeking somewhere to shelter when the mountain weather is doing its worst. The wooden boxed pews that once seated 100 people remain *in situ* and are packed in so tightly that there's no floor space to speak of.

In 2013, a painting of Soar y Mynydd by local artist Wynne Melville-Jones was sent to former US president Jimmy Carter, who had been impressed by the chapel when he visited the area in 1986 and is quoted as saying he'd never seen anything like it in his life. The artist himself has personal links with Soar y Mynydd – his father, the Reverend J. Melville Jones, regularly preached there.

We faced another steep ascent after the chapel. There was an option of leaving the unexciting farm track and continuing to climb across grassland. The latter was a more direct route and, as we'd been walking along track for most of the day, we opted to go for the cross-country route. We were soon regretting our decision and retracing our steps to the track over marshy ground.

What is it about Wales? We definitely seem to have more than our fair share of water here. Though I suppose frequent wet feet are what should be expected when you choose to walk across a country in lightweight running shoes rather than ankle-high hiking boots … you get wet feet! But no blisters … so far!

As we trekked past the farmhouse, a young dog came rushing at us, barking and nipping at our heels as we tried to walk. A woman appeared at the door with a baby and called him off apologetically. I laughed, saying the dog had probably mistaken us for a couple of stray sheep. If only we were right, she sighed, but unfortunately this mutt hadn't got the hang of dealing with sheep as yet. To her perpetual embarrassment, it seemed he preferred to concentrate his youthful energy into rounding up passing hikers.

We climbed steadily, pausing to watch the large-scale tree felling operation that was taking place on a nearby slope. We regularly walk through felled sections of forestry but had never before witnessed the methodical cutting down and removal of these huge fir trees.

Another hill climbed, we were soon descending into the steep-sided Doethie valley, one of the most scenic in mid Wales and a favourite of ours. We've walked this valley in both directions, yet it always seemed harder to determine the *right* footpath when approaching from the north. Fortunately, one of us was on the ball and we hadn't gone too far in the wrong direction before I cottoned onto our mistake. I don't have Harri's homing pigeon instinct, but I've learned to question any route that involves climbing and mud … just in case. Happily, on this occasion, I was right; we did an about turn and headed downhill again.

Harri was surprised how marshy and eroded the footpath seemed to be throughout the length of the valley. Last time we walked this way it had been firm underfoot and neither us recalled such a high level of erosion. I wondered if the current rutted and muddy ground might be the result of the valley's popularity with mountain bikers (the Doethie is frequently named among the top biking trails in Wales); however, Harri explained how it's a misconception that mountain biking causes

178

erosion. Scientific research has demonstrated that mountain biking actually compacts the ground so is more likely to prevent erosion than cause it. If it wasn't mountain bikers who were wrecking the footpath, the only other explanation was cows!

Despite being boggier than we'd have liked, this valley definitely deserves its place on 'O Fôn i Fynwy' – the scenery is simply stunning and we always enjoy walking here. Unfortunately, today it was a tough call whether to keep our eyes peeled on the ground, thus avoiding *really* wet feet, or just give up on the feet and instead concentrate on enjoying the gorgeous landscape.

We eventually emerged on a lane which would take us to Rhandirmwyn, but first there was the little question of a beverage. I'd enjoyed a 50th birthday drink at the Towy Bridge Inn and on that occasion, the owner told us he'd had to put the pub on the market because he couldn't make a living there. It's a lovely spot, right next to the Afon Doethie and with plenty of outside seating. At the time we thought it was a real shame that yet another country pub was likely to soon be closing its doors for the last time. Three years on, we fully expected it to have been converted into a house. What a happy surprise then to discover the Towy Bridge Inn was still alive and kicking – with the new owner waiting behind the bar to welcome two weary hikers in dire need of a drink. This establishment is always going to have the disadvantage of being slightly out of the village; however, we really hope the new owner manages to make a success of his business and is supported by the local community to do so.

While the Towy Bridge Inn has benefited from having new life breathed into it, the beautiful Grade II farmhouse and stone outbuildings of Broncwrt on the opposite bank of the Towy looked as empty (though not as neglected) as it had on our last visit. Such a magnificent home in a beautiful spot; it's crying out for children to run across that farmyard.

Stopping at a pub a mile or two short of the day's final destination is usually a mistake (yet still we do it!). I'd been flagging badly for the past hour and while we were walking through the Doethie valley I'd managed to overbalance and topple onto my knees. Add a glass of cider to the mix and Harri's proposed route through woodland and then along the riverbank sounded like a recipe for disaster. It seemed imminently more sensible to part company with one another for fifteen minutes or so and head into Rhandirmwyn on different routes.

The village name is derived from two Welsh words: *rhandir*, meaning area of land, and *mwyn*, meaning mineral, in this case referring to lead and zinc. The Nant-y-mwyn lead mine, after which the village was once named, is believed to pre-date Roman times and remained active until 1932.

These days Rhandirmwyn relies mainly on farming and tourism. Most villages and towns like to remember a favourite son, or occasionally daughter, and more than 400 years after his death, Rhandirmwyn remains proud of its own Robin Hood figure, the infamous Twm Sion Cati.

As with much folklore, historians have long struggled to separate fact from legend, but what does seem true is that Twm Sion Cati was born Thomas Jones in 1530 at Porth y Ffynnon (Fountain Gate) near Tregaron, Cardiganshire, and later became a Welsh bard, winning the Llandaff Eisteddfod in 1561. As a young man, he gained a reputation as a highwayman and trickster, though allegedly robbing only the rich and taking care not to seriously harm his victims. A Welsh Robin Hood.

Frequently forced into hiding, Twm Sion Cati would take refuge in a cave high above the Twyi river on the inaccessible and boulder-covered slopes of the Dinas Hill near Rhandirmwyn. His hideout was difficult to locate, helping him to escape the long arm of the law. In 2009, Carmarthenshire Council erected a wooden staircase to make it easier for people to clamber up the rocky terrain and peer into the graffiti-covered cave. The route of 'O Fôn i Fynwy' doesn't actually pass through the wooded RSPB sanctuary where the cave is located, but if you're keen to visit the cave, it's only a half mile detour.

After his colourful youth, Twm fled to Geneva in 1557; when he returned two years later he was granted a royal pardon by Elizabeth I.

I'm not sure about sleeping in a cave. After two nights of comfort, however, it was time for us to toughen up and put our tent up again. The campsite in Rhandirmwyn is run by the Camping and Caravanning Club and is beautifully laid-out and maintained. There were only two drawbacks: its location on the riverbank meant there were a lot of midges around, and, inexplicably, the tent field was located about as far away from the toilet/shower block as possible. Yes, all those people in huge camper vans and touring caravans *who wouldn't need to use the campsite's toilets in the night* were nonetheless located right next to them, whereas those of us with no en-suite facilities faced a long, unlit trek to the loos dodging said camper vans' electricity cables.

The inconvenience of the conveniences aside (though the toilet block was up there with Beddgelert in terms of facilities and cleanliness), this was a first-rate campsite in a stunning location. There's little likelihood of me ever becoming one of those hardy outdoor types who choose to camp even when there's a perfectly decent and affordable hotel across the road; however, it's good to know there are some pretty amazing campsites around for those occasions when we want to save our pennies. Shame about the midges.

For photographs visit uk.pinterest.com/thewalkerswife

JUNE 18: RHANDIRMWYN TO LLANDOVERY

We'd received a friendly enough welcome at the campsite last night but hadn't been able to pay due to the peculiarities of the electronic till system. This meant we had no choice but to linger this morning until reception reopened at 9 a.m. Not exactly mid-morning, I agree, but far later than we'd otherwise have set off on this perfect summer's day and only emphasizing further how far down the pecking order we long-distance hikers are when campsite owners are shaping the facilities.

I'd had a good night's sleep by camping standards; however, from the outset, and for no reason I could put my finger on, I felt completely drained, devoid of even an ounce of energy. The short climb from the valley bottom to the lane above seemed endless. My rucksack dragged painfully on my shoulders and I was tempted to check no one had slipped a sheep inside while I was sleeping. Despite jigging it this way and that in an attempt to shift the weight around and it more bearable, I couldn't get comfortable at all.

I was also starting to feel homesick, which was absurd because we'd be home within the week. The truth was that the sparkle of our project had dimmed and the notion of a middle-aged woman walking all day every day for several weeks now seemed faintly ridiculous.

Surely there were more useful things for me to be doing than rambling around Wales? Perhaps getting on with the novel I started last summer, or looking for the job I really needed. My mind was suddenly whirring with a list of pressing domestic chores. I should be gardening or decorating, or sorting out the kitchen cupboards. When was the last time I cleaned the oven? Or cleaned on top of the wardrobes?

There was so much to attend to back in Newport, yet here I was wandering through mid Wales with a rucksack on my back and a camera around my neck. In truth, I could barely be bothered to put one foot in front of the other on this sunny June morning and even the ironing seemed more appealing than hiking.

Sensing my weariness, Harri tried to engage me in upbeat conversation, but, try as he would, my mood refused to lift. It didn't help that the byway that had looked so solid underfoot at the outset had mysteriously transformed itself into one gigantic puddle. At one point we had no option but to climb into an adjacent field and follow the waterlogged track from the other side of the hedge.

One of the problems is that four-wheel-drive vehicles are allowed to use byways and their heavier weight often results in the breaking down of the lane's surface. The drivers aren't doing anything illegal, of course, but the increasing popularity of larger family vehicles at a time when councils have seen their road maintenance budgets drastically cut is bound to have a detrimental impact on the quality of many rural lanes. Unless action is taken, many of the byways hikers currently enjoy are going to become all but impassable to anyone who isn't driving a 4x4 or doesn't fancy a swim.

Everything felt such a massive effort this morning and nothing seemed to be going according to plan. We climbed a too-high stile (who installs these things ... eight-foot giants?) and followed a footpath down through two steep fields only to find it came to an abrupt halt at a muddy stream. I scowled at the cows who'd gathered to watch us and dragged myself back up the hill, all the while grumbling about having to scale said stile for a second time.

Tearful and exhausted, I finally blurted out what had been bothering me all morning. I was sick of hiking, sick of getting up every day and walking for miles, sick of mountains and rivers and bogs, sick of cows and sheep and even wild ponies. I'd had it with Wales's wet weather and the blustery winds and, yes, even the sunshine. Harri was clearly concerned. These were clearly not words he wanted to hear at this advanced stage of our journey.

You should never allow the floodgates to open, because when you do, you find it's impossible to close them. Every tired, muddled thought in my head came gushing out as an incoherent surge.

Why had he not warned me how tough this journey was going to be? How much it was going to cost? Didn't he realise there were other things in life apart from hiking? Things like family, friends, running, reading, lazy holidays (I must have been feeling low because I'd really, *really* hate a holiday that didn't involve lots of activity). On and on I ranted, growing more tearful and emotional by the minute.

My torrent included complaints about the many times we'd walked sections of the Cambrian Way, researched walking books in Wales, done AA work in Wales, walked across boggy Welsh land, etc., etc. As I let loose, it dawned on me that I'd spent both my 50th and 51st birthdays walking sections of Harri's precious Cambrian Way, which struck me as the pinnacle of selfishness on his part.

As if wishing to mock my human frailty, the Carmarthen Fans chose that moment to appear on the horizon, looming high and dark in the distance. It was our first glimpse of the Brecon Beacons, but instead of feeling excited, I just wanted to sit down and wail.

'Do you want to go home?' Harri asked me, gently. I shook my head.

'Right then,' announced my lovely, easy-going other half (who obviously knows me better than I know myself). 'This is what we'll do. When we reach Llandovery, we're going to call it a day. You're obviously exhausted. You need a rest and a proper meal.'

But there was no pleasing me in the mood I was in. Instead of just agreeing and thanking my lucky stars that I'd been blessed with such an understanding partner, I wanted to keep going, persuading myself that the more miles we covered each day, the quicker my ordeal – for at that point I really saw it as one – would be over. Of course, my completely irrational behaviour was simply down to overtiredness, and thankfully Harri realised that. He also knew that ever since the idea for 'O Fôn i Fynwy' had been hatched, I'd been completely on board and as enthusiastic about the project as him. I was just having a bad day ... a spectacularly bad day.

Still in disagreement over whether we were stopping at Llandovery or pushing ahead to goodness knows where, we paused briefly to look around the graveyard at Llanfair-ar-y-bryn where William Williams Pantycelyn is buried. Williams (1717–91) is acknowledged as a leader of the eighteenth-century Methodist Revival in Wales, along with Howell Harris and Daniel Rowland, and remained an important influence on Welsh-language culture long after his death.

He is undoubtedly Wales's most famous hymn writer and is responsible for the ever-popular 'Guide Me, O Thou Great Redeemer', sung at Princess Diana's funeral and Prince William's wedding. The song – colloquially known as 'Bread of Heaven' – is also a favourite at rugby matches in Wales.

As a young curate, Williams's application for ordination as a priest was refused because he was involved in the Methodist movement. Forced to decide between Anglicanism or Methodism, he chose the latter and devoted his life to it.

We headed into Llandovery, Harri keeping his eyes peeled for accommodation and food. I was feeling slightly calmer by now, so we decided we'd go for a pub lunch, forgetting that this is mid Wales and it was now just after 2.30 p.m. Today it wasn't so much a case of 'no room at the inn' as 'no food at the inn'. It really is rather exasperating; I don't know what overseas tourists must make of our very arbitrary serving hours.

No late pub lunch then; we concentrated our efforts into finding somewhere to stay. Spotting Llandovery's Tourist Information Centre, we headed inside. I could see Harri turning green with envy as he compared the spacious, well-laid out premises brimming with interesting reading matter and gifts with his own cramped and understocked workplace in Caerleon.

There wasn't, it transpired, a lot of low-priced accommodation in Llandovery town centre, but perhaps we might be interested in a nearby hostel? It wasn't too far away, just opposite the railway station (hence its name, The Level Crossing). Harri didn't bat an eyelid about the location (or not that I noticed) but it must have crossed his mind that being so close to a railway station wasn't necessary a good thing. As luck would have it, one of the hostel's employees was actually in the TIC so she telephoned and checked there was a double room available.

Phew! That was our bed for the night sorted. The kindly lady escorted us to The Level Crossing, a short walk away. We hadn't been sure what to expect, but we were pleasantly surprised. Our room was en suite and although it was basic, i.e. lockers instead of a wardrobe, no television, no tea-making facilities, etc., everything was very clean and modern. We had twin beds, but the room was so airless we saw that as a bonus … it's so much easier to sleep separately in the heat.

By now we were ravenous (no big cooked breakfast this morning). We'd had a family-run café recommended to us that carried on serving *all* afternoon, but before we could get going, something very strange happened. I popped into the bathroom and suddenly, I was sitting on the loo sobbing my heart out. Poor Harri. Llandovery train station was just across the road; if I wanted to bail, he knew I wouldn't get a better opportunity.

The truth was I really did want to walk the length of my country. I wanted to hike the full distance between Wales's traditional ends, see everything our beautiful country has to offer between Anglesey and Monmouthshire. It's just that exhaustion does strange things to people, and the accumulative effect of walking so many miles day after day had undoubtedly caught up with me.

Llandovery is actually a pretty little market town, located at the very western edge of the Brecon Beacons (maybe it was this perceived proximity to home that was the reason for my meltdown). George Borrow writes in *Wild Wales*, 'I have no hesitation in saying [it] is about the pleasantest little town in which I have halted in the course of my wanderings.'

Llandovery's Welsh name of Llanymyddyfri means 'church among the waters', the waters in question being the Towy, Bran and Gwydderig rivers.

Nestling on the slopes of the upper Towy Valley, Llandovery once lay at the junction of three droving routes and thus became an important meeting place for the drovers. And long before the drovers, the Romans arrived here, building a fort at Llanfair-ar-y-bryn around AD 50–60 as part of their plans to conquer Wales. In the end they stuck around for about four centuries in the settlement they called ALABVM, during which time they successfully held their fort against the Celts.

Present-day Llandovery sprang up around the twelfth-century Norman castle. The castle had been standing just 42 years when control was seized by the Welsh under Gruffydd ap Rhys. This state of affairs didn't last long, and control alternated between the Welsh and English for years, during which time there was also some infighting by Rhys's heirs. Edward I seized the castle in 1277 and, apart from a few months in 1282 when Llywelyn the Last took control, it thereafter remained in English hands, and over the centuries gradually fell into neglect.

Little of the original structure remains *in situ*, although castle stonework is dotted around the town thanks to numbers of 'recycling' enthusiasts over the centuries.

Occasionally, Llandovery's history becomes rather gruesome; it was here that wealthy local landowner Lord Llywelyn ap Gruffydd Fychan was publically executed in 1401 for supporting Owain Glyndŵr in his fight for Wales's independence. A blue plaque on the HSBC bank stating '*Llywelyn ap Gruffyd Fychan was executed near this spot on 9th October 1401*' now marks the spot where he died with King Henry IV and his young son (the future Henry V) looking on.

To be fair, the townsfolk of Llandovery have done their best to make up for the foul deed committed in their town (though emphatically not at their hands), and in 2001 they erected a 20-foot stainless steel statue of the Welsh resistance hero, created by St Clears sculptors Toby and Gideon Peterson.

The statue, commissioned to commemorate the 600th anniversary of Llywelyn's execution and standing on a 17-tonne limestone boulder quarried from nearby Llyn Brianne (and donated by Welsh Water), is certainly impressive. At first glance, it appears to depict Llywelyn wielding his helmet and Celtic spear, ready for battle; look closer and you will see there is no head inside the helmet. The Petersons' imposing statue is a stark reminder of the brutal nature of Llywelyn's death (he was hanged, drawn and quartered).

Given the impressive size of this stainless-steel sculpture, it's difficult to believe that it might never have happened were it not for a *tour de force* in the shape of Robert ap Steffan, who first convinced the people of Llandovery that they needed this tourist attraction and then raised the necessary £60,000 funding.

As well as its significance in terms of Welsh history, the area surrounding Llandovery is also significant from a geological viewpoint. In fact, the market town lies on the outermost edge of Fforest Fawr Geopark (the name means 'great forest'), Wales's first European geopark.

The rocks underneath Llandovery belong to the Ordovician period, a time around 500 million years ago when there was volcanic activity in Wales. Fforest Fawr's oldest rocks are the sandstones, mudstones and limestones in the Llandovery area. They were laid down horizontally when a sea called the Welsh Basin covered the region, but the 'Caledonia Orogeny' (Britain's mountain building era) catapulted them into their steeply tilting present-day position.

Interestingly, the most seismically active area in Wales today (as well as one of most active in the UK) is the Menai Strait. The 1984 earthquake measured 5.4 on the Richter Scale and was one of the largest recorded in the UK in the twentieth century. The earthquake was also unusual in being onshore – its epicentre was on the nearby Llŷn Peninsula.

One of my favourite exhibits at the National Museum of Wales was always the continental drift counter, which explained very graphically how America and Europe are steadily drifting apart at a rate of about one inch a year as a result of volcanic activity on the seafloor. And if you think that doesn't sound very much, remember it adds up to nearly eight and a half feet per century ... every century. Standing there gazing at that counter in Cardiff certainly made plate tectonics come alive for me.

Geopark status is not just about rocks. According to the official website, a geopark is 'a territory whose geological heritage is of European significance' with each adopting 'a holistic approach to their heritage and ... [promoting] all aspects of their region's natural and cultural heritage'.

I'm still struggling to understand what this actually means in practice and how the relationship between Fforest Fawr and the larger Brecon Beacons National Park works, but I'm certainly open to being educated and, besides, the more official statuses you can garner for a place the better, yes?

For no reason at all, I've just remembered a bus trip we took from Brecon to Craig y Nos a few years ago. Back then, the Brecon Beacons National Park ran an excellent summer bus service on Sundays and Bank Holiday Mondays with a knowledgeable tour guide on board.

Ours certainly knew her geology but she wasn't quite as hot on Welsh pronunciation (when Harri reads this be sure he'll be shouting 'pot' and 'kettle'!). Her mispronunciation of Welsh mountains and place names gave us much cause for merriment – particular favourites were Fan y Big, which she referred to as Fanny Big (it sounds more like Van er Beeg, but perhaps she was getting muddled up with US-finance giant Fannie Mae) and Pen y Fan, which she insisted on pronouncing as Penny Fan.

Sadly, the excellent service was reluctantly withdrawn in 2014 as a result of 'falling income from partners and concessionary fares, a significant rise in tendered prices for the coming year and to accommodate overall funding reductions of more than 13% over the next two years'. Its demise is certainly a great loss to visitors to the Brecon Beacons, particularly to hikers wishing to follow a linear route.

At The Level Crossing, Harri mopped up my tears and we headed to the nearby West End Cafe which happily lived up to its recommendation. My Thai fishcakes were delicious and Harri thoroughly enjoyed his curry. The restorative powers of good homemade food and a pot of good strong tea should never be underestimated.

When we emerged an hour later, I remembered why I'd loved Llandovery so much on my first visit here back in 2011. It's one of those places that's brimming with charm and quirkiness and independent shops; outside one, pairs of old jeans had been put to good use and transformed into unusual planters. There was a fabulous health food shop, Iechyd Da, overflowing with so many appetising-looking goodies that Harri had to once again remind me we were hiking, and one of those wonderful old-fashioned iron mongers that induce in people the sudden and inexplicable urge to buy hinges and clothes lines and a whole myriad of other things they never knew they wanted until they stepped over the threshold (please tell me it's not just me!).

There's a tale about how Twm Sion Cati once visited an ironmonger in Llandovery to purchase a pan for a poor man. When he heard the high price, he told the unsuspecting shopkeeper there was a hole in the pan. The ironmonger raised the pan and the trickster forced it over his head, declaring that there must indeed exist a hole if such large head could get inside.

One of my regrets about the timing of our Welsh expedition was it meant missing my youngest daughter's exhibition at college. She plans to pursue a career in film and television set design and has spent the past year on an art and design foundation course. Her final project was an ambitious installation piece, constructed entirely from old video cases, video cassettes and the unravelled tape.

At home, we don't tend to hang on to things we no longer use or need, so in spite of keeping our old video player (for the very few videos we still have *and never watch*), we certainly couldn't supply the hundreds our daughter now needed.

It didn't matter because as soon as I put word out to the wonderful running community that she was looking for old videos, we were inundated. Over the next month, I transported numerous boxes and bags of videos to her classroom; however, such is the secrecy shrouding a great artist at work that I'd never seen the actual installation taking shape.

My older daughters provided family support on the night; however, I was disappointed that I couldn't be there myself. Now photographs of the finished piece had been posted on Facebook and I was keen to view them. Except … yes, you've guessed it. Even in a town as big as Llandovery there was no decent internet access in our second-floor room. The lovely people at The Level Crossing suggested leaning as close as possible to the window in the (first floor) conference room where apparently the signal was strongest.

I managed to view the images and press the 'Like' button a few times before losing the Wi-Fi signal again. It wasn't ideal but at least I'd seen my daughter's finished artwork – and I was incredibly proud of what she'd be able to create with what was basically my friends' old rubbish.

We nibbled, drank cider and rested for the rest of the evening; in one way, perhaps we were wasting a beautiful balmy summer evening (and how many of those do we get in Wales?), but it was a nice change to do nothing and recuperate for a few hours. Harri had time to catch up with his notes while I sorted out the laundry then lolled around reading the day's *i* newspaper (which despite its price – 30p – and diminutive size is really rather informative and kept me occupied for over an hour). Note to self: sometimes it's good just to chill.

For photographs visit uk.pinterest.com/thewalkerswife

JUNE 19: LLANDOVERY TO DAN YR OGOF

I wish I could say we woke refreshed and raring to go, but that wouldn't be true; the combination of humidity, endlessly itching midge bites and constant passing traffic did not result in the most restful of nights.

Though yesterday's black mood had lifted, I wasn't in any hurry to rush out there and start climbing mountains, even ones as stunning as the Carmarthen Fans.

Just as well that the hostel served breakfast. The lady who'd brought us here last night had mentioned that she had a 9 a.m appointment, so we'd agreed to come down for breakfast at 8.15 a.m. Not that we'd have been able to linger in our room – after such a short day yesterday, Harri was hoping we'd be able to make up some miles.

We ate in The Level Crossing's bistro, an unfussy modern space with large windows and a nice airy feel. From our table, there was an unbroken view of the railway station. I think Harri was feeling more relaxed about its proximity this morning. We always knew 'O Fôn i Fynwy' wasn't going to be a walk in the park, that there would be days when we wondered why on earth we had embarked on this long-distance walk, but neither of us had imagined my tiredness would lead to such a dramatic and tearful meltdown.

In the great scheme of things, ours wasn't a spectacular distance to be walking over four weeks. Certainly not when you consider the thousands of solitary miles walked by Ffyona Campbell or the mammoth European hike BBC presenter Nicholas Crane undertook in the early nineties.

Harri and I have both read – and thoroughly enjoyed – the *Coast* presenter's book *Clear Waters Rising*, an account of his solitary walk of several thousand miles from Finisterre in Galicia to Istanbul.

Facing eighteen months on the road, Crane didn't have the option of luxury accommodation, frequently having to bunk down in wet, uncomfortable conditions. While I might occasionally lament the lack of facilities in the more rural parts of Wales, be assured they are first class compared to what the Balkans had to offer two decades ago.

A sole hiker had arrived at the neighbouring table and we struck up conversation while he awaited his companions. Life is full of coincidences. When Harri explained that the original catalyst for our project was the Cambrian Way, this Englishman told us he'd known the late Tony Drake and had himself walked several sections of the route.

Over breakfast, it also transpired that our breakfast chef and waitress was none other than the deputy mayor of Llandovery, Councillor Gillian Wright. She explained that she was helping out for a few days while her daughter, the manager of The Level Crossing, took a much-earned break. Only in Wales.

The bunkhouse and bistro is a community interest project rather than a privately owned enterprise. It's based in a former pub, the North Western, and caters for 35 people in rooms which sleep up to ten. Fortunately, there are smaller rooms for couples like Harri and me who prefer a little privacy.

Llandovery was in the midst of a mini heatwave, meaning we'd had no problem washing and drying clothes overnight in our room. The Level Crossing does, however, have its own drying room, which makes it perfect for those walking 'O Fôn i Fynwy' or any other long-distance route in mid Wales.

Once we'd cracked her 'disguise', Councillor Wright revealed that her 9 a.m. appointment wasn't with the dentist but was an official mayoral engagement. She had her chains with her in a small case, and a little group gathered around the table to admire them.

In the morning sunshine, Llandovery looked absolutely perfect, a charming small town that's delightful to wander around on foot. We'd be camping again tonight, so we needed to buy some supplies. Harri employed his long-practised supermarket avoidance tactics, announcing out of the blue that there was an alternative path into town he needed to 'check out'.

While he disappeared with his map, I popped into the centrally located NISA store rather than trek the full length of the high street to the supermarket, hoping there'd be less temptation in the smaller store. Rather annoyingly, the family-sized packs of Jelly Beans (on special offer yesterday) had vanished from display; it served us right for devouring an entire packet last night. Today's offer was half-price Frosties, so I grabbed a box, reasoning that would be breakfast sorted for the next few days.

As we climbed out of Llandovery, my spirits soared, so much so that after a few miles of walking through this wonderfully lush landscape, it was impossible to fathom yesterday's despair. True, some of the recent hiking had been tough and the days long, and, yes, we'd had some bad weather (though things seemed to be looking up now), but sobbing on the toilet? After more than two weeks, I was also missing my girls, but we'd been apart for similar lengths of time before and I'd survived. The explanation had to be tiredness, pure and simple.

Now I was thinking rationally, I was convinced Harri had made the right call when he'd insisted we stop overnight at Llandovery. The morning's hiking involved some of the steepest on-lane climbs we'd encountered so far, and I wouldn't have had the physical or mental energy to tackle them yesterday. As we walked, the splendour of the Carmarthen Fans beckoned ever closer, our first summits in the Brecon Beacons National Park. Yesterday morning their towering height had dismayed me; now I couldn't wait to climb them and look out on those amazing views.

As anticipated, Myddfai was as pretty as a picture, if strangely deserted. Apparently, over 400 people live in this exquisite locality, yet on this glorious Thursday morning in June not one of them was around to pass the time of day with us, and every one of those well-tended gardens was empty.

Not so many years ago, the village had a pub, a post office and a school – places where villagers would meet and socialise. The old village school is now a luxury five-bedroom, four-bathroom holiday home, equipped to sleep ten guests 'in great comfort'.

In his 1991 history of the village, *Myddfai: Its Land and Peoples*, author David B. James writes: 'The modern traveller visiting the village has only one inn to call at, the Plough. There is record of at least another two, the Kings Head which closed around 1925 and the Myddfai Arms which seems to have ceased functioning as a public house around 1880; its site is now occupied by The Manse.'

James reflected that: 'the demise of the inns was probably accelerated by the substantial decrease which had taken place in the population of the parish but allied no doubt to changing social conditions and attitudes. These changes were reflected and represented by the two nonconformist chapels, Seion and Bethania which had been built at the edge of the village but within sight of the old church – Llanfihangel ym Myddfai.'

At the time of writing, the Plough Inn was on the market for £330,000, its tradition of offering liquid refreshments a distant memory. The asking price suggests that it's unlikely to be bought by a local; property around these parts now attracts an altogether different class of buyer. In 2007, the Prince of Wales bought the nearby 192-acre Llwynywermod estate for a reported £1 million. At the time, an estate agent was quoted as saying that the arrival of a Royal neighbour would only push up house prices.

To be fair, Prince Charles's Welsh home is very modest by royal standards: it is the three-bedroomed coach house he and Camilla have refurbished and not the ruined mansion house. They also sourced local materials and craftspeople as much as possible. Historian Mark Baker details the history of the estate and its restoration in *A Royal Home in Wales: Llwynywermod*.

In 2011, Myddfai featured in the BBC One programme *Village SOS*, when villagers were supported in their long-term bid to raise money to build a new community hall and visitor centre. A Big Lottery Fund grant was secured, and locals' vision for a centre to revitalise the community was realised. The new centre is now selling the wares of talented local artists and craftsmen, while the Myddfai Trading Company (a social enterprise) produces and sells luxury beauty products, Welsh organic herbal teas and wooden toys. There's also an inviting-looking cafe, though with such a long day ahead of us we sadly didn't have time to investigate the cake on display.

It's great to know the little village of Myddfai is fighting back, and we really hope these modern-day entrepreneurs will be as successful and acclaimed as the legendary physicians of Myddfai, who were famed for their healing powers for centuries.

Like all legends, it's hard to disentangle the truth from the fanciful, and this particular story has more versions than most. What appears to be true is that the physicians existed as far back as the twelfth century and that their healing powers and herbal medicinal remedies were seen as very progressive.

Less believable is the story that the original physicians were the three sons of the magical 'Lady of the Lake'. This beautiful fairy being, said to live below the waters of Llyn y Fan Fach, agreed to marry a local farmer who had fallen in love with her, but eventually returned to the lake with all the livestock she had brought as a dowry when he broke a promise not to strike her three times. The couple's sons allegedly inherited their mother's magical powers and became known as the Physicians of Myddfai.

Historic records suggest that the first physician was a practitioner called Rhiwallon who tended the Welsh prince Lord Rhys at Dinefwr. Rhiwallon was assisted in his medicinal work by his three sons, Cadwgan, Griffith and Einion. The last of the Myddfai physicians was John Jones, who died in 1739; however, Sir John Williams, Queen Victoria's physician, also claimed to be a descendant.

Around this time, the new monastery at Strata Florida was being established, sponsored by the Lord Rhys. It's likely that the monastery became a centre for herbal healing and that successful remedies for ailments like headache, coughs and swellings were passed down to subsequent generations. For years it would seem, Myddfai was a centre of excellence for medical practice, its physicians in constant demand.

I just wished one of those celebrated herbal healers had discovered a remedy for midge bites – the itching from mine was driving me to distraction.

We bade farewell to the lovely ladies in the arts centre and carried on up the lane, standing to one side to let a *white* Royal Mail van pass. The scenery in these parts is so pretty that it's impossible to do it justice in words. The narrow lanes are almost traffic-free and the fields undulating and full of cows. With few visual reminders of the twenty-first century, it's easy to imagine how rural life might have been several hundred years ago.

We'd been walking about half an hour when the Royal Mail van drew up behind us again. The driver called out, asking where we were heading and adding that we were moving at a very brisk pace. Mid Wales may be short on facilities at times, but it's certainly not lacking in friendliness. We didn't keep the postie talking for long – he had letters to deliver and we had the Carmarthen Fans to climb – but it was nice that he'd bothered to stop for a brief conversation.

Harri had mentioned that we'd shortly be reaching the Red Kite Centre at Llanddeusant where there was a cafe. In view of the heat, we decided we'd push the boat out and treat ourselves to an ice-cold drink and/or lollies (we certainly know how to live!). For some reason, he was fancying a glass of Lucozade, but I doubted the range of drinks available would be *that* extensive.

Imagine our dismay when we rounded the corner to discover that the cafe was no more. The Red Kite Centre still appears to be open for kite feeding at certain times of the day, but this remote cafe on the outskirts of the national park clearly didn't attract sufficient regular custom to survive. It's a real shame, not just for us, but for all those who enjoy wandering off the beaten track. It's the age-old dilemma: holidaymakers and tourists flock to the places where facilities already exist. The infrastructure has to be in place *before* they will come, but all too often a rural business can't survive while it's waiting to be discovered by the masses.

Harri wondered if the resurgence of the red kite population in Wales – clearly a *good* thing – might to some extent have contributed to the demise of the cafe. If a species is rare, people are more likely to head to a known spot to see it. Twenty years ago, there were fewer than thirty breeding pairs of red kites; now there are over 300!

The Red Kite Centre attributes this population explosion in part to its regular feeding sessions (3 p.m. during British Summer Time and 2 p.m. at all other times). We were passing far too early to get involved, which was a shame, but with Harri alongside me frequently calling out 'red kite' or 'buzzard', I probably get to see my fair share of this graceful bird with its distinctive forked tail. (A word of explanation: Harri's childhood friend, Andrew, now a geneticist, has always been an avid bird watcher and throughout their teenage years shared his enthusiasm with Harri.)

Just before we reached the youth hostel at Llanddeusant (where we planned to eat our picnic lunch before venturing into the mountains proper), we got an insight into what Welsh farming life is all about. As we walked along a lane, we encountered a farmer who was moving a large flock of sheep from one field to another with the assistance of several sheepdogs. It was riveting to watch them work, running this way and that, nipping at the heels of any errant individual to keep the flock moving forward together. We stood right back in a gateway while the sheep were herded past, the occasional few pausing to inspect us before one of the dogs rushed up to hustle them forward.

The final climb to the hostel is an absolute killer – one of those hills that you know would be just as tough to walk down as up.

We stopped here three years ago when Harri was researching walks for *Day Walks in the Brecon Beacons*, so we knew there was a small camping field in front of the building where we could sit and eat. On that occasion, we'd been extended the use of the hostel's toilet facilities by the volunteer warden, so we were hoping the same kindness would be extended this time around.

One of the biggest hurdles you need to overcome when you're a serious hiker is the ability to pee outdoors. Completely unproblematic for men whose physiology lends itself to a discrete widdle, it's a slightly more daunting prospect for us women. For starters, we need more time to extricate our body parts from our clothing, do the necessary and make sure everything's back in the right place. Secondly, and more crucially, women (and I think I speak for most of us here) tend to be more prudish about flashing our flesh. Boys grow up using urinals, making it seem perfectly normal for them to wee in the company of others. Girls, on the other hand, have deeply ingrained notions of propriety and discretion. From childhood, we've been taught to hang on, legs crossed, for hours rather than risk being caught - horror of horrors - responding to the call of nature. I'm certain the queues in the ladies would reduce dramatically if we accepted that excretion is a normal physiological function and we don't need to remain inside the cubicle, door locked securely, until we can get the toilet to flush again.

Fortunately, years of hiking and running have made me less adverse to 'a wee with a view' than many of my gender. Even so, there are times when it can be difficult, e.g. on popular trails, open moorland, canal towpaths, etc.

We'd been following tarmac lanes for several miles by the time we reached Llanddeusant, without easy access to woods or fields. To put it bluntly, I needed that toilet!

My heart sank as we rounded the corner. Someone was cutting the grass in front of the hostel with a strimmer, scuppering our plans for a picnic on the lawn. Fortunately, the 'gardener' was none other than part-time manager Paul, who immediately stopped what he was doing to say 'hello' and offer us a cup of tea. What is it about we British and tea? Even on this scorcher of a day – when half an hour ago we were salivating about ice lollies – we weren't about to turn down a cuppa. The hostel's small-scale catering operates on a self-service and donation-basis, so we paid 75p each and headed for the kitchen area.

Then disaster struck. Paul couldn't find any teabags. A prolonged search followed, during which he pulled all manner of snack bars and cereal packs from the well-stocked cupboards. Eventually – and to everyone's relief – the elusive box of teabags was found and the tea-making operation started in earnest.

Paul is an interesting individual; a science teacher by profession, he'd got involved with the youth hostel after arriving one day on his motorbike. Before he knew what was happening, he was agreeing to take on a part-time management role at Llanddeusant. He clearly enjoyed his work and was enthusiastic about the future of the hostel.

We'd have been happy with chipped mugs, but this lovely man had decided to do things properly. To our surprise, he emerged carrying a tray laid with teapot and cups. If I was having afternoon tea on the lawn, I really should make an effort to dress up for the occasion, I thought. I rifled around in my rucksack and hurriedly plonked the sunhat on my head.

One of the other guests, a man in his early sixties or thereabouts, thought the scene was hilarious and asked if he could take a photograph of me sitting there at a table on the freshly mown lawn with my teapot and khaki hat. He told us he'd walked from Craig y Nos and across the Fans that morning, so had done the same route we were about to do but in reverse. It had taken him five hours and he looked pretty fit; it was time to get going if we were to reach our campsite at a reasonable hour.

Through necessity and the scarcity of shopping opportunities, we'd had to choose foods with a high energy to weight ratio and a long rucksack life rather than those we most enjoy eating. Today's lunch comprised of one Frikadellen each slotted into a fresh, unbuttered bread roll with Pringles as a side dish. Not the most exciting fare but substantial and filling.

It was time to say our goodbyes and head into the mountains. We couldn't have picked a more perfect day, warm and windless with nothing more threatening than the occasional high cloud floating overhead.

We soon joined the popular and well-walked Beacons Way, conceived by the late John Sansom and Arwel Michael at the height of the foot and mouth outbreak in the UK.

I was working for Monmouthshire Council at the time, and I remember clearly what a devastating effect the 2001 crisis had on rural tourism. While Tony Blair was busily assuring everyone that 'Britain is indeed open for business. The message is clear: go and visit the countryside but stay off the farmland,' the rest of us were coming to terms with the fact that the countryside was most definitely not open. With practically every handkerchief-sized piece of grass, woodland and open moorland out of bounds, it was pretty much impossible to go for a country stroll. Despite the Prime Minister's supposedly reassuring words, those of us who tried to visit rural Wales knew the countryside was taped off as securely as if it were one massive crime scene.

I remember travelling to the Brecon Beacons for a family day out. There was red and white tape everywhere. We ended up settling down on the rough surface of the Brecon Mountain Railway car park to 'enjoy' our picnic (there simply was no alternative except abandoning our picnic and heading to a cafe). This dreadful state of affairs continued all summer.

It was in this climate that the idea for a 'trans-park' trail was first mooted. As John Sansom explained in his introduction to the 2005 edition of *The Beacons Way*, it was during the devastating foot and mouth outbreak that 'the value of tourism to the rural economy became starkly apparent'. Fortunately, the Brecon Beacons National Park Authority was supportive, and the Wales Tourist Board was … well, on board … providing much of the grant funding.

The 100-mile route extends from Abergavenny in Monmouthshire in the east to Llangadog (near Llandovery) in Carmarthenshire in the west. Harri believes the more logical approach would have been to walk from west to east so as to avoid walking into the prevailing winds. The official guidebook by John Sansom and Arwel Michael splits the walking into eight tough but manageable day sections, some of which form part of Harri's much-longer 'O Fôn i Fynwy' route.

The Beacons Way is well waymarked for most of its length, less so on open hills and moorland (where it was rightly deemed that too much signage would be obtrusive).

We crossed the Afon Sawdde, a river whose source is the nearby Llyn y Fan Fach, the glacial lake (now dammed) from which the legendary Lady of the Lake mentioned earlier first emerged and later returned.

This legend should not to be confused with the much wider-known Lady of the Lake of Arthurian legend (she was the one who gave King Arthur his sword Excalibur). While various lakes are associated with this lady, Llyn y Fan Fach is not one of them.

So enticing is this small and remote lake that in 2011 it was placed in a list of one of the 1,000 must-see sights in the world by travel book publisher Lonely Planet – the only place in Wales on the list. Lonely Planet waxed lyrically about the lake, writing: 'This isolated drop of blue, beneath a cirque of raw Welsh hills, is enchanting – and enchanted.'

The book *Ultimate Sights* included 100 top ten lists, with Llyn y Fan Fach featuring in the most unusual lakes category. For whatever reason, ignorance perhaps, the editors chose not to include the towering overhead Fans in another pertinent list: the most vertigo-inducing cliffs.

As we were gazing down at Llyn y Fan Fach, Harri noticed what looked like a Madeiran levada following the contours of the landscape. I could tell from his rapt expression that he was already mulling over a possible book of Brecon Beacon levada walks.

Though popular with hikers, the Carmarthen Fans (or Black Mountain as it's also confusingly called) have never attracted the same number of visitors as the Central Beacons peaks of Pen y Fan, Corn Du and Cribyn.

The Carmarthen Fans is a term used to describe the peaks on the Carmarthenshire side of the Black Mountain range (not to be confused with the Black Mountains in the far east of the Brecon Beacons National Park). 'Fan' is Welsh for Beacon so basically we're just talking about the Carmarthen Beacons, which sort of makes sense. However, the highest peak in the Black Mountain range, Fan Brycheiniog, is actually in the former county of Brecknockshire – Brycheiniog in Welsh. Whether viewed from the north or south, the peaks have a distinctive shape which makes them instantly recognisable.

The 63-mile long River Usk, which has had such a massive impact on the development of our home town of Newport, originates on the flanks of the Black Mountain range, as does the Tawe (which flows into Swansea Bay).

As we climbed, I spotted what looked like a long line of sheep following the outermost edge of the Fans. I'm fully aware that sheep behave like ... well, sheep ... but this was following the leader on a grand scale. Where were all those sheep heading? It was only as we got closer that I realised that the sheep at the tail end of the convoy looked a bit square round the flank and none of them were actually moving! It transpired that these nice plump (if slightly angular) sheep were in fact large bags of stones, presumably airlifted to the elevated location in readiness for planned repairs to the heavily eroded footpath. Time for an eye test, maybe?

It's regrettable that those of us who love walking in the mountains are inadvertently contributing to the accelerated erosion of many footpaths, particularly those in high rainfall areas where the soil underneath is thin and gravelly.

Just a quick browse through the Brecon Beacon National Park's *Upland Erosion Strategy 2007* alerted me to the high cost, aesthetics (and sensitivities) involved in maintaining footpaths in these wild and very beautiful places. There's always a balancing act between making them accessible to as many people as possible without destroying the natural landscapes that those same visitors come to enjoy. Sections of Offa's Dyke Path already feel far too much like Dorothy's yellow brick road as far as we're concerned; however, erosion is a very real problem that has to be addressed if walkers are to continue enjoying Wales's natural beauty.

A horse rider passed us and waved; a small dog ran alongside her horse. The woman clearly had complete confidence in both animals to canter along the escarpment edge; one false move from either her mount or canine and I dread to think what would have happened.

The views are spectacular in all directions, but there's no denying the Fans can be tough going, and, as with all mountains, the weather at the various summits often bears little resemblance to conditions in the valleys below. For this reason, the Beacons Way describes an alternative low-level route to be used in bad weather or if your legs aren't up to the tough uphill slog, which is followed by an unexpected descent and a second hard climb.

Yep, the Carmarthen Fans have a real sting in their tail. At 2,631 feet, Fan Brycheiniog is the highest peak in the Black Mountain range and was also the highest summit that we'd scaled so far during our walk.

When I expressed surprise at this news, Harri reminded me that the summits of Snowdonia are optional on this walk. And while the Pony Path to the pass near Cadair Idris might have seemed high (perhaps because it was hot and we'd climbed from sea level that day), it was actually only 1,842 feet.

With the cairn of Fan Brycheiniog beguilingly close, we were now descending steeply again, keeping to the right of a line of what looked like steeplechase hurdles, but are actually part of the National Park's erosion prevention strategy. And then it was up, up, up, to the highest point of 'O Fôn i Fynwy' so far.

There were other walkers on the summit as we approached; however, they were long gone by the time we pulled ourselves up those last few metres. There's a rather nice slate wind shelter on the top so we took advantage of it; not because it was cold, but because it's easier to extricate things from a rucksack if you can get out of the wind.

We'd settled down to enjoy our mini cheesecakes (high calorie but after that climb we needed an energy boost) when all of a sudden, we became aware of birds swooping above our heads. There were lots of them, soaring before diving rapidly again, over and over. It's the first time we've ever seen such a spectacle on the top of a mountain and it took us by surprise. From the way they were swooping to catch insects, we guessed they were probably swallows, but if anyone knows any differently …

We've walked this section of the Brecon Way many times and in both directions. After the thrill and spectacle of the Fans, the west to east descent into the Tawe Valley always feels something of an anti-climax, to me anyway. Clambering down the steep rocky footpath from Fan Brycheiniog on tired legs demanded plenty of concentration. Here again, the popularity of the route has caused erosion. The path has undergone maintenance work with the result that there are now some very steep steps towards the lower part of the path which my short legs struggled with.

The last ice age (the Devensian glaciation) left its mark in a major way on this landscape. The second lake of the afternoon – Llyn y Fan

Fawr – was created when a rock hollow formed by a glacier was dammed by moraine. Though the clear waters of Llyn y Fan Fawr look enticing on a hot day, bathing is ill-advised unless you like sharing your swimming pool with leeches!

We continued to make our way down the slopes, following the contours of a moraine until we reached the Nant Tawe Fechan stream. Disappointingly, the towering escarpment of Fan Hir on our right completely blocked out the early evening sunshine, making it feel colder than it might otherwise have been.

At the valley floor, we were saddened to see that the Tafarn y Garreg pub at Pen-y-cae appeared to be closed for good. A few years ago we chatted to the pub's owner as he sat in a dilapidated caravan collecting dues for the car park opposite. At that time, he had grand plans for the pub; it seemed they'd amounted to nothing, which is sad.

It had been a hard day and we were longing for a pint, so we headed down valley to the nearby Gwyn Arms, a pub on whom fortune seems to have shined more favourably. To be fair, the success of this lovely spacious pub is undoubtedly down to the hard work of the couple who run it (the wife also happens to be the chef, which suggests she puts in an awful lot of hours!).

We'd managed to miss the first week of the football World Cup completely, but it seemed our luck was about to run out. Understandably in a valley where public houses are rare, the large television screen at the Gwyn Arms had attracted an audience, namely a large group of Duke of Edinburgh participants fresh from the hills. Despite positioning ourselves some distance away from the football fans, there was really no escaping the England–Uruguay game.

There's a long-standing joke in Wales about the Welshman who will support any team as long as it's playing England. It may sound mean-spirited, but many Welshmen take a certain glee in seeing the England football team getting slaughtered, and this was one such occasion. As we sipped Green Goblin cider and chatted to the cheerful landlady/chef about this and that, we kept hearing cheering in the background, mostly from her husband. No, England hadn't scored; it was Uruguay the landlord was rooting for.

Harri was also amused when the landlady twice instructed people to put their shoes back on! So many pubs display signs asking walkers to remove their boots, the poor Duke of Edinburgh kids (now yelling at the screen) must have thought they were doing the right thing by taking theirs off. Not at the Gwyn, apparently. We weren't sure what our host's objection to socked visitors was, unless it was the overpowering smell!

It was with great reluctance that we bid farewell to this comfortable historic pub and headed down the valley to the campsite at Dan yr Ogof, crossing over the boulder-filled but waterless Nant Haffes on the way. (Unless in flood, the water in this river flows mostly underground, through the permeable limestone rocks forming its bed.)

As is becoming our way, we arrived long after reception had closed, so we found a quiet spot and put up our tent. There were midges absolutely everywhere, making it impossible to sit outside on this otherwise warm and pleasant evening.

The number of Duke of Edinburgh students setting up camp around us was slightly disconcerting. Presumably these were the younger ones, as anyone old enough to order a pint was enjoying the World Cup at the Gwyn Arms. We needn't have worried; they settled down quickly enough and we didn't hear another peep from them all night. Probably exhausted after a hard day's hiking, poor things; I knew exactly how they felt.

How times have changed. When I was a teenager anyone over 15 (even 14 if they could get away with it) would have piled into the pub and been served alcohol, no questions asked. I make no moral comment here, I'm just remembering how things were back in the 1970s when most parents – and politicians – didn't get themselves particularly worked up about underage drinking. In fact, my earliest memories of getting tipsy were at family events.

I remember my Uncle Jack (a devout Catholic) buying me a glass of Babycham at a family wedding. My mother seemed far more upset that the eleven-year-old me had refused to be a bridesmaid at the wedding than the fact I was successfully persuading male relatives to buy me alcoholic drinks (it was always the men who went to the bar in those days).

Not that most of my family were massive boozers – certainly not compared with some of our neighbours – it was just that a family wedding was an occasion, a cause for celebration and we kids were automatically included. There seemed to be a much more European approach among the working classes back then. There was no need for young people to sneak off to drink illegally purchased alcohol when you could just get an uncle to buy it for you – or raid your parents' Christmas stash.

Dan yr Ogof is another example of a beautifully located campsite which is spoilt by zillions of midges. Tonight's swarms seemed intent on attacking our heads, necks, legs, arms; any slither of flesh on show or easy to access was a target. Unusually, Harri was as much under siege as me. As he struggled to get the tent up, he was besieged by mozzies buzzing relentlessly around his nose, ears and eyes and driving him crazy in the process.

I was interested to learn from Wikipedia that midges aren't one species at all, but a collective name for the small flies that exist 'on practically every land area outside permanently arid deserts and the frigid zones'. Some provide a food source for insectivores, others carry disease, and not all bite. Unfortunately, the ones we've encountered on this hike *do* bite as the marks all over my legs and body testify. In North America, they call them 'no-see-ums', but here at Dan yr Ogof they weren't exactly creeping up on us unawares. Frustratingly, all midges – and other biters like horseflies and mosquitoes – thrive in warm, humid weather like we were experiencing at the moment.

There's always a price to pay for a warm, dry spell in Wales, you see. *Always*.

For photographs visit uk.pinterest.com/thewalkerswife

JUNE 20: DAN YR OGOF TO THE STOREY ARMS

After a fitful night's sleep, we were wide awake before six o'clock so we headed straight over to the toilet block, eager to be showered before all those teenagers surfaced.

No matter how exhausted I am when I crawl into my sleeping bag, I never seem able to get a decent night's sleep in our tent. True, it's not the biggest tent around (there's not enough room to lie straight so I have to curl my legs around my rucksack), but the hardest part is trying to get comfortable on bumpy ground, not to mention the fact I'm almost always freezing.

Such is our regular discomfort that last night, Harri considered sleeping outside under the clear twinkling night sky. His extra height (and length) means he finds the tent claustrophobic; however, with so many biting midges around, he quickly changed his mind and joined me inside. We did that once – sleep under the stars – but it wasn't as restful as I'd imagined.

We were staying in an apartment in Paul do Mar in Madeira and had drunk too much Portuguese wine. It was a warm night so I persuaded Harri to drag our mattress on to the narrow first floor balcony, fondly imagining that we would doze off to the sound of the waves gently crashing on to the shore. Except the waves hadn't read the script and didn't know they were only supposed to be providing background sound while we snoozed peacefully on the balcony above. They crashed noisily onto the pebble beach all night, making it near impossible for us to sleep.

There's no doubt camping has gone upmarket over the past decade or so. Perhaps it's different in the summer holidays when more families are holidaying, but our experience on this long-distance hike has been that most campsites are now dominated by luxury camper vans and touring caravans. Those who still prefer to sleep under canvas now do it in style with commodious pavilions that ensure no one ever needs rough it again. Our two-person overnighter is almost always the only tent on the site where a head pokes out at knee height to greet the new day.

We left the campsite before 8 a.m., desperate to get away from the ubiquitous midges, which appeared to have multiplied still further overnight. Copying what I'd seen the youngsters doing, I zipped my hoodie to the neck and yanked the hood down over my head, pulling my Lliswerry Runners buff up to cover my mouth and nose. Only two eyes peered out. I'm not sure the emus we passed on our way out of the campsite even recognised me as human!

The plan was to head down the valley to Craig y Nos Country Park where we could stop to eat another Frosties breakfast. The upper Tawe valley looked glorious in the early morning sunshine, though unfortunately the cloudless night meant plenty of dew; my feet were soaked through from the outset.

Craig y Nos ('rock of the night') was deserted so we settled ourselves down at a covered picnic table alongside the lake and enjoyed the tranquillity of the hour. Just a few feet away, a sword of mallards were sleeping on the lakeside path, not stirring even when a wild rabbit emerged from the bushes and bounced around between them.

Just a few hundred yards away from our breakfast table was the Victorian neo-Gothic castle of Craig y Nos, a popular wedding venue and allegedly 'the most haunted castle in Wales' (on just one staircase, the castle's website promises, there are 'ghosts in abundance'). The long-time home of opera singer Adelina Patti is said to be haunted by the singer herself, her suitors, and children who died of tuberculosis there during the castle's spell as a TB hospital.

Reassured by the knowledge that 'things that are ghostly, ghoulish and haunted' (their words) don't habitually make themselves known in the early morning sunshine, I munched on Frosties and caught up with my notes while Harri disappeared to the toilet.

The castle, with its turrets and four pyramids shaping the walls of the roof, was built in the early 1840s by Captain Rice Davies Powell, a county magistrate and High Sheriff of Brecknock, whose own tenure was cut tragically short. His younger son died in 1851, followed by his wife and daughter. Powell himself died in 1862, and two years later his eldest son was killed in a hunting accident. His eldest daughter Sarah inherited the castle and moved in with her husband, until he died a few years later. It was said the family was cursed due to their family ties with the Dutch Overbeek family, who possessed an equally cursed bloodline.

Sarah sold her wretched house to the Morgan family of Abercraf, who lived there happily for several years. Then in 1878, the castle was purchased by Adelina Patti, the spectacularly talented and highly successful Spanish opera singer, who spent the last four decades of her life in the Tawe valley.

Adelina paid just £3,500 for the property and its 40 acres of parklands; however, she went on to lavish another £100,000 on renovations and additions. The magnificent property that exists today, with its private theatre seating 150 people, the clock tower, iron fountains fashioned as cranes, and spacious winter garden (Adelina presented the latter to the people of Swansea during the First World War where the restored Patti Pavilion remains) is testament to her efforts. By 1898, electricity had been installed, suggesting Craig y Nos was the first private house in Wales to be wired.

Adelina remained at Craig y Nos until her death in 1919, since which there have been tales of her benign presence being sensed (and seen) in the castle.

For decades, the Adelina Patti Hospital (as the castle became in 1922) functioned as a sanatorium, first treating children with tuberculosis and later elderly people. The hospital finally closed in 1986 and was rescued from dilapidation by Dr John Trevor Jones and his wife Penelope, who threw themselves into restoring the castle to its former glory. It reopened as a hotel at the beginning of the millennium.

We once stood opposite Craig y Nos Castle waiting hopefully for a bus that failed to materialise. Alright, that's not quite true. A bus did eventually turn up but so long after the specified time that it might well have been the next one if you get my drift. I might not have minded, but we'd run hard and fast so we wouldn't miss that bus. We ran along the river path and winding trails of the country park, our rucksacks bouncing on our backs, only to stand there like lemons for an eternity.

By the time Harri materialised, the mallards were swimming on the lake, the rabbit long gone. It was still chilly, but after yesterday's glorious weather, we were confident that we'd be basking in warm sunshine before the hour was up.

We were in familiar territory again today. Once upon a time, we used to hike in the Brecon Beacons for no reason other than pleasure, and we particularly enjoyed walking in this valley. Harri included two walks here in his book *Day Walks in the Brecon Beacons* (published by Vertebrate).

Predictably, the hills were alive with Duke of Edinburgh participants. I reprimanded Harri when he groaned alongside me. These were our future customers, young people who venture into the wilderness for the first time while still in their teens and resolve to spend the rest of their lives in hiking boots. Only the majority of this lot looked pretty miserable under the weight of their huge rucksacks; worse, despite having barely left their valley campsite, they were huddling together in that all too familiar way. They couldn't be lost already, Harri sighed.

In the shower block that morning, I'd chatted briefly with a tired-looking girl of about 16 who told me she was covered in bites and hadn't slept a wink all night. She hated camping, she concluded with vehemence. I'd clearly found a kindred spirit. Still, it could have been worse. The weather was holding and, so far today, the mountains had been dry underfoot.

We passed the distinctive stone terraced cottages of the South Wales Caving Centre, which provides bunkhouse accommodation for divers wishing to explore the extensive cave systems underneath. Ogof Ffynnon Ddu – one of the deepest caves in Britain as well as being the third longest – lies just a few feet beneath these cottages, though you have to walk to one of three nearby entrances if you want to investigate what's underground.

The cave system was first discovered by Peter Harvey and Ian Nixon in 1946, the year the club was formed, and it's been gradually revealing itself over the succeeding decades. The Ogof Ffynnon Ddu cave system is now known to be 1,010 feet deep, and there are around 30 miles of passages, chambers, formations and chasms waiting to be explored. Astonishingly, this cold, dark habitat has its own specialised wildlife, including a colourless species of underground trout and cave shrimps.

On this fine sunny June morning there were no cavers about, but in the past we've spotted several groups making their way across the rough moorland to those entrances. At first glance you'd be forgiven for mistaking them for deep-sea divers, but when you consider these limestone caves are formed by the raging underwater Ffynnon Ddu ('black spring'), then it's easy to appreciate why cavers and divers require similar kit.

For those of us who aren't too keen on squeezing ourselves through narrow, watery channels, there's always the National Showcaves Centre for Wales on the opposite side of the valley (next to the campsite). The first section of the eleven-mile Dan yr Ogof cave system is a popular tourist attraction, where visitors can wander into chambers with exciting names like Cathedral Cave and Bone Cave, where alongside various species of Ice Age megafauna human bones have also been found.

The Dan yr Ogof cave system was discovered by brothers Tommy and Jeff Morgan back in 1912; however, it wasn't until 1963 that anyone advanced beyond a narrow squeeze known as the Long Crawl. As with Ogof Ffynnon Ddu, much of Dan yr Ogof has been explored by cave divers, one of whom (Martyn Farr) claims that the system is likely to extend to at least 90 miles.

It's fascinating to think about what's going on right under our feet, but I'm a little too claustrophobic for caving. I turned down an opportunity to go underground in August 1993 when my sister married a member of the South & Mid Wales Cave Rescue Team.

In those days, there were only two options for getting married – church or register office. Wanting a day to remember, they decided to quickly attend to the boring legal stuff at Newport Register Office with just two witnesses before whisking a large group of family and friends off to the Llangattock escarpment. Here, braver members of the wedding party could enter Ogof Agen Allwedd to witness a mock wedding ceremony.

My brother-in-law's caving mates had already deposited champagne and nibbles in Aggy's first chamber, so all that remained was for bride and groom to wriggle their way to the altar.

Maybe it's me, but squeezing first into a wetsuit and then through a series of icy, wet passages is definitely not what I have in mind when I respond affirmatively to a wedding invitation. I'm asthmatic … and claustrophobic (on account of inadvertently getting myself locked in the bottom of my best friend's nanna's wardrobe as a child). I wasn't sure I fancied all those bats whizzing past my head either. I also had two children to look after, neither of whom had a wetsuit. And so I passed.

As you'd expect, the underground wedding photographs were spectacular, and I did experience a pang that I wasn't standing next to my sister as she said 'I do' for the second time that day. After all, not many people can say they got married in a cave (and are still happily married nearly 23 years later).

We soon overtook several more Duke of Edinburgh walkers – an all-girl group this time – and climbed steadily through the nature reserve studiously avoiding a number of the very obvious sink or shake holes, which are created when the surface layer of millstone grit collapses into the limestone cave systems below.

Interestingly, the southern edge of the Brecon Beacons National Park has more of these sink holes than any other part of Britain. While we were following the Beacons Way over ground, an underground line of caves was pursuing us! This is probably not the place to let your dog off the lead or to allow a small child to go running ahead.

Understanding the mortal peril we found ourselves in, I stayed close to Harri's side, occasionally noting a particularly shaky-looking shake hole or one that had collapsed to such an extent that it had been covered with boards. Who says that geology is the study of million-year-old rocks? It's all still happening here in south Wales!

To our right, a section of moorland was fenced off and an interpretation board announced 'Some pavements are more special than others', which might seem a rather bizarre thing to proclaim on top of a mountain until you realise that the 'pavements' in question are flat exposed limestone ones which seem almost to burst forth from the surrounding moorland. Most of the landscape here is grazed by sheep, hence the need for fencing around this 'special' section, which, according to the board, 'is packed full of rare and beautiful plants'. I looked hard, but it must have been the wrong season for the lily of the valley (the plant used to illustrate the board).

This once industrialised area (the remains of quarry workings, a former firebrick works, kilns and tram roads are clearly visible) is now a designated National Nature Reserve with lovely far-reaching views.

It was hot this morning, but the temperature hadn't yet reached the soaring heights of one particularly memorable visit here a few years ago. We'd been following the Beacons Way across the open mountainside in pretty uncomfortable conditions – for once too hot and sticky – when Harri suddenly turned to me and demanded, 'Where's the camera?'

I hate that awful sinking feeling you get when you realise you've lost something; though on this occasion the camera wasn't exactly lost. I knew exactly where I'd left it – a mile or so back on a nice rounded boulder where we'd briefly stopped.

Back in that long-ago era, I wasn't much of a runner – if I had been I'm sure it would have been me sprinting back across the parched landscape to recover the camera. As it was, I sat at the track's dusty edge watching Harri getting smaller and smaller until he eventually disappeared over the horizon. He was gone for what felt an interminable time. Most worryingly was the knowledge that we had very little water left; we generally carry one litre of water each, perhaps 1.5 litres on hot days, which is usually ample. If it's particularly hot and we have an opportunity to refill our bottles, e.g. at the source of a mountain stream or in a toilet block, we'll do so, but generally there's no need.

The Day of the Lost Camera was one of those rare occasions when we'd badly underestimated our water consumption. Earlier in the day we'd glugged carelessly from our bottles not anticipating how hot the day would become, and now our supplies were dangerously low. Though I was thirsty, I daren't take more than the tiniest sip because I knew how thirsty Harri would be when he returned from his undulating three-mile run across this unforgiving terrain.

After what felt like an eternity, a tiny figure reappeared on the horizon and gradually made its way back across the mountain. Hot and sticky, Harri resisted the urge to chide me for being the cause of his impromptu run and accepted just a few small sips from my bottle. At moments like these, it's easy to remember why I love my man so much.

We passed an outcrop where two young men appeared to be surveying the landscape as though looking for something – or someone. It transpired they were Duke of Edinburgh leaders and they'd mislaid their all-boy team! A little while ago, Harri had spotted a group of walkers in the far distance, but they'd been going at quite a speed and were no longer visible on the horizon. Could it be that we'd finally encountered a group of DoE participants who could read a map and knew where they were heading! The leaders shuttled on, remaining slightly ahead of us for a mile or so until they were joined by a third man, presumably another teacher/leader. They made no more attempt at conversation and we put their collective taciturn down to rising concern over their young wards rather than embarrassment at losing an entire team.

We parted company with the men when we reached a junction with Sarn Helen. The main 160-mile Roman road once ran from Aberconwy to Carmarthen. The section that we walked – an off-shoot of the main route – connected the Roman forts situated at Neath and Brecon. Today is little more than a badly eroded and potholed track, impassable in anything but a four-wheel drive or tank. Still, it was quite exciting to think that we were walking the same route followed by the marching Roman legionaries in the first century AD.

We might complain about the unaccustomed weight of our rucksacks on this hike, but what we were carrying (by choice) was nothing compared to the armour, daggers, swords and marching pack those poor legionaries would have been carrying, not to mention food and water. And if they even thought about slacking, they risked the wrath of the centurion or even stoning!

Fortunately, we were approaching Harri's favourite dipping stream, so the last thing on his mind was increasing our pace. Nedd Fechan is shallow, clear and easy to enter. While Harri was having fun splashing around in the icy water with all the enthusiasm of a Labrador pup (he claimed he was washing his tee-shirt!), I tentatively dipped a toe in. Alas, the water was just a wee bit cold for me to be tempted, so I just lazed around on the river bank, enjoying the sunshine and munching Frosties.

While we were descending into the river valley, Harri had spotted a group of walkers climbing the track on the far side of the stream; we guessed these were the 'missing' DoE kids, but, sod's law, the leaders were now nowhere to be seen, having carried on when we turned downhill towards the stream.

Harri dried himself off and we headed straight up 'killer hill', which seemed surprisingly easy this time around (perhaps confirmation that all this hiking actually is improving my fitness levels?).

The next stretch of walking brought back memories of the Day of the Forgotten Teabags, a cold day's walking when Harri remembered to pack the flask of hot water but I forgot the essential teabags. Rather

213

than pointlessly carry the flask all day, Harri hid it against the fence and we retrieved it at the end of the walk. It appears there is a trail across the Brecon Beacons linking my various senior moments and Harri is determined *never* to let me forget them.

There's a large Forestry Commission car park at Blaen Llia so there were suddenly people everywhere. Well, everywhere in the immediate vicinity of the car park and the sparkling stream that runs alongside it.

The summit of Fan Llia is 2,073 feet above sea level, but we were starting from a relatively high point so the ascent shouldn't have felt as tough as it did. I'm not a big fan of this Fan for several reasons; the terrain tends to be quite wet underfoot, and as is often the case when the ground is boggy, people wander around this way and that, trying to avoid the marshiest areas with the result that there is no obvious footpath. This leads to more wandering about and plenty of backtracking when what looks like a reasonably solid path suddenly turns into a bog. If a hundred people a day were to desert their cars and climb Fan Llia (perhaps when pigs fly), I doubt a single identifiable footpath would be created. There's just too much bog!

My other reason for disliking this mountain is that the climb just goes on and on, with several false ridges and very little reward in the sense of views. Sure, you can look down into the valley and marvel at how tiny all those glittering cars have become; however, ahead of you, where the views really matter, there's nothing save moorland and sheep.

Grey clouds were gathering overhead. Not that we were too concerned about the possibility of rain, but the overcast sky did nothing to dispel my gloomy mood as we plodded up and up, finally following something that resembled a firm path.

At last we reached the summit and the views opened up. The twin peaks of Pen y Fan and Corn Du looked just a stone's throw away, belying the fact that there was another valley hidden away down there. Behind us, the Carmarthen Fans were sloping off into the distance. Hard to believe we were walking along the escarpment only yesterday afternoon – it's amazing how far two feet can carry you in a day.

Our game plan was to descend Forest Fawr and catch a bus to Brecon opposite the Storey Arms. We'd briefly debated whether this would constitute a break in our long-distance hike or not. Other than the brief and unavoidable bus journey across the estuary from Penrhyndeudraeth, our journey through Wales had been entirely on foot. It wasn't as though we'd be skipping any of the actual walking – we'd be returning in the morning to start out from the same spot – yet somehow it still felt like we were cheating.

With the youth hostel at Llwyn-y-celyn fully booked for the weekend, our only other option was wild camping at height, and our experience in the Carneddau was too recent for either of us to risk repeating it anytime soon. A bus to Brecon it was then.

Earlier in the day, it looked like we might be set for an early finish, but as many have learned to their peril, the mountains can often dupe and deceive. Conditions change rapidly. Timescales protract, itineraries shrink.

Our sojourn alongside the sparkling mountain stream belonged to another day as the clouds darkened and the light breeze grew gusty. We wandered across the wide ridge seemingly heading nowhere, our only companions the wild ponies grazing on the mountainside.

Yesterday's high spirits had gone missing again as I grumbled my way across uneven moorland, convinced Harri had mislaid the Beacons Way. We come close to hating each other at times like this. He resents the voice in his ear that keeps demanding to know why, where, what, when. I, on the other hand, feel aggrieved that I spend so much of my leisure time cold, wet, exhausted and muddy. What would be so awful about spending a long weekend in Rome, or Barcelona, cities I visited years ago and adored? Or heading down to the Mediterranean for a week's wall-to-wall sunshine? What was it with Harri Roberts and his Welsh mountains?

Despite its name, the sprawling upland area of Fforest Fawr was never forested (at least not in historic times), but was rather an ancient hunting ground. In 1819, this Welsh mountainside was sold by the Crown (which had owned it since 1521) to help pay for the humongous cost of the Napoleonic War, which had soared to £831 million.

One of Fforest Fawr's more bizarre incarnations was as a large-scale commercial rabbit farm. In a time when wild rabbits were far rarer – and their meat and fur more popular – a series of cigar-shaped tunnels were erected on the mountain side at Cefn Cul (above Crai Reservoir). These flat-topped mounds were lined with stone to give them a warren-like appearance, thus duping the rabbits into burrowing in what would otherwise have been soil that was too thin. They obliged and were soon doing what rabbits do best!

In 1984, the Brecon Beacons National Park purchased 9,300 hectares of common land, including much of the Black Mountain and Fforest Fawr. The Countryside and Rights of Way Act (launched in May 2005) gave people the right to walk across registered common land, mountain, moor, heath and down.

We finally seemed to be heading downhill when it occurred to me that I recognised this path; we'd been here before. Far below us was Craig Cerrig-Gleisiad, an impressive natural amphitheatre (or cirque) created during the last Ice Age around 20,000 years ago. The snowfield which collected on the north-facing slopes eventually turned into a glacier, which in turn carved the landscape of high cliffs and escarpments visible today.

Harri included a walk through Craig Cerrig-Gleisiad in *Day Walks in the Brecon Beacons*, and though the climb through the nature reserve is quite steep and little sunshine seeps into the cirque, it's a stunningly beautiful spot with several rare arctic-alpine species clinging to the ledges and crags. One – the purple saxifrage – does not reappear again in southern Europe until the Alps themselves.

From Craig Cerrig-Gleisiad, we followed the narrow escarpment footpath teetering high above the busy A470. Far, far below, articulated lorries snaked through the valley like Dinky toys, while tiny specks queued in front of a burger van. From here, it was easy to spot the well-trod tourist route up to the summit of Pen y Fan.

The footpath we were following, though generally solid underfoot, had a tendency to teeter precariously close to the edge, rendering it somewhat vertiginous in places. All that gazing down was resulting in the occasional wobble. Not wishing to end my days squashed by a Dinky toy on the A470, I forced myself to focus on the route ahead.

As we gradually lost height, the gradient of the slope became gentler and it was easier to relax and enjoy the scenery, once again bathed in sunshine. There's a wonderful small waterfall on the route, and several small children were having fun splashing around in the shallows. Seeing our faces, their grandparents urged us to abandon our footwear and join them. It was tempting, but we were conscious of the time (buses to Brecon aren't exactly frequent), and I was certain that once I'd taken my shoes off and enjoyed the feeling of cold water on my bare feet, I'd struggle to put them on again.

The car park opposite the Storey Arms was full, as one would expect on a sunny June afternoon, with the majority of those parked there heading straight up Pen y Fan (as we ourselves would be doing tomorrow).

It was late afternoon by now, but we hadn't actually got around to eating lunch, so we settled down on a grassy verge next to the bus stop, munched our food and waited. And waited. And waited. The bus's stated arrival time came and went; the minutes ticked by. Once or twice we mistook a coach for the bus and stepped forward eagerly only to discover our error when it whizzed straight past. Harri rang his mother to double-check the timetable (we'd been right) and I rang Traveline Cymru to check if there were any timetable changes (there weren't).

We consoled ourselves with the fact that there was one later bus, albeit a good two hours after we'd arrived at the bus stop. Of course, that was if there hadn't been a blanket cancellation of Cardiff to Brecon buses (you never know).

I'd long given up on any idea of strolling around Brecon; now all I wanted to do was arrive in time to find a room for the night then pop into Morrisons (sad that I am, I was once again really excited by the prospect of a proper supermarket).

We were just on the verge of giving up when the bus sailed around the bend and ground to a standstill in front of us. The driver explained that his monumentally late arrival was down to road works in Merthyr, which were, quite frankly, causing complete chaos. We could hardly grumble when the poor man was so apologetic; besides, while he'd been sitting in stationary traffic, his engine revving, we'd been basking in sunshine at the foot of south Wales's highest mountain. We were hardly in any position to complain; it wasn't the bus driver's fault that the powers-that-be had decided to dig up the roads at the start of the tourist season.

In many ways – perhaps if we'd had a larger tent and more comfortable sleeping mats – it would have been rather nice to have camped in the mountains overnight. In 2012, the Brecon Beacons became the first International Dark Sky Reserve in Wales (and only the fifth in the world). Thanks to the low levels of light pollution, the skies above the mountains are so dark it's apparently possible to 'see the

Milky Way, the major constellations, bright nebulas and even meteor showers'. There's even a Brecon Beacons Dark Sky video, which emphasises what we missed out on by being softies who opted for a hot water shower over a meteor shower.

I maintain you need a certain kind of mind to memorise constellations, quite possibly the kind that remembers complex patterns or makes you good at chess, which rules me out on both counts. Perhaps it just comes down to we city dwellers getting so little stargazing practice; though, as councils opt to turn off street lights in a bid to balance their budgets, the brightly-lit towns and cities of the past are fast becoming a distant memory.

In *Classic Walks in the Brecon Beacons National Park*, Chris Barber explains that the naming of the mountains dates back to the fourteenth century when 'a chain of intervisible hill beacons was established'. Back then, it was the French who posed a risk, and news of an impending attack could be conveyed by a series of fire signals on high points located six to eight miles apart. Pen y Fan would have undoubtedly been the site of one of these beacons, hence the origins of the name.

We arrived in Brecon about twenty minutes later (it would have taken hours to walk) and headed straight for the Markets Tavern a stone's throw away. We'd stopped here for a drink in the past (yes, while waiting for a bus), and it always seemed friendly enough.

Thankfully nothing had changed. While we enjoyed a drink, the landlord regaled us with tales of his own hiking days. His appearance certainly belied the claim that he was an avid walker who'd three times completed the Camino de Santiago in northern Spain (he added that Galicia – a place we've always fancied visiting – is gorgeous but lacks any decent facilities). While we were busy being impressed with this feat – feats, if he'd really done it the three times he claimed – he also dropped into the conversation that he'd walked from Wales to Rome. If he'd started in Brecon, that's almost 1,230 miles! It makes hiking *through* Wales pale into insignificance in terms of an endurance walk.

The Markets Tavern, it transpired, was popular with other walkers (probably due to its proximity to the bus station and the fact that it was amazingly good value). The inspirational Welsh sailor, runner and charity fundraiser Rosie Swales Pope had stayed here, we were told. Rosie was older than I am now when she embarked on a 20,000 mile-run around the world in 2002, the longest unsupported run ever. I feel exhausted just thinking about it.

Our genial landlord revealed he was counting down the days until his tenancy ended and he could go travelling to India. I trust he didn't intend to walk there too!

The Markets Tavern is one of those huge old public houses with a massive bar that looks like it was built in the times when public houses were packed every night and whole communities celebrated at their local (like in *Coronation Street*). Their vast size – the Markets Tavern is three storeys high – means maintenance and redecorating is a costly affair with the result that many seem stuck in a time warp.

To be fair, despite several flights of stairs, our twin bedroom, when we reached it, was extremely comfortable. It wasn't en suite (all the superior – and double – rooms having been let while we lingered at the bus stop), but we had exclusive use of a spacious bathroom just along the landing (though, as we later discovered, the only way of 'locking' the door was to drag a wooden unit across it).

Brecon felt positively tropical after Fforest Fawr. Harri settled down for a session of note-writing while I bounced enthusiastically off to the supermarket.

We rarely go out in the evening after a day's hiking. First, it's usually well into the evening by the time we arrive at our accommodation. Secondly, we're too exhausted to bother (or care) about a social life. Honestly, hiking's one of the best weight-loss programmes I've ever come across, and not just because you burn calories walking. At the end of a long day's hike, neither Harri nor I care a jot what we eat, or, in my case, whether I eat *at all*. A glass of cider and a packet of crisps is absolutely perfect nine times out of ten.

On this occasion, Brecon's entertainment came to us. Unbeknown to us, the Markets Tavern holds weekly karaoke nights, and tonight was *the* night. With all windows open, upstairs and down, we had no alternative but to listen to every singer's rendition of their chosen song. To be fair, the music wasn't too bad, though when you're two floors up it's very noticeable when someone is flat or singing out of tune. It was all very reminiscent of our two-week holiday in Setubal, Portugal. Eager to experience the real Portugal, we stayed in an apartment in the middle of town, on a narrow street lined with bars and shops. At weekends, those same establishments which opened as coffee bars and sleepy little drinking holes by day were transformed into noisy karaoke bars. With heat and humidity forcing us to keep our windows open, we would lie in bed listening to rendition after rendition of the same few Portuguese hits with that same booming beat. Finally, we'd fall asleep exhausted in the early hours, our hearts thumping in time with the beat, the now-familiar tune infiltrating our dreams.

Maybe it was because we recognised more of the songs here in Brecon, but on the whole we enjoyed a pleasant evening's musical entertainment. And we didn't even have to leave our room.

It's just as well the Markets Tavern partying didn't go on all night because we needed as much energy as we could muster. Tomorrow we would be tackling the highest mountain along the route of O Fôn i Fynwy: the towering 2,907-foot Pen y Fan.

For photographs visit uk.pinterest.com/thewalkerswife

JUNE 21: STOREY ARMS TO CWMDU

Now we've reached the Brecon Beacons it's really starting to feel like we're nearing the end of our walk through Wales. Mindful of my 'wobbly' in Llandovery, last night Harri suggested we make a 'final push' over the next few days in terms of effort and miles walked. We'd originally thought it would take us up to 28 days to walk from Holyhead to Chepstow, but now it seems we're on schedule to complete the entire route in less than 25 days. Harri will work out the exact mileage when we get home, but he thinks we'll have covered around 380 miles in total.

We still have some tough walking ahead of us in terms of terrain, and although I have been longing for the sunshine to return, there's no denying it is far tougher climbing mountains in the heat. I woke up wondering how I would get myself and my rucksack to the summit of Pen y Fan. Still, it was the longest day of the year so we had plenty of daylight hours ahead of us.

Our late arrival in town meant we didn't get a chance to look around Brecon properly, which is a shame as the market town has plenty to see: a cathedral, some lovely old Georgian and Jacobean buildings, a military museum, and the Monmouthshire and Brecon canal basin. The stretch of canal from Pontymoile to Brecon was actually one of two waterways which now comprise the Monmouthshire and Brecon Canal. The Brecknock and Abergavenny arm ran 33 miles from Pontymoile in the south to Brecon in the north; construction began in 1796; however, it wasn't until February 1812 that the canal was completed.

Early one morning in October 2007, a section of the 200-year-old canal collapsed, and eight people had to be rescued after a torrent of mud and water flowed into their homes in Gilwern. Three houses were damaged and there were several road closures. Two months later, after draining sixteen miles of the canal, British Waterways announced their early investigations had identified over 90 leaks between Talybont and

Gilwern alone. This was going to be one big renovation job. The canal eventually reopened in March 2009, but I still remember how strange it was to walk in the area and look down on to the drained canal where once there had been a waterway full of wildlife and activity.

The Markets Tavern might have been fully booked last night, but we seemed to be the only guests tucking into breakfast. The service was casual but friendly, and there was certainly plenty of food. In fact, the chef popped out with extra portions of cooked breakfast while we were eating our cereals (he was so quick off the mark with the cooked breakfasts we had to shuffle the various courses around).

I really do enjoy visiting old-fashioned unpretentious pubs like the Markets Tavern where they believe in offering you a decent bed/meal for a reasonable price. We've stayed at some places where guests are all seated at one table and encouraged to socialise with one another over breakfast. I prefer this friendly set-up to the separate tables and hushed dining rooms of olden days, though I do agree with Harri that it encourages the talkative among us to linger over breakfast for far too long.

While we were waiting for our bus back to the Storey Arms, I noticed that a man standing near us was wearing a polo shirt with a HF Holidays logo on the breast. HF is the company Shane works for in Beddgelert, and as the man was on his own, I struck up a conversation with him. He told us he volunteers with HF Holidays ten to twelve times a year, enjoying free accommodation and food in return for taking holidaymakers on walks which are suitable for their ability. It sounded like the perfect job for Harri and me, if only it was paid.

The man told us his company had organised a media trip to Ystradfellte today; had we been heading in that direction rather than to Pen y Fan who knows which famous travel writer we might have teetered on a footpath with, or followed behind the Sgwd yr Eira waterfall?

Pont ar Daf car park was almost full to capacity when we disembarked from our bus twenty minutes later. We shouldn't have been surprised; it was a warm, sunny Saturday and Pen y Fan is the biggest draw in the Brecon Beacons National Park – and not just for regular hikers. The highest mountain in south Wales attracts lots of charity walkers. One large group was raising money for someone's teenage daughter to take part in an African expedition while other walkers were fundraising for the children's cancer charity LATCH. Some of those involved in organising the charity walks hadn't realised they were supposed to register the event with the National Trust until they were approached by a lady member of staff who pointed this out.

Curious, I later checked the National Trust's website for clarification. A page titled 'an event on the Brecon Beacons' refers organisers to guidelines provided by the Institute of Fundraising code of practice for outdoor fundraising events. The National Trust adds 'we also request events adhere to certain conditions relating specifically to the Brecon Beacons'. I'm none the wiser what these 'certain conditions' might be, however, because the link on the page took me to a blank black webpage. Maybe it's a cunning ploy on their part to deter inexperienced hikers from taking to the hills.

While we had to admire the fact that so many kind-spirited people were prepared to do something outside their comfort zone for charity, it was mind-blowing to see how inadequately equipped many of them were: women wearing flimsy fashion shoes and leggings (even jeans), numerous people carrying nothing except a 50 cl water bottle, very few sunhats being worn despite the cloudless sky and lack of shade. They'd probably get away with their casual attitude towards the mountains on this lovely warm day, but seeing people setting off up Pen y Fan with no supplies, suitable clothing, maps or equipment gives you some idea what the mountain rescue teams are up against.

After weeks of relative wilderness, I wasn't altogether happy to find myself in the middle of this noisy scrum. Harri, who hates crowds at the best of times, was even more dismayed that our relaxed schedule had resulted in us scaling Pen y Fan at the weekend.

We walked at a steady pace, gradually overtaking many of the walkers who'd set off much faster than us. The morning was warming up nicely and several red-faced people were already on the side of the path taking a breather. Perhaps they were belatedly realising that walking up this mountain – any mountain – was not a walk in the park.

The paved road we had been able to see so clearly from Fforest Fawr yesterday runs almost to the top of Corn Du – the smaller of the twin peaks – the large flat slabs being laid by the National Park Authority to prevent further erosion of south Wales's most popular mountain. In essence, the ascent to Corn Du and Pen y Fan has been urbanised, and a stone conveyor belt now panders to the thousands whose sole purpose for coming to the Brecon Beacons is to conquer its highest, most iconic summit. Maybe there's an argument for insisting mountains remain the domain of those who are willing to clamber over moorland and boulder, bog and stream; to consult maps, get their boots muddy and their feet wet?

On the summit Corn Du, there were people everywhere – hugging, taking photographs, eating sandwiches, drinking from flasks. It occurred to us that some people may have confused this first summit with the big guy just across the col – at 2,907 feet, Pen y Fan towers 43 feet above its neighbour; it's just not that obvious when you're up close.

Harri said it was proof of our vastly improved fitness levels that we'd walked from the car park to the summit of Corn Du without stopping once. Thanks to last night's £30 shopping trip we were well and truly loaded down, yet the additional weight hadn't posed the slightest problem to either of us.

As always when I'm on this mountain, I paused to reflect upon the tragic story of five-year-old Tommy Jones who died on the ridge above Llyn Cwm Llwch after going missing on August 4 1900. The story has haunted me for decades simply because it's so terribly sad.

Tommy lived in Maerdy and was on his way to his grandfather's farm at Cwm Llwch when he vanished without trace. The little boy had run ahead with his 13-year-old cousin; however, for whatever reason, perhaps the rapidly descending darkness or a fear of farm animals, he started crying and headed back to find his father alone. Tommy was never seen alive again.

Despite an extensive search of the area involving police, troops, farmers and local people, Tommy's father never set eyes on his son again. As you can imagine, the story reached the national news and the *Daily Mail* newspaper offered a £20 reward to anyone who could solve the mystery. The paper also sent a special commissioner to Brecon to work on Tommy's disappearance. An early theory that the little boy had been abducted by gypsies was now dismissed, and it seemed more likely that Tommy had been taken by a childless woman or couple (though the mountainside would seem an odd place for abduction).

Now comes the part of the story that I find so fascinating. A lady called Mrs Hamer – the wife of a gardener at Castle Madoc near Brecon – read about Tommy's disappearance and the ongoing search for him and dreamt of the exact spot where Tommy lay. On September 2, four weeks after Tommy went missing, and with Mrs Hamer's help, his body was finally found at 2,250 feet above sea level.

The newspaper reports of the day did not hold back. 'They had reached the top of the ridge immediately above Llyn Cwm Llwch and were making their way towards the peaks across some open ground when suddenly Mr Hamer, who was a few yards in front of the others, started back with an exclamation of horror, for there in his path lay the remains of a body.' It was identified as the little boy's and brought down the same day. Sadly, no one had expected the little boy to walk so far or climb so high; the various searches had concentrated on lower ground.

From the summit of Corn Du, you can just about see the obelisk that marks the place where Tommy's body was found (paid for from a donation by Mr Hamer, jurors at the inquest, and members of the public). The inscription on it reads: 'This obelisk marks the spot where the body of Tommy Jones aged 5 was found. He lost his way between Cwm Llwch Farm and the Login on the night of August 4th 1900. After an anxious search of 29 days his body was found on September 2nd.

Tommy died over a hundred years ago, and yet I still feel profound sadness whenever I think of that terrified little boy alone and lost on this mountain.

We headed down and up again to Pen y Fan, where the splendid views distracted from the badly eroded summit. It wasn't always this way. We – the hikers who trample the mountain day after day, week after week as though this peak alone is worth climbing – have created this disintegrating peak.

In *The Beacons Way*, John Samson & Arwel Michael write, 'Fifty years ago the way to the summit was not nearly so well defined. The summit was covered with grass and the now crumbling eastern approach to Pen y Fan was hardly eroded at all.' Hard to believe, isn't it?

In those halcyon days, the Storey Arms had a cafe serving hot meals and you could even travel to the area by train (the nearest station was four miles south at Torpantau – it closed in 1964).

When you're standing on Pen y Fan under cloudless skies and warm sunshine, it's nigh on impossible to imagine this busy and popular place can be transformed into a perilous mountain top in bad weather, which is, of course, exactly the danger. Familiarity breeds contempt and all that. We should remember Pen y Fan is a very high mountain. Low cloud, poor visibility, high winds, rain, even hot weather can easily result in walkers getting lost, disorientated, exhausted or injured.

Even experienced, well-prepared hikers get caught out, so there's absolutely no excuse for setting off without proper gear and supplies. Okay, I'm on my soapbox now, but it really annoys me when we see people heading up a mountain dressed as though they're going for a stroll around the park. Has it never occurred to them that the weather might change for the worse while they're out walking? Or that their lack of forethought could end up putting others at risk.

I was surprised to learn that only the police have the authority to call out a mountain rescue team; then, it's generally in response to a 999 call or if someone who is known to be on the mountains is reported missing. These courageous men and women will turn out at any time of day or night and in any conditions. Sometimes other resources are also required, e.g. other teams, search and rescue dogs, even a helicopter.

By August 2014, Brecon Mountain Rescue Team had already responded to 55 recorded incidents that year. While some were straightforward and were resolved without having to embark on a full search and rescue mission, it's sobering to consider the risks the rescue teams face when venturing onto the mountains in often appalling conditions.

At the end of July, 34 selfless volunteers joined the hunt for a frail man who disappeared around four in the afternoon; when he was finally found, cold and dehydrated but otherwise unhurt, it was nearly midnight. And it's not only walkers who need assistance; mountain rescue teams are sometimes called out for incidents involving cyclists and mountain bikers, paragliders, horse riders and climbers. It's not unusual for them to search for people who have gone missing from home. Despite the large numbers on the mountain today, I'm pleased to report that no one got lost, injured, dehydrated or otherwise debilitated (I couldn't resist checking the call-out log).

We still had a long walk ahead of us so decided not to hang about despite the perfect conditions on the summit. Harri's far too cool to risk being mistaken for a tourist! With the big ones behind us, he expected the crowds to peter out as we followed the base of Cribyn before heading up Fan y Big.

How wrong can you be? Not only had we inadvertently chosen to climb the most iconic mountain in south Wales on a hot, clear *Saturday* morning in June, but we'd also managed to clash with the annual WAAT4 Challenge, a team navigation challenge event now in its fifth year.

Our first inkling that some kind of team race was taking place was on the lower slopes of Pen y Fan when four extremely athletic Nepalese young men came racing down the mountain in matching tee-shirts.

It didn't immediately click. The Nepalese team long gone, there were no more runners on the mountain, just a lot of hikers coming up Pen y Fan from the opposite direction. We'd started noticing there was a team element to whatever was going on – several people passed with the same number pinned to their front – but still had no idea what was going on.

It gradually transpired that those we'd passed close to the summit of Pen y Fan were the front runners. For the next hour or so we passed many wearier participants, frequently red-faced and panting. These mountain challenge events are tough. We guessed many had underestimated the difficulty of the terrain in soaring temperatures – possibly overestimating their own fitness too.

The WAAT4 Challenge offers participants a choice of distance – 30km or 40km. When you consider that the shorter distance is nearly 19 miles, a far greater distance than the average hiker will cover in a day, it's not surprising so many people of the people we passed looked ready to drop. Incidentally, the Brecon Nepalese Youth took first prize in the 30k race, completing the route in an incredible 3 hours 50 minutes.

The longer route (nearly 25 miles) is particularly tough and includes 'elements of two Special Forces selection routes' (the 'Fan Dance' and 'Point to Point'). Incredibly, that one has been completed in a record 3 hours and 45 minutes. Of course, we didn't know any of this at the time so we just resigned ourselves to repeating 'hello' *ad infinitum* as the WAAT4 participants trekked red-faced up the mountain path towards Pen y Fan and we trekked down towards Fan y Big.

You've got to take your hat off to the 97 teams who signed up for this annual fundraising event on the longest day of the year. Despite the promise of soaring temperatures, only five teams failed to record a finish time (and who knows, perhaps they never made it to the start).

At the base of Fan y Big, I psyched myself up for the steepest climb of the day. To our left the ground fell away into Cwm Cynwyn, to our right the slower WAAT4 teams continued plodding up the gentler slope crossed by the 'Gap Road'. Harri voiced his doubts that some of them would have the stamina to reach Pen y Fan, but I guess it's all about having the right mental attitude and just keeping going (not being a great fan of hill-climbing myself I am more sympathetic to other tortoises than the hare-like Harri).

Fan y Big means 'peak of the bill', which probably alludes to its pointed shape. The scramble to the summit from this side is an absolute killer despite the well-established 'steps' which get you halfway up before petering out.

At 2,359 feet, Fan y Big is best-known for its spectacular 'diving board' – one of the most photographed rocks in the Brecon Beacons. It's amusing to watch people step cautiously onto the dramatic outdrop for that obligatory photograph and then watch the relief flood their faces when they return to solid ground.

Today, it was a young boy who was keen to have his photograph taken and you could hear the fear in his mother's voice as she directed her offspring onto the jutting slab and instructed him to 'stop there' before he'd shuffled more than a foot forward. The 'diving board' is actually something of an optical illusion. While the drop certainly looks terrifying from certain angles, the grassy slope isn't all that far below the 'board'. If the boy had toppled off the edge, he'd probably have been able to stop himself rolling long before he reached the distant valley floor.

Whether you're courageous enough to venture onto the diving board or not, the views from Fan y Big are pretty incredible. Behind you Cribyn, Pen y Fan and Corn Du line up on the horizon, while hundreds of feet below is the steep-sided valley Cwm Cynwyn.

Today the air was so clear we could see for miles. Harri, with his homing-pigeon instincts immediately spied Twmbarlwm. Our local mountain pretty much dominates the skyline and can be seen from just about anywhere in Newport and Cwmbran, yet from this height it looked like a tiny distant hill, a bump on the landscape.

Not wishing to be outdone, I spotted a familiar-looking escarpment some miles away.

'Look, Hay Buff,' I pointed excitedly.

'It's Hay *Bluff*,' Harri immediately corrected me. He scanned the horizon, looking baffled. 'Where?'

'Over there.' I pointed to a distant ridge.

He burst out laughing. I'd identified the Black Mountains alright, but from our viewpoint Hay Bluff was completely hidden.

Talking of the Black Mountains, what on earth were our ancestors thinking of when they were bestowing place names on this region's mountains? Two days ago we were walking across the Carmarthen Fans in the Black Mountain range and now we were looking out at another range, this time called the Black Mountains. If that's not confusing enough, there's a summit in the Black Mountains called Black Mountain (or Twyn Llech), and just across the border in England another one called Black Hill (known locally as Cat's Back). It's hardly surprising that some of us get a little disorientated at times when we're surrounded by so much blackness.

We wandered along the Craig Cwm Oergwm escarpment and followed the steep rocky path down to Blaen-y-glyn car park, where an oddly incongruous burger van was doing surprisingly brisk business on this hot afternoon. If only it had been an ice cream van.

There's a rather nice natural pool at the base of the waterfall here and as we'd approached from above, Harri was toying with the idea of a dip. Unfortunately, a group of young lads had got there first and as they cavorted in the shallow waters, wincing as they tiptoed across the sharp stones underneath, Harri turned into a sensible adult and reluctantly decided not to bother on the grounds that he didn't want to go into the water without shoes but neither did he want to get his only shoes saturated.

Distracted by thoughts of unwanted burgers and yearned-for ice creams, we somehow managed to miss the stone arch marking the entrance to the 150-year-old Torpantau tunnel. At 1,313 feet above sea level, the tunnel was the highest standard gauge tunnel in Great Britain and the station at Torpantau the highest on the Brecon and Merthyr Railway. It's more than fifty years since trains last steamed through the darkness, but it seems the tunnel is still possible to enter on foot. Recalling the gusto with which Harri greeted the numerous levada tunnels in Madeira, I'm rather relieved he didn't notice that arch.

I had nothing to complain about in terms of hilliness or crowds for the next few miles. We followed the wide and flat Taff Trail to Talybont Reservoir in almost complete solitude. This wasn't the most exciting walking of the day, and the views were limited to the track ahead and occasional glimpses of Talybont Reservoir glittering in the sunlight in the distance, but after the morning's hard climbing, the easy terrain gave us an opportunity to get some miles under our belts.

After three weeks on the road, we'd developed an almost complete disregard for time-keeping and now allowed our rumbling tummies to dictate when and how much we eat. Hence it was nearly four o'clock when we succumbed to our hunger pangs and settled down on a familiar bench overlooking the reservoir. Surprisingly – or maybe not – we seem to be eating far less now we're not following arbitrary meal times, and feel much healthier as a result.

Knowing we had hours of daylight ahead of us, we decided to stop for a quick cider at the Coach and Horses in Llangynidr before pushing on to Bwlch. The former coaching inn alongside the Monmouthshire and Brecon Canal has a lovely and very popular beer garden, but for once we were happy to disappear inside for half an hour. Settling down in the shadowy lounge, it would have been so easy to have hung around for a few hours. However, this duo is nothing if not determined. With monumental resolution, we dragged ourselves from the low leather sofas, heaved our rucksacks onto our backs and braced ourselves for more dazzling sunshine.

Now we were back in south Wales I had a better grasp of the terrain – not necessarily a good thing! Without doubt, the final five or six miles of the day were going to be tough going – and two halves of cider had left me feeling less than energetic.

Bwlch (meaning 'pass') is one of those Welsh place names that I struggled to pronounce for years. It probably didn't help that I always confused it with Builth Wells in mid Wales, meaning that mid word my brain would switch from one to the other and I'd end up blurting out something that sounded like 'bullith'. Fortunately, Harri's patient coaching (read constant ridiculing) finally worked, and the name now trips off my tongue like a local.

I came across these rather sardonic instructions on a BBC webpage while researching this book. The page is no longer online so I'm presuming the organisation eventually came to its senses and realised that providing a platform for a narrow-minded, Anglo-centric journalist to spout derisory nonsense was not a good idea.

> The word itself [Bwlch] was designed by 15th Century Welsh linguists so they could laugh at the feeble attempts of English invaders at pronouncing the word. To pronounce it, practice a sort of phlegm-inducing 'cchhchchchhh' sound at the back of your mouth. Then say 'Buwl-chch', sneezing as you finish. That's more or less it. If you cover the listener with spittle, you probably have the pronunciation right.

The web page was dated September 1999 and was presumably written when the Welsh language – and Welsh people – were considered fair game for anyone wanting to raise a cheap laugh. The brainless author goes on to describe the local pub (the Farmer's Arms) as 'a typical Welsh pub, full of farmers brawling about rugby, Young Farmer's rugby, and local rugby teams' and concludes, 'Bwlch imports tourists, pensioners and farmers; and exports phlegm and Women's Institute choir singers'.

I suspect the comedian who wrote this patronising and offensive drivel did so solely for comic effect; however, the Welsh continue to be seen as fair game for xenophobic diatribes by national journalists and commentators as another fatuous pre-NATO summit in Newport blog by a well-known right-wing writer demonstrates.

Back to Bwlch (did no one ever consider calling the village Black?). Having mastered the pronunciation, my next challenge was to pinpoint its equally confusing location because for some unfathomable reason I could never quite remember where it was. My recollections of travelling to mid Wales frequently included passing through Bwlch – but not always. In recent years, we'd arrived in Llandrindod Wells on several occasions without as much as a glimpse of this pretty little village of sloping gardens.

We strolled along a delightfully traffic-free B road and I pondered the enigma for some time before voicing it to Harri. Clever clogs immediately explained that we only pass through Bwlch if we're travelling to Brecon on the A40. As we're mostly heading further north, we generally follow the A479 Talgarth road, leaving the A40 before we reach Bwlch. I'd be dangerous if I could read a map!

Well, I for one had missed Bwlch during the years of bypassing it in favour of Talgarth so I was quite happy to meander along its narrow lanes, admiring those gorgeous undulating gardens and noting there was a rather wonderful aroma wafting around our nostrils. After dragging ourselves away from a country pub replete with interesting ciders, we now found ourselves having to resist the aromatic offerings of a pub barbecue in the New Inn. Never let it be said that Harri and I lack self-discipline.

It would have been so, so easy to succumb and spend the rest of the evening munching pub grub and swilling back pints. It was Saturday night and we'd climbed the highest peaks in south Wales on one of the hottest days of the year then pushed ahead for miles. No one could criticise us if we called it a day right here and now and put in our orders for those delicious-smelling beef burgers. With two bunkhouses in town – Beacons Backpackers (located at the New Inn) and the Star Bunkhouse – we'd be assured of a cheap bed for the night.

We exchanged glances, neither of us wishing to be the one to succumb to temptation but willing to be persuaded by the other. Except no one did any persuading. We had set out to walk to Cwmdu today and if that meant walking six or seven miles more at the end of a long and exhausting day, then walk it we would. And yet it was so tempting ... the smell of those burgers, the convivial atmosphere of the beer garden, not one but two conveniently located bunkhouses. Everything was set for that perfect summer evening .

We exchanged glances, then slowly and very definitely, we shook our heads. We crossed the road quickly, suspecting any hesitation would be our undoing, and charged up a lane signposted to Penuel Chapel. Like many other rural chapels of its era (*c.* 1830–50), the Presbyterian stone chapel is no longer used for worship and the stone building has been sold for conversion to a residential dwelling.

As we climbed steadily, we began to regret our stoicism; our cider-induced exuberance had all but diminished and right now we couldn't think of anywhere we'd rather be than sitting in a beer garden in Bwlch. And a bunkhouse would have been far more comfortable than a tent.

The track grew ever steeper, usually my cue for a tirade of grumbles, yet as we walked across Cefn Moel common, my enchantment with my surroundings grew. The last vestiges of the setting sun had imbued the landscape with warmth and a faint pink hue. Behind us the now black peaks of Pen y Fan and Corn Du already appeared distant, and it was hard to believe our day had started on the far side of those towering mountains.

Over the past few days, we had conquered all the high peaks of the Brecon Beacons; now all that remained were the ridges of the Black Mountains. It was hard not to feel a sense of achievement, of pride in what we'd achieved. Neither of us is a seasoned backpacker; however, our shoulders and legs were growing stronger every day, as was demonstrated this morning when we tackled Pen y Fan with relative ease and without stopping. Okay, in the great scheme of things our walk isn't up there with Nicholas Crane's solitary trek across Europe or Ffyona Campbell's epic walks across various continents, but in a few days' time we would have walked the entire length of Wales, and how many people can claim to have done that?

As the sun sank still lower, we came off the mountain, passing the two familiar and very different farmhouses of Blaen-y-cwm-uchaf and Blaen-y-cwm-isaf at the top of a small valley (the one dwelling is extremely dilapidated, the other rather grand).

The campsite at Cwmdu was farther away from the main road than we remembered; however, it's situated on a lovely elevated spot away from the river. While this meant there was no desperate need for the Jungle Formula I'd belatedly purchased in Brecon (fortuitously on a half price offer at Morrisons), the absence of great swarms of midges was definitely cause for celebration. As with the campsite at Dan yr Ogof, reception had closed by the time we pulled up, so we found what looked to be a quiet spot before enjoying an evening meal of bread and cheese on a conveniently placed picnic table.

Having hoped for a good night's sleep, we were dismayed to belatedly realise that we had set up camp a stone's throw away from a large family group with several tents and even more young children. Their tender age suggested that they they'd soon be tucked up in sleeping bags; however, as we frequently find on campsites, we're usually ready for our beds long before the little ones. On this occasion we had a treat in store. While we lay in our sleeping bags, the group decided to have an impromptu sing-song. Their repertoire, it transpired, was limited, the children collectively knowing only a few lines of one hymn. But know it, they did, and they sang their little hearts out for quite some time. We were beginning to fear this one song might be repeated *ad infinitum* throughout the night when one of the adults began interjected with the popular campfire song 'Kumbaya'. Soon the rest of the party had joined in and very pleasant their musical efforts sounded from the inside of our tent.

For years, I believed 'Kumbaya' to be Welsh in origin, probably because the first syllable sounds like 'cwm' and also because it was so popular here (I recall singing it endlessly on my first and last Girl Guide camping trip). It seems I was way off mark because the song originated across the pond in the United States.

In 1926, an ousted English professor called Robert Winslow Gordon set off in search of Negro spiritual songs. On the South Carolina islands, he heard H. Wylie singing the song in Gullah – a Creole language. The lilting lyrics, calling upon God to help people in despair and urging him to 'come by here', captured Gordon's imagination, and he recorded his own version. The song was later taken to Angola by American missionaries and its origins forgotten. In the late 1950s, it was 'rediscovered' and returned to the States where its popularity soared.

And so it came to pass that two weary long-distance hikers were lulled to sleep by the joyous singing of young children. A perfect end to a perfect day.

For photographs visit <u>uk.pinterest.com/thewalkerswife</u>

JUNE 22: CWMDU TO LLANTHONY

A clear starlit sky in the Welsh mountains generally means a nippy night. Last night was no exception. No matter how hard I tried to snuggle up in my single sleeping bag, there was no escaping the fact that my feet were *freezing;* in normal circumstances I'd have gone in search of socks, but attempting to locate anything in our tiny tent in the blackness would have meant clambering over Harri and almost certainly waking him. And, despite my nocturnal restlessness and frequent wriggling, Harri remained sound asleep. Frostbite it was then.

We have camped far fewer times on this trip than we intended. Truth is, wild camping is far more romantic in theory than in practice; having tried it three times in the past month (twice on this trip), I must conclude that the life of a canvas-carrying nomad is not for me.

Fortunately, sunrise arrives early this time of the year, so my fitful night's slumber ended around 5 a.m. Next to me, Harri too was stirring. While he headed over to the shower block, I commandeered the picnic bench we'd used last night … just in case anyone else decided to rush in first, you understand. As yet there wasn't a soul around, but you can never be too careful. Like any good hostess I spread out the breakfast options: Frosties, Frosties or … Frosties.

There was no sign of the Van Trapps at this early hour, and I resisted the urge to start a breakfast sing-along. We had enjoyed the children's singing, but it had continued well after ten, and there was no attempt by their parents to hush them lest other campers be weary and trying to sleep. As early risers, Harri and I frequently find ourselves creeping around so as not to wake those who like a lie-in on holiday, and yet other holidaymakers rarely extend the same courtesy to those of us who crawl into bed before ten, physically exhausted.

For the second time in three days, we found ourselves leaving a campsite that was still sleeping. Back on the main road (Cwmdu is located on the A479 Talgarth to Tretower road which links up with the A40), we were surprised but delighted to spot the tea rooms were open (we hadn't allowed ourselves to hope, this being a Sunday in Wales). The tea rooms are popular with bikers and even at this early hour there was already a group sitting outside eating.

The sign above the premises always pains Harri. It's emblazoned with the words Mynydd Ddu, Welsh for Black Mountain; yep, the cafe's as imaginatively named as the rest of the area. Unfortunately, my Welsh-speaking and very grammatically correct other half tells me that the noun *mynydd* is masculine and thus the adjective *du* ('black') doesn't demand a mutation in the form of a second 'd'. For a Welsh speaker, Mynydd Ddu is as big a bloomer as an English speaker referring to 'an coffee' or 'a orange'. The mistake was unforgiveable in Harri's eyes; worse, it had blatantly and shamelessly been printed on business signage.

I half expected Harri to veto the premises on the grounds of bad grammar but fortunately his need for a morning cuppa overcame his pedantic streak. The Mynydd Ddu (it pains me to write that) is renowned for its good-value, great-tasting food, but having recently eaten our fill of Frosties we decided against a cooked breakfast and shared a large piece of carrot cake instead – quite delicious it was too.

Like so many rural facilities, Cwmdu's public toilets closed years ago; however, non-customers are permitted to use Mynydd Ddu's own for 20p a visit, which seems perfectly reasonable under the circumstances (someone has to buy the toilet paper and clean them).

The restorative powers of a strong cup of tea are quite incredible. Within half an hour, I felt myself being transformed from a grumpy, tired woman who was convinced she hadn't slept a wink into an energetic and enthusiastic long-distance hiker raring to climb the next mountain. Or maybe it was the carrot cake?

We headed out into the sunshine, aware we had a long day ahead of us but excited to have reached the familiar and very beautiful scenery of the Black Mountains.

On this occasion, we didn't bother to visit the wonderfully named Church of the Archangel Michael, but for first-time visitors to Cwmdu, it's well worth a detour. The church dates back to the fifteenth century but was extensively rebuilt in the early 1830s at the cost of £2,000 (using existing stonework). This major restoration was at the behest, indeed the determination, of the then incumbent, the Reverend Thomas Price. Price was a major Welsh literary figure of the time, though he's better known by his bardic name of Carnhuanawc. His accomplishments are impressive: orator, naturalist, educationalist, artist, musician, linguist … the list goes on. When the Reverend wasn't organising the rebuilding of churches, he was spearheading the revival of the Eisteddfod or helping Lady Charlotte Guest to translate the mythic Mabinogion tales from Welsh into English. I wonder what Carnhuanawc would have said about the cafe's linguistic blooper?

The Reverend Price's greatest achievement was his *Hanes Cymru* ('History of Wales'), in which he attempted to trace the origin and development of Wales as a nation. Price is buried on the north side of the church.

John Sansom certainly wasn't a man who liked straight lines. The late creator of the Beacons Way managed to make places that look relatively close on an OS map become a hard day's hiking apart. When Harri asked if I wanted to push ahead to Llanthony today rather than come off the mountain for an overnight stop at Crickhowell, I'd based my (affirmative) response on the fact that it didn't look all *that* far from Cwmdu on the OS map.

When I quietly voiced my displeasure at having to cover all those extra miles, Harri retorted Samson's intention was to showcase the Brecon Beacons not to devise the fastest route from A to B. That was me told!

Actually, despite my grumbles, it would be hard to improve upon John Samson's route through the Black Mountains. We've walked this section before, albeit in the other direction, yet despite my familiarity with the landscape, I found myself stopping every five minutes or so to wax lyrically about the views, specifically the view towards nearby Mynydd Troed.

Thirty miles away, my older daughters were running the second Caerphilly 10k race. If it was airless up here in the mountains, the heat rising from those wide tarmac roads would surely be unbearable.

We snaked around the common boundary, crossing a stream and passing above a conifer plantation. From time to time, we found ourselves sharing the footpath with sheep who chased ahead for a while before disappearing into the ferns.

Mention Table Mountain to someone who doesn't come from south Wales and they'll probably assume you're talking about the towering Cape Town peak. But here in the Black Mountains we have our very own Table Mountain. At 1,480 feet, the flat-topped Welsh mountain is diminutive compared to its namesake, which soars 3,338 feet above sea level and measures roughly two miles from one side of its steep-cliffed plateau to the other.

The Welsh hill is formed from old red sandstone and its distinctive shape is believed to be the result of a landslide back in the Devonian period. Fast forward several hundred million years and the flat summit provided the perfect location for an Iron Age hill fort, the remains of which are still visible today.

On this warm Sunday morning the summit was teeming with local hikers and holidaymakers, many of whom had taken the steep path from Crickhowell below, a town which took its name from Crug Hywel (the mountain's Welsh name).

We watched with amusement as a remarkably confident sheep wandered from group to group, presumably hoping to steal a morsel. A couple sitting perilously close to the edge seemed oblivious as the animal approached them from behind, looking for a moment as though it was about to nudge them over the edge. The incident reminded us of a film we hired a few years back; in fact, *Black Sheep* – a comedy horror film about infected zombie sheep –might have been conceived and produced in Wales had the New Zealanders not got there first. What was our verdict on the film? We had second thoughts about watching it after my youngest daughter declared it to be terrible.

As the hours passed, the temperatures soared until eventually Harri was left with no option but to plunge into the nearest river. This happened to be the deliciously cool Grwyne Fechan, a tributary of the Grwyne Fawr which marks the Powys-Monmouthshire border, but I suspect he'd have happily plunged into a cattle trough by this point. I'm not a big dipper myself, though Harri did manage to coax me into the River Monnow in my underwear two summers ago. Splashing around in the water was great fun – exhilarating and liberating – although I was less enthusiastic about the post-dip shuffle in wet pants.

Last time we called into Partrishow Church my camera batteries had run out so I wasn't able to take any photographs. This time I was determined to capture the so-called figure of doom painted on the wall (and later whitewashed over). With an hourglass in one hand, a sickle in the other and a spade on his arm, the skeleton in the medieval wall painting is a chilling sight and one which simultaneously reminded me of my own mortality and how death played a greater part in people's everyday lives hundreds of years ago.

Undoubtedly, it was the church's remote location that saved it from a post-Reformation fate similar to many others. Had the Puritan iconoclasts reached St Issui's, there's no doubt the exquisite intricate rood screen carved from Irish oak would have been smashed to smithereens and other antiquities wrecked.

Having avoided the worst ravages of the Protestant reformers, this remote little church found itself facing another 'enemy' at the beginning of the twentieth century. And this time, it was the very fabric of the building that was threatened. St Issui's – erected on made-up land – was in imminent danger of collapse. As the rebuilding programme got underway, human remains were found under the south wall of the chapel, leading to supposition that this wasn't the first time the church had subsided. It's now accepted that the south wall was rebuilt in the fourteenth century and that sometime between its collapse and the rebuild, the ground was used for burial.

Nearby is an ancient well, its approach marked with a pilgrim stone incised with the eight-pointed Maltese Cross associated with the Knights Hospitaller. The story is that a holy man called Issui had a cell nearby from where he spread the Christian faith. Issui was brutally murdered by a passing traveller to whom he had extended his hospitality. After Issui's death, his cell became a place of pilgrimage and the well purported to have healing powers (they didn't appear to do Issui himself much good).

Visitors still visit St Issui's Well and occasionally toss in coins and twigs – some even sipping the healing waters (with hindsight, I rather wish we'd stopped at the well to partake ourselves). In the early eleventh century, a wealthy pilgrim from the continent was allegedly cured of his leprosy by the water in the well; it was he who gifted the gold which enabled the church to be built.

While I was inside taking photographs, Harri was relaxing in the graveyard and striking up a conversation with two Dutch hikers. He was amazed to learn that the two men had travelled to the UK overnight, headed straight to Crickhowell, and immediately set off along the Beacons Way. Their ultimate destination was Hay-on-Wye, but, like us, they were today heading for Llanthony, where they planned to camp before joining the well-trodden Offa's Dyke Path tomorrow.

By coincidence, the taller of the two men (we never did discover his name) worked in electronics and had had reason to visit Newbridge Electronics in Newport on several occasions. This being the same Newbridge Electronics where I had worked for one *whole* week back in the late 1990s, having just escaped a miserable hourly-paid admin job and been willing to try anything (though actually it might only have been four days; it was Christmas week after all).

We bade our farewells and were soon passing the impressive Ty'n-y-llwyn, a fifteenth-century stone house which has remained in the same family for four centuries. As you pass in front of this incredible building with its terrace of huge flagstones, it's not difficult to let your imagination wander and be whisked away to the earlier times when life was much tougher physically but far, far simpler in so many ways. For example, no one worried too much about sleeping arrangements; when it was rebuilt in the late sixteenth century, Ty'n-y-llwyn boasted a lower byre, enabling the humans and their livestock to live side by side under one roof.

In Snowdonia, we'd longed for summer to arrive. When we were squelching across waterlogged upland areas in waterproofs, I'd fantasised continually about sunshine and being warm. Now it wasn't just pleasantly warm, it was scorching … and far too hot to be hiking across open moorland with virtually no shelter from the sun's rays.

The heat sapped our energy, slowing us down just at the time of day when we needed to be pushing on to get to Llanthony. Worse, our water bottles were almost empty, so that we were reduced to taking tiny sips as we snaked across the ridge in soaring temperatures.

We flagged, acutely aware that the Dutch hikers were rapidly closing the distance between us. It wouldn't be long before they would catch us up and overtake, or worse, adjust their pace to walk alongside us (I have no objection to strolling with strangers but Harri is generally less keen as he thinks it slows me down).

What to do? Summon every last ounce of energy and up our pace dramatically in the likelihood they'd fall behind? Or should we slow down to a very un-Harri-like amble, enabling them to catch up and quickly pass? Of course, just a few hundred feet behind us, the men were undoubtedly weighing up the options too. Slow down or speed up? Trail behind convoy-style or overtake?

Who would believe the level of strategic planning and diplomacy needed to circumnavigate human traffic on a mountain? Regrettably, no walkers' equivalent of *The Highway Code* exists to guide you through every imaginable manoeuvre, meaning you can't fall back on the rule book.

The absence of clearly displayed speed limits would help. If you knew the speed limit was, say, four miles per hour, you could safely assume that a momentary breaking of the law, perhaps quickening the pace to four and a quarter miles per hour, would see you breezily sailing past the hikers in front. Conversely, if you slowed to three and three-quarter miles an hour, you'd know there was no chance of catching them up.

Of course, this assumes that hikers – like car drivers – always travel at the maximum speed permitted in any given conditions, which is patently untrue of me. Anyway most roads are so busy that unless someone cuts you up or tears through a red, we mostly don't notice what other drivers are doing.

When we're walking we frequently see no one for hours; occasionally, we go all day without seeing another soul. So when we do encounter other hikers we're very aware of each other. And there's a certain etiquette of the hills which demands that every hiker must acknowledge another with a massive smile, generic greeting and an inane comment about the weather turning out far worse/better than the morning's forecast.

It's the insincere enthusiasm with which walkers first greet one another that fuels the awkwardness when you then find yourself shuffling along in the same direction; not actually walking together, but sufficiently close to prohibit normal conversation and the *other* stuff. We'd been friendly enough with the Dutch guys but we'd already said farewell. Now they were hot on our heels and we seemed destined to launch into another conversation about what a scorcher of a day it was.

The Beacons Way takes a tortuous (some might say masochistic) route from Partrishow to Llanthony, climbing steadily when any right-minded person would expect to be descending to the valley below.

As we trudged ever higher, I pointed in the general direction of the Vale of Ewyas (that's all you can do on these wide ridges because you're not able to glimpse the valleys below).

'If we're supposed to be heading down there,' I demanded. 'Why are we walking uphill?'

'Because we're following the Beacons Way,' Harri said. 'And this is the waymarked route.'

I didn't know whether to cry – or to throw something at him. I know he's a stickler for walking every inch of any route that goes into the digital pages of our hiking ebooks, but there are limits. By this point, I was so tired I could barely lift one foot in front of the other. Tired and very, very thirsty. The change in weather had been cause for celebration, but as we were now discovering, the relentless heat and lack of shade can make the going extremely tough.

On a trip to Las Vegas several years ago, we took a boat trip on the Colorado River. This wasn't a white-water rafting trip – my daughter was too young for that – but just a nice scenic meander along the great river accompanied by two experienced guides. Something shocking had happened the previous week, they told us. Two hikers had been found in a gully, disorientated and suffering from severe sunstroke and dehydration. Tragically, both men later died and yet it wasn't their deaths *per se* that had stunned local people – the guides said people frequently died while walking in the area. No, what had astounded everyone was that these men were local and, as such, were fully aware of the risks they were taking and so should have been equipped for the hostile conditions.

And if you think it can't happen here in Wales, it can and, tragically, it did. Three Army reservists died on a training exercise in the Brecon Beacons in July 2013. Despite being young and fit soldiers, they'd collapsed due to heat stress on the hottest day of the year. It can happen to anyone.

We took tiny sips of water and wondered why we hadn't availed ourselves of the medieval well or stopped at a farmhouse to ask to fill our waters bottles. There were no signs of habitation up here. Our new friends were walking just a few hundred metres behind us. The fact that they'd also run out of water only highlighted how easy it was to seriously underestimate your water consumption when temperatures rise. We weren't unduly burdened by the weight we were carrying now. With food supplies running low, much of our clothing abandoned in Brecon (including my only 'best' top, one of Harri's bamboo tee-shirts and several manky pairs of socks) and toiletries fast running out, our loads were probably as light as they were going to be on any long-distance trek.

The Dutch duo finally caught up with us just as we turned to leave the ridge and finally began our steep descent to Llanthony. Goodness, it was hard going for a downhill route. The path is steep and stony, and proved a challenge for my tired legs – a challenge I could happily have done without.

By now, the only thing that was keeping me going was the knowledge I would soon be having a nice hot shower followed by a good night's sleep in a comfortable bed. There isn't a huge amount of accommodation in Llanthony, but this being June we thought we'd be able to get a room without too much trouble.

Our first port of call was the Half Moon Hotel, where a 'Vacancies' sign hung in the window. We ventured inside and found the public bar completely deserted. By now, we were desperate for drinks and we had no intention of giving up easily. We called out time and time again until eventually the chef emerged from the kitchen. He served us willingly enough but had no idea if there was an available room or not, which seemed a bit odd given the 'Vacancies' sign. He'd find out for us, he promised. When he returned, the news wasn't good. It seemed a large group was expected later this evening. There was no room at the inn for us tonight.

The danger of stopping, of course, is that it's almost impossible to get going again. When I was hopeful that we'd get a room here, while I was drinking my half pint of cider, my body had decided enough was enough and it wasn't moving again today. Of course, staying put in the bar was out of the question; we needed to find somewhere to stay overnight.

We had ruled out camping on the grounds that the site at Llanthony is as basic as it gets – just one toilet and a cold water tap. The prospect of having to spend another night under canvas without even a lukewarm shower for consolation filled me with despair. At £3 per person per night, the campsite was the cheapest we'd come across, but I just didn't think I could do it. Not again.

Every now and then Harri surprises me by transforming himself into my knight in shining armour. Now was one of those occasions. Understanding how exhausted I was, he announced that we were heading straight across the grass to the Llanthony Priory Hotel to see if they had a room available. This one was likely to be expensive, but in his current frame of mind, he didn't care what it cost. As long as we had hot water and a soft (or hard) mattress, it would be worth every penny, he declared.

Having made the decision to part with his money, Harri was devastated to learn that this hotel was also fully booked. We'd always known that we were taking a risk in not booking our overnight accommodation ahead; however, we'd been confident it wouldn't be too difficult in Llanthony. Now it seemed our optimism had been misplaced.

We were heading for the campsite when Harri recalled reading about a bunkhouse at Llanthony. Not that a bunkhouse sounded like the ideal place to plonk my weary self, but it had to be better than a two-person tent crammed with two persons who were very smelly because they'd walked in the heat all day and now couldn't get a bath, shower or even hot water. I think I might have been tempted to drink myself into oblivion in the Llanthony Priory Hotel's bar if a night in our tent was the only option.

Our hopes rising ever so slightly, we headed to the bunkhouse. (This is the beauty of Llanthony: as well as being historic and scenic, the hamlet is so tiny you can limp from one place to another within minutes.) To my dismay, everything was locked and the only people around were a couple who were feeding dogs in several outbuildings. The man looked up and this genial soul must have recognised a damsel in distress when he saw one because he immediately stopped what he was doing and offered to go in search of Sue, the lady who ran the oddly-named Llanthony Treats. He couldn't promise anything but if he brought her over to see us, at least we could ask.

Nearby, the bare-chested Koen (one of the Dutch hikers we'd met earlier) had courageously washed under the single cold water tap and, intrigued by our attempts to secure a bed for the night, he now wandered over to join us in the wait for Sue.

At first, we were convinced she was going to turn us away. This brisk no-nonsense former English teacher told us in no uncertain terms that she'd just finished cleaning up after an extremely busy weekend and wasn't expecting any arrivals at this late hour. She looked pointedly at the adjacent field where there was oodles of grassy space for a small tent.

Harri and I exchanged glances. Despite his best efforts, he had drawn a blank. Llanthony Treats had been our last chance of securing a roof for the night, but Sue was tired and she wanted to put her feet up.

We've walked from Cwmdu today, I wanted to shout. *You can't possibly be as exhausted as we are.* And after a long, hot day in the mountains, we were facing a stand up wash in cold water, dry bread rolls and another night in a cramped tent.

Then, unexpectedly, Sue nodded. Whether she recognised desperation when she saw it, or she just didn't want to turn down business, it was going to be okay. We wouldn't be sleeping under the stars, after all. I could have kissed her.

By now, Koen's friend had joined us and, on witnessing Sue's capitulation, the two men immediately indicated their own interest in swapping a field for some comfortable bunks.

Ten minutes later, after agreeing to fight off any campers who dared to venture anywhere near our private shower rooms under the miscomprehension that they could enjoy free warm water, all four of us were all settled in two lovely spacious bunkhouses with flagstone floors and simple furnishings. The room – though simple – was clean and ample for our needs. There were tea and coffee making facilities (with plenty of teabags) in ours so we had a quick cuppa, showered, then had a second cuppa, relishing every mouthful. Sue and Llanthony Treats had saved the day. Unbelievably, these wonderful facilities in a stunning location were costing just £12 per person per night and the price even included a full English breakfast.

It's mostly hikers who use the bunkhouse so Sue only provides duvets upon request (the per person charge then increases to £15 per night) If only there were more bunkhouses like Llanthony Treats in Wales – perhaps offering smaller rooms for couples as well as the six-berth ones for larger groups. I long for the day when accommodation providers wake up to the fact that long-distance hikers like us require very few luxuries, just somewhere to shower and rest their weary feet. Oh, and tea-making facilities are always appreciated.

I later learned that Sue operates the business all year round; though she did admit that some visitors have found the bunkhouse a little cold for their liking at cooler times of the year (and have demanded heaters). For me, having fully expected another night curled up in our little tent with feet like icicles, the bunkhouse was bliss and exactly the kind of business I could see myself running if only I had a stable block to convert.

We joined Koen and companion (someone else whose name we never asked!) in the bar of the Priory Hotel just as they were finishing their meals. We'd already eaten, if you could describe what was becoming our staple diet of bread and cheese as an evening 'meal'. I tried hard not to drool at the homemade pies and wonderful *hot* gravy and reminded myself that we had a cooked breakfast to look forward to in the morning.

The hotel's tiny bar is located slightly below ground level and always reminds me of the extraordinary cave houses dotted all over Spain's Andalusia region. The Priory's shadowy bar isn't the result of rock eruptions but is believed to have been the prior's cellar in the original twelfth-century priory. I suspect there has been many an alcohol-fuelled mishap as beer-loving hikers attempt to lift stagger up those steep stone steps out into the fresh night air.

Exhausted but captivated by our historic surroundings, we ended up having one of the most enjoyable nights of this whole trip. Our new friends were well-travelled, interesting people and, better still, they spoke perfect English

Koen manages a large Dutch outdoor shop and our three men to one woman ratio meant we were soon discussing hiking equipment … specifically *our* equipment. Koen was of the opinion that we'd enjoy camping far more if we went 'upmarket' and invested in some decent kit. He was rendered almost speechless when I said I slept on a basic foam camping mat and was unimpressed with Harri's 'posh' self-inflating three-quarter one.

He pointed out that we'd be less inclined to opt for expensive bed and breakfast accommodation if we bought better sleeping mats, saving ourselves a fortune in the long run. He's right, of course he is. We promised to investigate his top-of-the-range recommendations when we got home.

The beer and conversation flowed. Over several rounds of drinks, we discussed footwear, British television, off-the-beaten-track European holiday destinations and linguistic skills (or lack of) and laughed a lot. It's quite humbling when you consider they spent the whole night talking to us in English and neither batted an eyelid. Koen, especially, was completely fluent and at ease conversing in English.

We strolled back to the bunkhouse under a perfectly clear, starry sky around midnight. I'm pretty certain I didn't imagine the men offering us a whiskey nightcap, which we very sensibly turned down.

Our long and very hard day's hiking in the Black Mountains had unexpectedly ended quite perfectly.

For photographs visit uk.pinterest.com/thewalkerswife

JUNE 23: LLANTHONY TO MONMOUTH

Llanthony Priory must surely lay claim to one of the most wild and beautiful settings of any historic building in Wales. It was difficult to tear my eyes away from its impressive stone arches as we made our way up onto Hatterall Ridge; from every angle, the Augustinian ruin is compelling.

We'd woken really early – before 5 a.m. – fortunately no worse for wear after last night's drinking session. Remembering my earlier half at the Half Moon, I'd sensibly stopped at two in the Priory. Less mindful when it comes to the beer, Harri managed to down four pints and wasn't feeling quite as lively as me on this beautiful June morning.

It was hard to believe we only had two days of hiking left. Sometime tomorrow evening we would walk into Chepstow where Harri's good friend, the Newport poet Goff Morgan, would be waiting to drive us home. After just over three weeks and nearly 400 miles, our journey would finally be over.

Lying there in the morning light, it hit me with sudden force that I didn't want this experience to end. We'd been soaked and parched, burnt and bitten, exhausted and exhilarated, happy and homesick, hungry and (a certain person who shall remain nameless) hungover. Walking 'O Fôn i Fynwy' hadn't been easy, but despite everything, we'd come through and kept going. And, once I'd caught up with my family, I wanted to carry on walking – possibly for the rest of my life.

I was barely fifteen when I stood on Newton beach in Porthcawl and announced to my father that I intended to walk the coast of Britain one day. That was in June 1976. We'd arrived at my Auntie Min's caravan in torrential rain, but a day or two later, the sun was shining and the longest hottest summer most Brits can remember was well underway. My father and I had walked along the beach for a mile or two from Trecco Bay Caravan Park but were prevented from going any farther by the fast-flowing River Ogmore which provides a natural obstacle between Newton and Ogmore.

I can still remember how I passionately I wanted to cross that river and continue walking along the coastline. What lay beyond and just out of reach looked enticing, far more intriguing, in fact, than the stretch we'd already walked (which I now believe is the essence of long-distance walking or at least the long-distance hiker's mentality).

I almost certainly exhibited a certain amount of teenage stropping, right there on the beach, but a river is a river and eventually I had no option but to turn around. (with hindsight, I suspect my dad was keen to get back to the pint of Double Diamond that awaited him at Dirty Duck pub).

As is the way for most people, life didn't pan out quite the way the 15-year-old me anticipated. Fast forward nearly forty years (and looking back it feels like those decades have indeed whizzed past) and, while the idea of walking around the UK still appeals, I have done a reality check. Doing such an epic hike requires a great deal of sacrifice and a *lot* of understanding from your family. We are, after all, talking 11,073 miles. And that's a long, long way. Even if you manage to cover 16-20 miles every day, you still need to allow between 692 and 553 days to complete the challenge. And if you're a purist and insist on including the coasts of the larger outlying islands the distance nearly doubles.

One of the issues is the 'wiggliness' of our coastline; it's high, much higher than countries like Spain, Australia and South Africa. Of course, there are long stretches of relatively straight coastline in the UK, but toss Scotland into the mix and you have a coastline that is much longer than similar-sized countries.

Wiggliness, it would seem, has shattered my life's ambition. Already in my prime, I just can't see me ever finding the two-year window of opportunity that is needed to walk the UK mainland in one go, let alone its islands. And, let's face it, given the tortuous journeying to certain parts of this country, it would be madness to attempt to do it any other way.

As you might imagine, there is one positive to all this wiggliness. Our lengthy coastline means that nowhere in the UK is more than 70 miles from the sea. Even Cwmystwyth, the centre of Wales, is not much more than a sixteen-mile drive from Aberystwyth on the Ceredigion coast. The Wales Coast Path passes through the university town and, at 870 miles, it's infinitely more achievable. Definitely one for the bucket list!

After breakfast, we bade our farewells to Koen and co. (we never did learn the other man's name, only that he preferred walking in minimalist shoes, had two children, and coordinated large-scale IT projects for a living). We were heading in opposite directions today, their destination being the book town of Hay-on-Way and ours Monmouth.

On this glorious Monday morning, we thanked our lucky stars that we weren't heading to the office to sit in front of a computer all day. Instead, our waking hours would be spent meandering through beautiful landscapes, living the nomadic and much more natural (and healthy) existence of our forefathers. At the end of the day, it would be our legs and feet that ached and not our souls.

It's always a wrench to leave behind the beautiful and tranquil Vale of Ewyas, though according to the late chronicler of Monmouthshire, Newport-born Fred Hando, the hamlet Llanthony wasn't always quite as sleepy as today. An 1880 map includes a corn mill, a saw mill, a smithy, a boys' school, the church, and two inns (one being the Half Moon).

Llanthony Priory's history begins around 1100 when the Norman nobleman William de Lacy stumbled across a small chapel dedicated to St David while hunting in the remote valley of Ewyas, a Welsh district which had been held by the de Lacy family since shortly after the Norman Conquest.

Impressed by the sanctity of the place, William decided to renounce the world of Norman power politics and settle there as a hermit. The world would not leave William alone, however, his example attracting a religious following which settled in the area and built a church dedicated to St John. The powerful Augustinian order also became interested in the site, and by 1118 there was a priory in the valley housing some forty English monks. Such was the spell of enchantment cast by Llanthony that one prior, Robert de Béthune (he was appointed Bishop of Hereford in 1131), described his forced removal from the valley as akin to Adam's eviction from paradise.

Paradise or not, the local Welsh populace were justifiably upset by this foreign intrusion onto their lands, and resented the monks' appropriation of their labour and produce under the tithe system. Repeated Welsh attacks on the priory led to its abandonment in 1135, with the monks retreating first to Hereford and then Gloucester, where a second Llanthony (Llanthony Secunda) was established in 1136.

Contemporary accounts, which recall bitterly cold winters spent 'singing to wolves', suggest that not all monks were as heartbroken as Robert de Béthune at having to leave the Vale of Ewyas. Despite the establishment of a second Llanthony, the de Lacy family continued to support the original monastery. A series of violent campaigns in Ireland poured more money in the family coffers, enabling them to fund the rebuilding of the priory church on a much grander scale.

Work on the new priory began around 1180 and continued until around 1220. The result was one of Wales's great medieval buildings and a striking example of transitional Norman/Gothic architecture. The priory prospered for at least a century after this, with further work being completed around 1325. For reasons unknown – though perhaps related to Owain Glyndŵr's war of independence – the priory entered a long decline during the fifteenth century. By 1481 – and long before its final closure in 1538 – the building was no longer functioning as an independent priory and had come under the control of its daughter cell, Llanthony Secunda.

In the centuries that followed, wind and weather took their inevitable toll; the antiquarian Richard Colt Hoare witnessed the collapse of the great west window in 1803, and on Ash Wednesday 1837 all five central arches fell. Fortunately, the remoteness of the priory meant that its stones were not plundered for building materials. In 1807, Llanthony was bought by the English poet Walter Savage Landor. Landor had grand plans for reviving the estate, but succeeded in upsetting all he had dealings with, landowners and tenants alike. Brought to the brink of bankruptcy, Landor was forced to leave Llanthony and hand over management of the estate to trustees.

Yet his heart remained in his beloved Welsh valley, and in Italy he wrote a poem to the Reverend Cuthbert Southey called 'Llanthony'.

> I loved thee by the streams of yore
> By distant streams I love thee more
> For never is the heart so true
> As bidding what we love adieu.

Today, the priory and adjoining hotel remain in private hands, but as Grade 1 listed buildings are under the protection of the Welsh historic environment service Cadw. Under its management, the site has been made safe and accessible, enabling visitors to appreciate the full splendour of this majestic ruin.

We climbed gradually, me twisting around every few minutes to get another glimpse of those wonderful high arches. For once, my preoccupation with the timeless splendour and romanticism of the abbey suited Harri; while I waxed lyrically about stones and monks, he was keeping mum about something he'd spotted – there was a bull in the field we were walking through.

He's learned over the years that pointing out one of these bovines is not the best strategy if he wants me to stay calm. On one momentous occasion a few years back, we were following one of Newport council's publicised countryside walks when my beloved suddenly realised we had unwanted company.

Keeping his voice low, he chose his words carefully: 'Don't look up and don't stop walking. There's a bull in this field. And it's watching us.'

Well, what would you do? I didn't look up and I didn't stop walking ... I ran! I ran as fast as my legs would carry me (and this was long before I joined a running club so it wasn't very fast). When I reached the gate on the far side of the field I hurled myself at it with such ferocity that the gate shuddered and I whacked both shins against its metal bars.

Harri was laughing his head off when he caught up with me. The young bull had apparently done nothing more than tap its front hoof on the grass before losing all interest in us. Rather than risk a bull charging me, I'd taken off and charged a metal gate. I was nursing bruises for weeks!

From the Vale of Ewyas, the footpath follows the contour of the mountain, climbing steadily but not too steeply until you have wonderful valley vistas. Last time we were here the path was quite muddy in places, but today it was nice and firm underfoot, which is exactly how I like my footpaths.

At the top of the ridge, just as you join the Offa's Dyke Path, there's an incredible rocky outcrop where the ground seems to fall away and all your hard work is rewarded with extensive views of the gorgeous and entirely underrated Monnow Valley below (we explored this peaceful valley in *Castle Walks in Monmouthshire* on the walks from Grosmont and Longtown castles).

Until the Wales Coast Path opened, the Offa's Dyke Path was probably the best-known long-distance walk in Wales. This National Trail – one of only three in Wales – opened in 1971 and follows the Wales–England border from Sedbury Cliffs near Chepstow in the south to Prestatyn in the north, passing through eight counties on its way. At just 176 miles, it's less than half the distance of O Fôn i Fynwy.

We have walked sections of the path in Monmouthshire, the Brecon Beacons and north-east Wales; however, it's never appealed to either Harri or me as a long-distance challenge for several reasons. First, it's just *so* popular in the summer months (and we do like to escape the madding crowds occasionally). Second, the border-hugging route also misses out on much of Wales's spectacular mountain scenery, such as the whole of Snowdonia. Thirdly, we prefer the idea of a walk that remains in Wales for its entire route like the Wales Coast Path or 'O Fôn i Fynwy' (though at this point I have to admit that Hatterall Ridge occasionally strays into Herefordshire as does tomorrow's Wye Valley Path … however, the incursions onto English soil are so brief we swear you'll barely notice them!).

Boy, does Offa's Dyke Path draw in the crowds, possibly because it's easily walkable in a fortnight's holiday or maybe its location pulls in walkers from both sides of the border it crosses no less than twenty times. Whatever the reason, erosion is all too evident in some parts; in a steeply-sloping field approaching Hay-on-Wye from the south, the route was so well-worn that very distinctive grass-free 'steps' had been formed.

It has also been known to attract the occasional display of exhibitionism as a friend who has hiked it *twice* alone discovered.

She recounts: 'I was a few miles out of Monmouth when I spotted a bare-chested guy cutting back vegetation with a knife. It wasn't until I got close that I saw his chest wasn't the only thing that was bare … the man was completely naked apart from a pair of knee-high wellington boots. He warned me about an electric fence and asked if his nakedness embarrassed me. I was very polite and assured him it didn't, but I didn't look down!' (I really do take my hat off to her – just my hat

– because I really don't think I'd have remained so calm if I'd encountered a naked knifeman whilst out walking on my own!).

For much of its length, Offa's Dyke Path follows or stays close to the ancient dyke which gives it its name – an eighth-century linear earthwork built by King Offa of Mercia to protect his land from invasion by the Welsh. The traceability of the dyke varies dramatically along its 82-mile length; in some places a great earthwork bank rises up to 25 feet high with a deep ditch on the Welsh side, but in other parts there is very little to see on the ground.

Offa's Dyke has caused historians headaches for years. Whether it had a defensive role or was merely symbolic, whether certain shorter sections of earthworks were built by King Offa or not, and whether Offa did in fact ever complete what King Alfred's biographer Asser referred to a hundred years later as 'a great dyke built between Wales and Mercia from sea to sea'.

It's not even certain whether some sections of the dyke were part of the master build or just happened to be dug nearby. The truth is that earthworks are difficult to date precisely. Take the 40-mile Wat's Dyke which runs east of Oswestry; it was once thought to be constructed before Offa's reign (757–796), but excavations in 2006 suggest it was built later, possibly in the 820s, when the Mercian king Coenwulf was again fighting the Welsh.

Another stretch of dyke has turned out to be about 200 years older than thought, meaning that Offa could not have built that part either. That particular carbon-dating exercise was only made possible due to the cavalier actions of a new landowner, who inadvertently flattened about 50 yards of the historic earthworks near Llangollen.

The man – referred to in newspaper reports as Danny – claimed he'd not been told the price of the field included an ancient and protected monument. As he wanted to build stables on the land, he hired a digger and didn't waste any time in removing what must have looked to him like an elongated mound of earth.

It was this local man's self-acclaimed ignorance that saved him from a £5,000 fine or, worse, a six-month prison sentence (it's a criminal offence to damage Offa's Dyke under the Ancient Monuments and Archaeological Areas Act 1979). No one it seemed could prove he had criminal intent or knowledge that he was committing a criminal act. Proof indeed that being dumb can sometimes be a blessing.

Up here on Hatterall Ridge where we were now walking, the Offa's Dyke Path and the Beacons Way follow one and the same well-walked route. Reach the bottom of the hill and they briefly separate before merging once again for about a hundred yards. The Beacons Way then heads towards Llanvihangel Crucorney. I can imagine lesser mortals getting very confused in this neck of the woods, but fortunately I had my secret weapon: Harri. And having pored over the two routes, he declared that we would be following the Beacons Way fork before continuing along Offa's Dyke Path to Pandy.

It being a Monday morning during term-time – and still relatively early – there were very few walkers around, so when I heard a sudden thud behind me, I spun around startled. There was no one there, just something lying on the ground. From this distance, it looked like a wine glass in a plastic bag.

My instinctive reaction – and Harri is still incredulous about this, so maybe there is something in the whole men/Mars and women/Venus thing – was to scan the sky (subconsciously, I think I might have been remembering an episode of *Six Feet Under* where a woman in her garden was killed by a block of ice falling from a plane overhead).

So there I am gazing up at a cloudless, plane-free sky trying to work out where this flying object might have originated from, while Harri is urging me to pick it up and see what's inside. I hesitated; it seemed an inherently risky thing to do. What if it wasn't a wine glass, after all? Harri was doing his whole 'I'm getting impatient' shuffle thing, so I slowly edged towards the bag. I picked it up and tentatively peered inside.

What greeted me wasn't a glass – or even a large slab of ice – just my mobile phone charger.

I laughed so much I had tears streaming down my face. If Harri had suspected I was deranged before, there could now be no doubt in his mind. While I roared with laughter, he kept asking me how on earth I'd imagined a wine glass might fall off a plane *mid-flight*. Perhaps a passenger, regretting choosing red over wine, had opened the toilet window and tossed it, glass and all, into the skies, he mocked?

I was still chuckling to myself as we started the long descent from Hatterall Hill. After several hours of solitary walking we were suddenly joined by clusters of young people heading in our direction. Duke of Edinburgh participants these youngsters were most definitely not! There wasn't an 80-litre rucksack in sight. In fact, judging from their fashionable clothing, we wondered if this was an impromptu class outing up a local hill. One girl, puffing and panting, approached us to ask if they were nearly at the top; Harri had to tell her unfortunately not.

As we neared the bottom of Hatterall Hill, we passed an unusual sight: the words of a poem painted on the side of a barn.

> To-day I want the sky,
> The tops of the high hills,
> Above the last man's house,
> His hedges, and his cows,
> Where, if I will, I look
> Down even on sheep and rook,
> And of all things that move
> See buzzards only above:-
> Past all trees, past furze
> And thorn, where naught deters
> The desire of the eye
> For sky, nothing but sky.

It's the opening lines of the poem 'The Lofty Sky' by Edward Thomas. The last three lines were hidden from us by a drystone wall but I'm assuming they were there, emblazoned on the corrugated steel barn in pale yellow paint.

Born in England to Welsh parents, Thomas spent many holidays in Wales and was himself a keen walker. A prolific book reviewer and novelist, he wrote 140 poems between 1914 and 1917, when he was killed prematurely at the Battle of Arras.

I was surprised to learn that Thomas was a good friend and mentor to Newport poet W. H. Davies, who also wrote about the countryside and nature. In fact, Thomas's untimely death prompted the grief-stricken Davies to write 'Killed in Action (Edward Thomas)'.

The day was turning into another scorcher, and as we bade farewell to the Black Mountains and headed towards Pandy, we started fantasising about ice lollies and ice creams (we never learn). Shockingly, we hadn't treated ourselves to either since Penmon on Anglesey – let's face it, with the exception of Barmouth, the opportunities for indulging have been rather thin on the ground. Once the idea had taken root, however, we were desperate for something cold. Harri thought there might be some kind of shop in Pandy so we hung onto that thought until we got there and saw our hopes dashed yet again. How anyone in rural Wales gets enough nourishment is beyond me; nothing is ever open!

It was barely noon and already I could feel my energy levels waning. With the Black Mountains behind us and the terrain promising to be a little easier than of late, we had planned to cover lots of miles today, but we hadn't counted on how much hotter it would be away from the mountains. As we crossed the busy A465 just north of Abergavenny, I wondered if we would have the stamina to reach Monmouth today.

We meandered through field after field, surprised by how flat everything looked. The landscape reflected my mood. After struggling up mountains for two weeks, I hadn't expected to miss them. Penultimate day syndrome had struck – as it always does on a holiday. You've finally left the stress of work/family/home behind and are beginning to enjoy your new surroundings when suddenly it's all over. The last day is too busy to reflect on the big questions; however, the last but one day … that's when the philosophising is done and you find yourself wondering if there's another way of getting through your designated time on this planet. Some way to perhaps avoid going back to the humdrum of daily life …

There's only one thing to do at such times and that's to head for the pub – the place that all the best philosophising gets done. Fortunately, we were just approaching Llangattock Lingoed, another sleepy little village with no one around, despite the fact Offa's Dyke Path passes through it. As recently as the early twentieth century, the Hunters Moon Inn operated its own cider mill. Sadly, that side of the business has disappeared, but we had no complaints about the Addlestones cider on offer … and stayed for a second.

We'd already decided to stop for lunch at White Castle, a place that will forever hold a place in my nightmares after the 2013 Rack Raid. On an airless morning in early June, I took part in a 14-stage, 100-mile relay race from Grosmont to the Castell-y-Bwch pub in Henllys (coincidentally, Harri's parents local). My leg saw me running from Skenfrith to White Castle, just under seven miles of almost constant climbing two short days after I'd walked fifteen miles in the area with Harri. On Friday, we had tackled what locals respectfully refer to as 'heart attack hill', and though my heart had survived, my legs were now reminding me very forcibly of what I'd put them through. I hobbled along country lanes far behind everyone else with only the St John ambulance for company; it was, without doubt, the most humiliating experience of my running 'career'.

White Castle is one of the three castles – the others are Grosmont and Skenfrith – which formed a strategic triangle to control the area. The original castles were built of timber and earth. In the late twelfth century, all three became royal castles and in 1201 were granted to Hubert de Burgh by King John. De Burgh rebuilt Grosmont and Skenfrith in the new defensive style but not White.

The three Norman castles provide the focal points of a popular waymarked walk – the 20-mile Three Castles Walk – which we walked several years ago. I remember my line manager at the time telling me she'd completed the whole route in five hours, something we struggled to believe even before we had walked the undulating route for ourselves.

Harri devised a two-loop seven-mile walk from White Castle for *Castle Walks in Monmouthshire* and when we were checking the route, I asked the Cadw employee at the gate if she would mind if I stepped inside the barrier to take a photograph of the castle. She refused point blank and in such a haughty manner you'd have thought she was a member of modern-day royalty who lived there herself.

We were a little taken aback by her downright refusal to help us promote *her* castle but didn't give the matter another thought until Harri was rereading *Mr Vogel* by Lloyd Jones a few months later. The Welsh author based his first novel on his own experience of walking around Wales. He arrives at White Castle before its fierce 'guard' has arrived for work so he vaults over the surrounding fence to take a quick look around (page 85). Alas, he lingers too long and as he's retrieving his rucksack from behind a portable toilet, she spies him.

At first Jones denies having entered the castle. When the woman doesn't believe him, he pretends he's a member of the fictional Collwyn ap Tango [sic] Re-enactment Society. The woman appears impressed, but still won't let the matter of payment drop. It's only when he hints at his 'real' reason for going into the woods that she finally relents.

'I liked her,' he concludes. '... she was guarding her castle to the best of her ability, as all those poor dead sods did six hundred years ago.'

Presuming it was the same woman, we didn't like her one little bit and so we were quite relieved to see her little hut was closed today.

If you like your castles, White Castle is not one to miss. Interestingly, in its early days it was known as Llantilio Castle. I had always wondered about this; castles are generally named after their location and 'white' didn't ring any bells. In the case of White Castle, it apparently got its long-time name from the white rendering to its exterior walls (still visible).

White was probably built for military rather than residential purposes, and it is remarkably well preserved. The outer bailey defences are there, as are the gatehouse, various towers, towering curtain wall and inner courtyard. There is still water in much of the deep moat and visitors cross over a modern wooden bridge to enter the castle through the late thirteenth-century gatehouse.

We were aware from our previous visit that there's nowhere to picnic in the immediate vicinity of White Castle so had it in our minds that we'd start looking for somewhere once we'd passed it. What we hadn't anticipated was the wonderful generosity of the couple who live just off the footpath that runs alongside the castle grounds.

As we approached, these lovely people were providing glasses of cold squash to two men who were walking Offa's Dyke. When the woman noticed two more hikers heading her way she immediately offered us drinks too. When we mentioned we were planning to stop for lunch soon, her husband suggested we make use of their garden bench, water tap and toilet.

Which is how we came to find ourselves drinking tea and eating our lunch in a stranger's garden overlooking a great Norman castle. I'm not a particularly gushy person, but it's really heart-warming to come across such big-hearted people. Not only did they invite us into their garden, but also their home … and what a magnificent view from that downstairs throne.

As we chatted, the woman revealed they were hikers themselves and had just returned from a walking holiday. Back home, they were extending the same kindness to fellow hikers that they hope to receive themselves; which is exactly the way it should be.

For the rest of the afternoon we felt like characters in a soft-filter film titled 'A Perfect British Summer'. We wandered in dazzling sunshine through an undulating and impossibly pretty landscape full of hay bales, wheat and potato crops.

'Such lovely colours,' I exclaimed, realising belatedly that I sounded just like Bridget Jones after her accidental magic mushroom experience. I skipped excitedly through a field of towering pink grasses in much the way of a five-year-old, clearly addled by my two halves of Addlestones.

We had it in our heads that we would reach Chepstow tomorrow evening; however, that meant pushing on to Monmouth today. Having done so much coastal and mountain walking over recent weeks, we'd assumed walking in undulating countryside would be a doddle. We'd forgotten how much the heat saps one's energy, making climbing up even the smallest hill a tough slog. By late afternoon, we were lagging far behind our self-imposed schedule, and finding excuses to stop every few minutes: needing to remove a stone from my shoe, checking the map, needing a drink, etc.

Maybe it was our subconscious at work, slowing us down because deep down we didn't want our journey through Wales, this experience of a lifetime, to end. Back in Llandovery, I'd been overcome by exhaustion and homesickness; however, I'd mustered up the mental strength to carry on and now I just wanted to keep going, for the rest of the summer at least, maybe for the rest of my life.

Rather than feel euphoric that we were going to achieve what we set out to do, i.e. backpack the length of Wales, I found myself constantly glancing over my shoulder to look back at the rapidly-diminishing outline of the Black Mountains. True, I'd missed my family, my girls, but right then if Harri had wanted to turn round and head back to Holyhead I'd have been hot on his heels.

Our slow progress through Monmouthshire's countryside wasn't only down to hot weather and low spirits. My feet – blister-free for the toughest, wettest parts of our hike – had decided enough was enough with the result that I was sporting a painful blister on the little toe of my right foot. After my disastrous five-day hike in May when I'd amassed five on two toes, I'd planned ahead this time around and packed my seven-year-old Brasher sandals to take the pressure off the blistered toes. Unfortunately, after two days of walking in seven-year-old old sandals, the soles of my feet were now aching horribly. As the hours rolled by, my walk became more and more of a hobble, while Harri grew concerned that we wouldn't cover the miles necessary to reach Monmouth before darkness.

The country lanes, though undulating, were so blissfully peaceful in the evening sunshine that we nearly jumped out of our skins when a gunshot went off within close by; in fact, far too close for comfort. We looked around nervously and that was when we saw him: a gentleman of advancing years wearing a silk smoking jacket was just lowering his rifle in a sprawling walled garden. We presumed this 'nature lover' was trying to kill the birds and/or squirrels who dared to venture into his extensive landscaped grounds. Casting us a glance of contempt, he stormed back into his equally large house.

The last three miles took us through King's Wood, a pretty wooded area close to Monmouth which is crisscrossed with footpaths and bridleways. Normally I'd have loved this kind of trail walking, but by now it was so painful to put my feet down on the stony, uneven path that I barely noticed my lovely surroundings. Instead, I sought out the much softer grass verges and probably added another half mile to my route!

I limped into Monmouth behind Harri. There was a certain synchronicity to arriving in this border town on the penultimate day of our walk through Wales. The Rack Raid had taken place the day before we started to walk 'O Fôn i Fynwy', and this year my eight-mile stage had seen me running across the Monnow Bridge and into Monmouth town centre. Three weeks later, I was walking across the same bridge, although on this occasion there was no cheering from my fellow Lliswerry Runners and it wasn't ice cream I craved but my bed.

Whichever way you look at it, it's a long walk from Llanthony to Monmouth. The former is in the Black Mountains, the latter on the

Wales-England border. We have really pushed ourselves these past few days, clocking up miles while the sun shone, walking from breakfast to bedtime with very few breaks. My blistered toe and current weariness aside, I was bronzed, fit, and half a stone lighter than I'd been at the outset.

But with just one day to go, the glorious weather we were starting to take for granted was threatening to break down. A huge black thunder cloud loomed overhead as we walked down Monmouth's main street, keeping our eyes peeled for accommodation signs. We trailed past the Robin Hood pub and the town's many independent shops. It was barely 8.30 p.m. and yet Monmouth's main street was completely deserted. No traffic, no people.

Monmouth's most famous son is undoubtedly Charles Rolls, co-founder of Rolls-Royce in 1884. Rolls is infamous for being the first Briton to be killed in an air accident involving a powered aircraft (his was the eleventh such death in the world). The death of the 32-year-old on 12 July 1910 was reported in a Tennessee newspaper. Under the headline 'Daring Aviator Dashed to Death', the report provided the following account of the incident:

> The first flying tournament of the year in England was brought to a tragic close this morning by the dramatic death of the most daring and popular British aviator, the Hon. Charles S. Rolls, third son of Lord Llangattock. In the presence of a great company of spectators, a majority of whom were ladies and children and many personal friends of the young aviator, The Wright bi-plane, on which he was flying, fell suddenly with terrific speed from a height of 100 feet. It struck the ground close to the crowded grandstand, smashed into a tangled mass and before the doctors could reach the spot, Rolls was dead.

A bronze memorial statue of Charles Rolls stands in front of Monmouth's Shire Hall in Agincourt Square. Once, when I was trying to frame it against the background of an unusually cloudless sky, a local mistook me for a tourist and offered to take a photograph of Charles and me together. I declined, obviously.

We had hoped we wouldn't need to walk as far as Agincourt Square this evening, but our hunt for accommodation wasn't going well. I recounted our regrettable experience at the Coach House Inn on TripAdvisor so I won't go into details here; suffice to say, it's very unusual to encounter such outright rudeness in the hospitality sector these days.

Having wasted a good fifteen minutes waiting, only to learn there were no rooms available, we had little alternative but to hobble to the far end of town. Fortunately, our faith in humanity was quickly restored by a very pleasant young bartender in the King's Head, a seventeenth-century coaching inn now run by Wetherspoons. None of their 24 rooms were available but he helpfully directed us to the nearby Queen's Head, where unfortunately Neil too was fully booked. I don't know if it was the exhaustion/pain written all over my face, but this genial innkeeper took one look at us and told us not to move, that he would find us a bed for the night come what may.

We settled ourselves at the bar and ordered a much-needed half of cider. One of Neil's staff was sitting alongside us at the bar and we got into conversation with her while he disappeared to make some phone calls. She recognised me immediately from one of my public sector jobs; it also turned out she was related to a Henllys family that knew Harri's parents well. It's a small world indeed.

After a while, a smiling Neil reappeared from behind the bar. True to his word, and despite it being well after 9 p.m., he had found us a double bed for the night. All we had to do was hobble a few hundred metres down the road and present ourselves to Penny at Ebberley House.

Now the challenge was to get moving again.

For photographs visit <u>uk.pinterest.com/thewalkerswife</u>

JUNE 24: MONMOUTH TO CHEPSTOW

The homeward leg. Chepstow nestles on the bank of the River Wye seventeen miles downriver from Monmouth – not that we were planning on rowing. No, we'd be walking every inch of the way as per norm. Barring a catastrophe, by early evening our long journey would be at an end; after nearly 23 days, we would at last be hanging up our boots.

Over breakfast, Harri asked me if the experience had made Wales seem larger or smaller in my eyes. I pondered his question, uncertain how to respond. True, it would be impossible to walk the length of most countries in just over three weeks, which – I guess – confirmed that Wales was a rather diminutive place. On the other hand, experiencing the diversity of this country's landscapes, from the wonderful Anglesey coastline to the high summits of Snowdonia, the 'green desert' of mid Wales and the bustling summits of Pen y Fan and Corn Du, had helped 'fix' the geography of my native country firmly in my mind, with the result that Wales now presented itself as a vast and infinitely diverse country.

So, after considering Harri's question at length, I told him it was irrelevant. The thrill of this end to end walk was seeing Wales laid at my feet like the Mappa Mundi. Day after day we had explored every contour of the ever-changing landscape. Big or small, Wales's size did not matter; its beauty had captivated me.

We were ravenous this morning. Penny had graciously received two hobbling hikers well after nine o'clock last night, by which time we were far more interested in our beds than our bellies. After desperately needed showers, we propped ourselves up against the pillows and munched, for the umpteenth time in the past three weeks, bread and cheese.

There was an alarming nip in the air this morning. Over the past two weeks, we'd become accustomed to walking in warm, sunny weather, and the prospect of anything other than perfect summer weather to finish our long journey was a little disheartening.

Walking from Land's End to John O'Groats (or vice versa) must be on every long-distance hiker's bucket list; however, at anything from 874 miles for the road version to 1,200 miles for a more scenic route, it takes time. Far longer than the average two weeks' average leave, probably the reason so many people choose to cycle the distance rather than walk it.

One such man was now sitting at an adjacent table in the high-ceiled dining room of Ebberley House. From Bristol and looking to be in his late 50s/early 60s, he had first cycled down to Land's End before heading back north. The most difficult thing so far, he told us, was setting off from home then passing very close to it a few days later. Having reached Cwmdu only to veer east towards Monmouth, we could certainly empathize with this sentiment.

The man's son, a slightly rotund young fellow, had originally planned to accompany him, but an injury had scuppered his plans and he would now be providing the vehicular back-up instead. Secretly, neither of us thought the younger man looked up to cycling great distances each day, but we said nothing. We certainly didn't envy him sitting behind a car wheel all day.

Neither of us was much looking forward to returning to wheels as our usual form of travel – as we had discovered, you experience and see so much more when you travel at a walking pace.

After the briefest of food shops in Iceland, we headed across the River Wye and out of town. It was only a matter of minutes before we hit the first climb of the day up to the Kymin. This morning, Monmouth-born Penny had ended years of uncertainty over its pronunciation by confirming it is called the 'Kim-in'. Not Kigh-min or Come-in (and I've heard it referred to as both) but like the girl's name, Kim-in. Thank you for sorting that one out, Penny.

Much of the steep climb to the Kymin is through woodland so the distant views were limited. We weren't too bothered because the sunshine was filtering through the trees and making our surroundings quite enchanting. We were killing two birds with one stone as we passed huge mossy boulders; not only were we walking Offa's Dyke Trail but we'd also joined the 55-mile Wysis Way which links it to the Thames Path, a National Trail which passes through the heart of

London. The name Wysis originates from the Wye River where the route begins and the Isis River, the name given to the upper part of the River Thames above Iffley Lock on the outskirts of Oxford.

The Kymin has been a local picnic spot for over two hundred years and its name is likely to originate from the Welsh *cymin* or *comin*, meaning a common. The eighteenth-century Round House and Naval Temple that make the climb worthwhile were built in 1794 and 1800 respectively. The latter was built by public subscription to commemorate the second anniversary of the British naval victory at the Battle of the Nile in 1798, and as a contemporaneous plaque declares: 'to perpetuate the names of those noble admirals who distinguished themselves by their glorious victories for England in the last and present wars'.

England? The historic county of Monmouthshire – and by extension Monmouth – is located close to the England–Wales boundary, leading to centuries of debate about whether the county was in fact part of England or Wales. You'd have thought the issue would have finally been resolved by the Local Government Act 1972 which clearly stated that any reference to Wales (subject to any alterations of boundaries) included 'the administrative county of Monmouthshire' (and the nearby county borough of Newport), but oh no. Sadly, there are still those citizens who still insist Monmouthshire is in England – the English Democrats fielded a candidate Stephen Morris in the 2015 general election (he garnered 100 votes in total) – and so the whole unhappy saga about Monmouthshire's nationality is likely to rumble on *ad infinitum*.

The quaintly named Monmouth Picnic Club built the Round House as a banqueting venue for its members – presumably the late-eighteenth century idea of picnicking was more genteel and involved less grass than today's version.

In *Hando' Gwent*: Volume II (edited by Chris Barber), the author describes how in the nineteenth century 'the summit had been developed into a showground, with bowling green, stalls, swings and donkey rides. Transport from the railway station to the summit cot 6d. by donkey and 1s. by pony'.

The Kymin has undoubtedly come down in the world since its halcyon days. An information board reveals how Lord Nelson breakfasted at this spot with Sir William and Lady Hamilton in August

1802, by omission hinting at a decorous social occasion. What the circumspect wording fails to mention is that by August 1802, Emma Hamilton and Nelson had been enjoying a passionate affair for the past four years and had an eighteen-month-old daughter, Horatia. Such was the public interest in the couple, the newspapers of the day carried regular reports on their infamous living arrangements (Nelson lived openly with the Hamiltons in what was undoubtedly a *ménage à trois*). Fast forward two centuries and the merest mention of their torrid relationship is a no-go ... on the Kymin's information board, at least.

While the picnic tradition continues, it's no longer the upper classes munching crust-free cucumber sandwiches on the lawn but local children with their teddy bears.

No matter what its *raison d'être*, the Round House with its whitewashed walls presents an appealing sight perched on its hilltop above Monmouth. We strolled over to the railed viewpoint to soak up the incredible landscape. It's been claimed that on the clearest of days you can see nine counties from the roof of the Round House: four Welsh and five English. The day was certainly clear, but as the National Trust keeps the Kymin locked we weren't able to verify the claim. It didn't matter: we were perfectly content to gaze towards the Black Mountains and marvel that only yesterday we'd been setting off from Llanthony. Twenty-four hours later, those same mountains looked an awfully long way off.

Of course, eighteenth-century tourists couldn't be trusted to look and admire the Wye Valley in a *proper* manner, so William Gilpin, originator of the idea of the picturesque, took it upon himself to educate the people on exactly how they should do so. Gilpin believed nature was rarely capable of perfection. His attempt to evaluate every landscape – and propose improvements – is encapsulated in *Observations on the River Wye*, published in 1782.

Preposterous as it now seems, visitors were instructed how to appreciate the views from the Kymin in the correct 'picturesque' way: 'the most perfect river-views are composed of four grand parts: the river itself, two side-screens, which are the opposite banks and lead the perspective; and the front screens. The other ornaments of the Wye ... are ground, wood, rocks, buildings ... and colour.'

In local running club circles, the Kymin is known not for its panoramic views, rather for the popular – and extremely challenging –

Kymin Dash. This seven-mile cross country race takes place at the end of April. My older daughters took part this year and loved it; but with just 50 metres of flat running before ascending *that* hill, I think I'll give this one a miss.

Anyone walking between Monmouth and Redbrook farther downriver has the choice of following either Offa's Dyke Path or the Wye Valley Walk. Harri decided to stick to Offa's Dyke Path, largely because it's the more interesting of the two (the Wye Valley Path hugs the river all the way to Redbrook). Neither did he want people to miss out on those incredible views from the Kymin.

Both paths veer into England at Redbrook, with Offa's Dyke Path continuing along the English side of the River Wye. We chose to cross the river and re-enter Wales on the Wye Valley Walk at Penallt, where the fabulous Boat Inn was just about to open its doors for the day. If only our journey had been scattered with inns like the Boat … though, on second thoughts, if it had, we'd still be on Anglesey!

The pub sits on the Welsh side of the River Wye but attracts its locals from the English side (where the houses are). Fortunately, a footbridge links the two banks or otherwise the Boat Inn might be one of the most dangerous places to drink in Wales … for the English!

This is a pub that takes its cider seriously, though with it being barely noon and we still having a fair few miles south to wander, we felt it best to steer clear of our favourite Old Rosie. Allowing our heads to rule our thirst, we ordered halves of the (slightly less alcoholic) Boat Special before settling ourselves at a riverside picnic table. Basking in warm sunshine, we watched strings of canoeists paddling past and chatted amiably to two retired couples at a neighbouring table who were touring Wales by car and expressed their amazement that we'd walked from Holyhead in little more than three weeks. All the while, observing this serene and pleasant scene from his vantage point on a beer barrel was the Boat Inn's resident terrier. Despite our celebratory mood, after half an hour or so, we demonstrated remarkable willpower and reluctantly heaved the rucksacks onto our shoulders. Wales needs more pubs like the Boat Inn. Hell, the world needs more pubs like the Boat Inn.

We were now deep into tourist country. The Wye Valley has been a popular destination since the eighteenth century and remains so today. Unhappily, many of the exalted views have all but disappeared as a result of overzealous tree planting. Like W. H. Davies, I like to stand and stare, but for miles the only thing to stare at was trees. Better than goats perhaps, but it can become a little tedious. Harri's argument is that the older a forest becomes and the taller its trees, the more pleasant it becomes. Perhaps we should return in thirty years' time when we'll be able to see out!

The sun was now high in the sky so it was fortunate that the terrain had at last levelled off; we enjoyed a long level stretch for several miles before eventually starting to climb again. Level trails through woodland may not be great in terms of scenery, but they can be life-saving when you have large distances to cover in hot weather.

Nothing good lasts forever, however, and at Whitebrook our route began to head uphill again. It's hard to imagine that this sleepy little hamlet used to be a thriving centre of industry a few centuries ago. In those days, much of the energy needed was produced by water mills, and some of those mill buildings remain, several converted into rather nice houses.

My fitness levels had improved dramatically over the course of the past three weeks, yet still my heart sank each time I spotted a footpath sign pointing towards a stile and the field beyond. You could bet your bottom dollar that within minutes we would be scaling first the stile and then a steep, or muddy – often both – field. Today was no exception. We had no sooner left the nice hard surface of the lane than we were clambering steeply through woods on a narrow path to the hamlet of Pen-y-fan (not to be confused with the mountain).

The lane at the top was dotted with impossibly pretty detached houses and cottages in little clearings in the woods. Near the idyllically-located Sarah's Place (which since our hike has sadly closed) a small barefoot girl emerged with her mother.

Our cider-induced euphoria fast diminishing, we decided to stop for lunch earlier than usual. Though referring to our nibbles as lunch is perhaps an exaggeration. Over the past three weeks, the concept of meal 'times' has been lost; now we eat only when our hunger pangs can't be ignored any longer. Our food input has reduced dramatically; yet those small meals of bread, cheese and crisps, supplemented with cooked breakfasts and the occasional evening meal, have provided us with sufficient energy to cover decent distances every day. It just proves that when food is plentiful we all tend to eat far more than our bodies need.

We wandered into the curiously named Bargain Wood and followed a gloriously undulating trail through dappled woodland strewn with moss-covered boulders and fallen branches. Before long, Tintern and its great Cistercian abbey was just a whisker's breadth away.

Tintern Old Station is a very popular tourist attraction, particularly with families. Located on the now defunct (and mainly dismantled) Wye Valley Railway track, the station opened in 1876 and closed for passengers in 1959 (though it was still used for freight trains). Five years later, the line was closed completely.

Fortunately, Tintern Station was not snapped up by a property developer keen to transform it into an unusual home, but was bought by the forward-thinking local county council for £1,500. It's now a very pleasant spot to while away a sunny afternoon without spending a lot of money.

We really liked the Circle of Legends wood carvings by Neil Gow and John Hobbs. King Offa, Sabrina and King Arthur need no introduction, but lesser known is King Tewdrig, a sixth-century king of Gwent who relinquished his kingdom to his son Meurig so he could live as a hermit at Tintern. Hermitage may have suited Tewdrig, but when the Saxons attacked, he was persuaded out of retirement by Meurig and was mortally wounded in battle. According to legend, Tewdrig died at Mathern en route to Flat Holm, on the very spot where a fountain sprang up to refresh him. There are also carvings of Eleanor of Provence and Geoffrey of Monmouth.

We had a few minutes of fun taking daft photographs of us standing next to the huge figures and then it was time to get going again.

Tintern is another of those strung-out villages like Capel Curig, with its houses, shops and pubs lined up along the busy A466 and barely any other streets. Its curious elongated shape could be due to the fact that Tintern was historically two villages: Tintern Parva (where we once stayed at the very comfortable Parva Farmhouse Riverside Guesthouse and worried all night that our car would be swept away by the unusually high tide) and Chapel Hill at the southern end near the abbey.

The peaceful wooded valley of today seems an unlikely place for industry to take hold, and yet industrialisation arrived here long before it did in the Welsh mining valleys, attracted by the tidal River Wye and its tributary, the fast-flowing Angiddy stream. At that time, Chepstow was the biggest port in Wales, and its proximity made Tintern a very attractive location for any industry which needed to bring raw materials in and ship finished products out. The area's ready supply of wood and charcoal was another bonus.

In his book, *Wales: 100 Places To See Before You Die*, the late historian John Davies tells how the Company of Mineral and Battery Works established wireworks in the Angiddy Valley in 1566. Back then, high-quality wire was a sought-after commodity used for knitting needles, fishing hooks, bird cages, buckles and guns. Wire even had a crucial role in ladies' clothing; it was used in farthingales, which held the skirts out, and stomachers, which held the bellies in!

Within 35 years, the Angiddy works employed more than 600 people, many trained by skilled German workers, making it the biggest industrial workplace in Wales by some margin. A special type of iron called osmond iron was needed to manufacture wire, so Abbey Tintern Furnace was built to supply cast iron to a nearby forge, where it was transformed into osmond iron, a process which involved heating and heavy hammering.

Things chugged along nicely for the next few hundred years until steam power arrived on the scene and the wireworks was replaced by a tinplate manufacturer. In 1895, this too was dealt the death knell, with a local newspaper reporting that 'Tintern Tin Works, which have been going irregularly for some time past, closed up last Sunday with no hope of an immediate restart.'

Fortunately, manufacturing's loss was tourism's gain. The Victorians had embraced the Wye Tour, and with a railway in place there was nothing to stop them arriving en masse to admire the natural beauty and Tintern's *pièce de résistance*, its Cistercian abbey.

While the abbey towers above the River Wye and the ruins of Abbey Tintern Furnace have been excavated and restored, little remains of the former wireworks, and only the one waterwheel survives at the point where the Angiddy stream joins the River Wye. The restored Abbey Mill is now a bustling visitor centre where coachloads of visitors come to eat, drink, shop and gaze at the old waterwheel as it is turned by the gurgling Angiddy stream.

Of course, Tintern was settled long before people arrived to work at the wireworks. The abbey was founded by the Cistercian Order in 1131 and extensively rebuilt in the following century. When Henry VIII dissolved the monastic orders in England and Wales in 1536 it was abandoned and much of the stonework removed. Five hundred years later the roofless, window-less abbey presents an impressive sight, especially at sunset.

With sufficient miles under our belts to secure an early evening arrival in Chepstow, we decided to risk another Old Rosie at the Abbey Hotel. My memories of this place stretch back to when I was an 18-year-old trainee tax consultant for Mann Judd, later taken over by Touche Ross and some years later absorbed by Deloitte UK. It's hard to imagine the present-day me ever working for an international financial firm. Fortunately, I realised pretty early on that a life spent helping wealthy dowagers to minimise their tax liabilities wasn't for me. I lasted just three months in that mirthless, conservative environment. Now we're living in an era where young people need degrees and masters to do the lowliest jobs, it's incredible to think that I was taken on with my A level results pending and that no one kicked me out when I scraped through just one – in English.

Back in 1979, Mann Judd was one of those forward-thinking companies that believed people worked better if they were occasionally whisked away from the office for a bout of team-building. Thus, a dozen grey-suited men, a handful of secretaries, and an 18-year-old trainee tax consultant were bussed across the Severn Bridge to tour the Harvey Bristol Cream Sherry distillery and sample its wares. As I recall, this incongruous excursion concluded with dancing (and more drinking) at the Abbey Hotel in Tintern.

So Tintern and I go back a long way, though maybe not quite as far as the late eighteenth century when Wordsworth penned his famous poem 'Lines Composed a Few Miles above Tintern Abbey; On Revisiting the Banks of the Wye During a Tour, July 13, 1798'.

Wordsworth was returning to the Wye Valley after an absence of five years, hence the 'revisiting' in the poem's title. Unsurprisingly, the poet conjures up the magical landscape much better than I ever could, writing of the 'steep and lofty cliffs' , 'the deep and gloomy wood' and 'wild secluded scene' and proclaiming himself 'a lover of the meadows and the woods'. It's a long poem, but Wordsworth seems to be saying that he garners strength from nature and, at times when he cannot experience it at first hand, his memories of nature's beauty sustain him.

Despite its title, Wordsworth's poem doesn't actually mention the long-abandoned Tintern Abbey, which was surprisingly quiet on this Tuesday afternoon.

The party mood mounting and with just seven miles walking left, we lazed around in the Abbey Hotel's pretty – and unusually deserted – beer garden in glorious sunshine. Harri headed back to the bar for a second drink and I'd probably have indulged in another myself had I not spotted a sign for homemade fudge. Old Rosie or homemade fudge? A tough call indeed. On this occasion, the fudge won; it was my first since Beddgelert. In the shop, I couldn't make my mind up between the delicious-sounding maple and walnut and the equally delicious-sounding chocolate and honeycomb. Throwing caution to the wind – and mindful that my grand entrance into Chepstow would be marred should my by-now-very-loose shorts actually slide to my knees – I plumped for both.

Whether it was the Old Rosie and fudge, or just a subconscious desire to draw out the last few hours of our walk for as long as possible, we were in no rush to leave our enchanted surroundings. It was well after 5 p.m. when we finally dragged ourselves from the beer garden. By any reckoning, seven miles is no distance at all, but when it's early evening, still extremely warm and you've been idle for more than an hour, believe me it's pretty hard to get going again.

We'd sent texts to close family members with our estimated time of arrival; however, it seemed unlikely our welcome committee would comprise anyone other than Harri's long-time friend, the poet and raconteur Goff Morgan (with or without their other mate, author and historian Paul Busby). Goff is a larger-than-life character who became Newport's first – and only – town poet in 1997 (when the city was still a town). If you're looking for a lively host for any event, Goff's definitely your man (here he is performing at Caerleon Arts Festival).

For whatever reason, the last few miles to Chepstow felt endless. After leaving Tintern there was a steep climb of the kind you'd rather avoid towards the end of the day. We passed a sign to the local lime kilns, which once burned limestone to temperatures of over 1,000 degrees centigrade and produced lime for agricultural and industrial purposes.

Upwards and onwards we trudged, feeling wearier of mind and body with every passing minute. It didn't help that we were soon back in mature woodlands, and though the immediate vicinity of light-dappled leaves was very pretty, the views were limited to trees, trees and more trees.

Harri has always enjoyed talking about time travel. If it ever became possible, he asks me frequently, what era would I like to visit? It's not a question I've ever felt the need to dwell upon, but as I wandered through the leafy woodlands high above the River Wye I did think I might like to visit the valley in Wordsworth's time, back in 1798. Then, the trees would not have dominated the landscape, and the vistas from up here would have reached down to the River Severn and beyond to England.

We clambered up a particularly steep section in Black Cliff Wood and eventually emerged in a meadow where, confronted with the painfully engorged udders of an entire dairy herd, our spirits plummeted still further.

After what felt like monumental effort, we reached the highest point on the Wye Valley Walk, a spectacular viewpoint known as Eagle's Nest where you can gaze down at the Wye as it curves around Lancaut Peninsula. High above on the plateau and mostly hidden by trees is an Iron Age fort called Spital Meend, parts of which experts believe were incorporated into Offa's Dyke.

In *Excursion Down the Wye* (1799), Charles Heath describes the scene from Eagle's Nest thus: 'Here let me pause, as the eye surveys this terrestrial paradise … the winding of the river … the farm on the peninsula, the waving woods … contrasted with the bare and ragged rocks, the town, the castle and the bridge of Chepstow … the splendid course of the Severn and the hills of Gloucester and Somerset.'

If the Heritage Lottery Fund hadn't stepped in five years ago, it's unlikely there would even be a viewpoint at Eagle's Nest because the entire structure was in danger of toppling over the cliff. Thankfully, disaster was averted, and a specialist rope access team were able to carry out essential repairs as they dangled from ropes. Sounds like my perfect job … not!

Offa's Dyke Path itself passes to the east of Lancaut, which seems a shame because what hiker wouldn't want to stop to explore a deserted medieval village?

Now in Gloucestershire, England, the tiny village remained under Welsh control until the middle of the tenth century (the 'Lan' in its name is a corruption of the Welsh *llan*). The ruined St James Church dates back to the twelfth century and has been linked to the Cistercian monks at Tintern Abbey. All that remains today is the roofless church and a working farm.

Lancaut's small congregation diminished until, in 1865, the church was abandoned, stripped of its roof and interior fittings, and deconsecrated. It is now owned by the Forest of Dean Buildings Preservation Trust, which purchased it from Poundland. Only joking! Though the Trust apparently did pay the same for Lancaut Church as I handed over for my last box of Maltesers.

What is really exciting is that in 2014 the trustees secured conservation funding for Lancaut Church, and they plan to promote 'an appreciation of the self-sufficient village community that once existed at Lancaut' and look at the religious history of this alluring place. (Harri has agreed to take me there sometime soon.)

Above Lancaut is Wintour's Leap, where the Royalist Sir John Wintour allegedly drove his horse off the cliff into the river below and survived to tell the tale. It's not true, of course; though Sir John escaped the Roundheads on two occasions, he did so by entering the river at a place far closer to sea level.

Eagle's Nest also marks the start (or finish) of Valentine Morris's Piercefield Walks, the section of the Wye Valley Path that would lead us into Chepstow.

The popularity of *Observations on the River Wye* (1782) saw travellers flocking to the Wye Valley to enjoy the two-day boat trip from Ross-on-Wye to Chepstow. While a rather less energetic way than ours of viewing the natural landscape and romantic ruins of Tintern Abbey and Chepstow Castle, the Wye Tour nonetheless pulled in the tourists. Gilpin himself wrote, 'if you have never navigated the Wye, you have seen nothing'.

The wealthy, it seemed, were queuing up to be part of 'picturesque tourism', and many disembarked at Wyndcliff to cover the three miles to Chepstow on foot.

Having praised the Wye Valley to the hilt, Gilpin was unable to suppress his schoolmaster tendency to criticise. The views of Piercefield Walks were not sufficiently picturesque, he declared, adding: 'They are either presented from too high a point, or ... they do not fall into such composition as would appear on canvas.' Lessening the blow slightly, he conceded, 'But they are extremely romantic, and give loose to the most pleasing riot of imagination.'

But that's enough of Gilpin. We owe the wonderful Piercefield Walks to Valentine Morris, son of Colonel Valentine Morris, who bought Piercefield House in 1736. Inspired by the natural beauty of his estate, Valentine Junior set about transforming some of its 300 acres into the wonderful woodland walks and viewpoints that remain today.

Fred Hando wrote, 'He cleared some eight viewpoints, laid down walks through the forest, along the clifftops, and sometimes down the cliffs.'

We didn't have much time to stand around and admire the views if we were to reach Chepstow before Goff, but as we hurried past the Grotto, the Giant's Cave and the Platform we gained a real sense of the huge undertaking involved to create so many charming views.

The historic tour journal entries reproduced on a notice inside the Grotto made us chuckle. In 1803, J. T. Barber described the views with Gilpin-esque glee: 'The distant Severn and its remote shores form an excellent termination, and complete the picture.'

An earlier visitor – Jon Byng in 1781 – was either overcome with romantic inclination or had stumbled upon a courting couple, for he noted: 'The quiet situation ... must inspire in youthful pairs every tender sensation.' Indeed, it would appear that the Grotto's peaceful setting was continuing to encourage bad behaviour 35 years later when Dr S. H. Spiker visited: 'We found the grotto full of gay ladies and gentlemen, and could not therefore examine its interior.'

Our route didn't take us directly past Piercefield House, but there is an alternative route into Chepstow if you are keen to view this roofless, windowless and presumably roomless ruin at close quarters (though if you continue that way it does mean missing out on the Grotto and other viewpoints).

As we emerged from Piercefield Park, the views towards the Severn Bridge and across the Bristol Channel suddenly opened up before us. We were instantly reminded of our five-day reconnaissance walk in May, when we attempted to walk from Chepstow to Minehead for another e-book *The England Coast Path: Chepstow to Minehead*. Fortunately, I'd avoided such painful blisters this time around, but as I got my first glimpse of 'home' I suddenly felt very weary.

There was no doubt we'd achieved what we set out to do. We'd walked from Anglesey to Monmouthshire in 23 days. We had hiked almost 400 miles over often tough and almost always undulating terrain in all weathers, each of us carrying the equivalent of a small child on our back. We'd pitched our tent on an ancient burial site high in the Carneddau, camped in style in Rhandirmwyn, and enjoyed a taste of luxury at our Dylife retreat. We had completed 'O Fôn i Fynwy' and were about to hang up our shoes on this perfect summer evening.

Tomorrow we would be waking up in our own bed and life would return to normal. Taking a month of work without pay was a big decision for Harri, something he couldn't do again anytime soon. While we might love the freedom of walking long distances day after day for weeks, like most people our reality involved a mortgage, bills and family commitments.

We were running late. Goff, who has never been on time in all the years we've known him, decided to break the habit of a lifetime and arrive in Chepstow ahead of schedule. We, of course, had assumed he'd be late, so when Harri got his text we were still meandering along the Piercefield Walks.

Feeling a little guilty now about the time we'd loitered in the beer garden, we stepped up our pace until we were practically marching past the leisure centre and towards Chepstow Castle.

Chepstow was the first Welsh place conquered by that most famous of conquerors, William. Having taken control of the town in the first year of his reign, William wasted no time in building an imposing stone fortress on high cliffs above the river. Work on Chepstow's Great Hall began in 1067, making it the oldest stone building still standing in Wales and one of the oldest Norman buildings in Britain.

Chepstow Castle may have been built on William's express order; the Great Tower – completed *c.* 1090 – is closely modelled on his birthplace, the Château de Falaise in Normandy.

The irony – if you can call it that – is that having successfully conquered England and built a whole lot of castles there, William shot off to the Continent again. It seems he didn't want England and the Welsh borders after all … he just didn't want anyone else to have them. Anyway, I don't intend to dwell on those barbaric times when anyone who fancied a shot at the throne – any country's throne – just waded in with murderous intent, but it's worth remembering it was the megalomaniac tendencies of rulers like William which 'earned' the more recent monarchs their reputed 'blue' blood.

As we limped into Chepstow, Harri grabbed my hand suddenly and said with urgency: 'Let's not stop, let's keep walking. Along the coast to Devon and Cornwall, let's keep going.'

Even now, I'm not sure if he was entirely serious, though I suspect that had I agreed, Goff would have spent his evening alone. As it was, our poet friend waited nearly an hour for us, and after taking the obligatory photographs on Chepstow town bridge – the start/finish of the Wales Coast Path (depending on which direction you're walking) – we set off to find him.

Endings often have a certain anti-climactic feeling and tonight was no different. Having focussed on nothing but completing our journey for weeks, our arrival in Chepstow felt disappointingly low-key. It wasn't Goff's fault – one person, however enthusiastic, doesn't really amount to a welcome committee – and our families were busy with their usual midweek commitments.

To be fair, Goff feigned as much enthusiasm for our venture as any non-walker could and listened patiently to endless tales of our travels. But we knew, deep down, that only two people truly understood how special our experience had been, how intimate our relationship with Wales had become, and how our long walk had changed us: Harri and me.

To plagiarise Fred Hando (*Hando's Gwent*, Vol II, ed. Chris Barber): 'The walker gets to know his countryside intimately because the villages – aye, the cottages – mark stages on his sensibly slow journey, but the motorist notes the beginning and end of his run and has but a sketchy idea of the places en route. Believe me, in an idyllic county like Gwent [or country like Wales], the journey is at least as fascinating as journey's end.'

And our journey on foot *was* fascinating, and the many different landscapes of Wales are idyllic (with the exception of the boggy bits). I daresay we'll walk through other countries, but none will be quite as memorable as our first walk through Wales.

We have been humbled by the beauty of our country. To quote a (translated) verse from the Welsh national anthem:

> Old mountainous Wales,
> Paradise of the bard,
> Every valley, every cliff,
> To my look is beautiful.
> Through patriotic feeling,
> So charming is the murmur
> Of her brooks, rivers, to me.

I couldn't have put it better myself.

For photographs visit <u>uk.pinterest.com/thewalkerswife</u>

SUBSEQUENT ROUTE CHANGES

When you're devising a new long-distance trail there are bound to be certain sections which, having walked and experienced firsthand, you decide against including in the final route.

After more than three weeks of hiking, we were mostly very happy with the route for 'O Fôn i Fynwy'. There were just a few sections in mid Wales (between Machynlleth and Pontrhydfendigaid) that we felt weren't really up to scratch and for various reasons.

First, there was the bleakness of Pumlumon in bad weather and/or poor visibility. Secondly, the unrelenting forestry in certain areas, which not only robbed walkers of distant views, but also made navigation difficult. But worst (in my opinion anyway) were the long stretches of walking across potentially very wet ground.

Deep down, we knew we needed to make some adjustments to the middle sections if we were to showcase the best of Wales and promote a long-distance route that's walkable in as many weather conditions as possible.

In early July, we returned to mid Wales with a proposed new route. The plan was to retrace the nicest bits of our June walk, e.g. climbing from Machynlleth via Glyndŵr's Way, while avoiding some of the sections which hadn't panned out so well, e.g. the Borth–Pontrhydfendigaid Linear Trail. We regretted losing the incredibly pretty scenery of this trail, but the appalling condition of the footpath alongside the River Mynach – when it had all but disappeared under water – absolutely ruled it out.

For ease of travelling from one place to another, we agreed Harri should walk alone this time round, covering eighteen miles each day. We were travelling from our south Wales home so it made more sense for him to walk the sections out of sequence, with the most southerly miles walked first (Ponterwyd to Pontrhydfendigaid) and the northerly ones (Machynlleth to Ponterwyd) tackled on the second day. Harri's guidebook suggests splitting these stretches into four days' walking but, as Harri demonstrated, with a good level of fitness (and fine weather), it's possible to cover all 36 miles in two days.

While Harri was yomping over the mid Wales landscape for the second time in a month, I would act as his chauffeur. I love hiking, but occasionally I've thought how nice it would be to hang up my boots and have a proper look around one of the little villages or towns we pass through. With two whole days to kill, it was time to seize my opportunity to be a proper tourist.

For photographs visit <u>uk.pinterest.com/thewalkerswife</u>

JULY 8: DEVIL'S BRIDGE AND HAFOD

For some reason, the drive to mid Wales on the A470 felt even longer than usual, and it was almost noon when I dropped Harri off at the George Borrow Hotel in Ponterwyd.

I am not the most confident of map readers. Harri is well aware of this – possibly because he's twice had to come looking for me when I've gone out walking alone locally. Today I had no choice in the matter. I had been entrusted with an old copy of OS Landranger 135: Aberystwyth & Surrounding Area and had committed to memory the route to my first stop of the day, Devil's Bridge.

We didn't pass through Devil's Bridge in June, but instead crossed the river Rheidol (the Mynach is a tributary) on a narrow footbridge farther up the gorge at Parson's Bridge. Now that the revised 'O Fôn i Fynwy' route was going to pass directly through what the Devil's Bridge Falls website describes as a 'world famous tourist attraction', we needed some photographs of those three bridges, stacked one on top of the other.

Harri prefers me to take charge of photography; I'd like to believe it's because he recognises my superior talent for getting that perfect shot, but I suspect it's more likely to be that he would prefer to walk uninterrupted.

Devil's Bridge was heaving when I arrived – hardly surprising on a warm July afternoon. People were milling around and spilling on to the road as they gazed down into the gorge and wandered to and from car parks (there are two – one next to the entrance to the falls and one in front of the public toilets – and surprisingly both are free).

I'd no sooner left the car park when I spotted the Great Western steam engine waiting at the end of the line. The popular narrow gauge Vale of Rheidol Railway opened in 1902 to transport lead ore, timber and passengers from Devil's Bridge to Aberystwyth, $11^3/_4$ miles away. Now popular with tourists, it clings to the hillside as it travels through woodland and rugged mountain scenery, stopping at Capel Bangor and Aberffwrd en route.

There were lots of people photographing the Great Western and others sitting outside the cafe waiting to board the train. I soon got talking to a couple from Hertfordshire who visit Wales regularly and were planning to climb Pumlumon the following day. I hope I didn't put them off when I said it was hard going! I did rave about the views, but my most recent memories of the endless clamber up that particular massif are still too fresh in my mind for too much positivity (or objectivity).

I was shocked to learn the entrance fee for the Nature Trail, Waterfalls and Three Bridges trail was £3.75 during the hours it was manned by an attendant (like now), though only £2 during winter and out of hours. The B side was just £1. I checked with the attendant that I could obtain my desired shot from the £1 side (belatedly noticing it was labelled Punchbowl and Three Bridges). She assured me I could indeed, so feeling smug about saving £2.75 so effortlessly, I headed for the unmanned turnstile which seemed to be posing great difficulty for a gentleman of advanced years.

The problem, it transpired, was one of co-ordination. In essence, anyone wishing to pass through the turnstile had to co-ordinate three actions. First, you had to balance your £1 in the correct slot (there were five slots in all, but four didn't appear to be working). Next, you had to slam the drawer shut without dislodging the £1 (quite a challenge). Finally, you had to push your body firmly against the turnstile gate. You needed to be doing the last two things simultaneously because the turnstile's timer was set at precisely five seconds. This poor Australian tourist had failed to co-ordinate his actions sufficiently fast meaning that his five seconds were up by the time he tried to push the turnstile!

He endured his £1 loss with magnanimity and produced a second coin. His wife (already on the other side) helpfully suggested I join her husband in the turnstile, presumably so he could push while I simultaneously operated the coin drawer. We quickly concluded, however, that trying to squeeze the two of us – and my daypack – into such a narrow space might result in mechanical breakdown and a close encounter of the most embarrassing kind.

The incident only reinforced my previously aired view that the storyline in the first episode of Welsh drama *Hinterland* bordered ever so slightly on the ridiculous. Were we really supposed to believe that the slim, female murderer had carried a body through the turnstile and down numerous steps to the bottom of the falls *at night?* My new Australian friend and I had just demonstrated how near-impossible it was to manoeuvre a *live* person through that metal contraption, let alone a body. I guess I should learn to suspend my disbelief when I'm watching television drama, but, on occasions like this, it's a big ask.

At last, we had all shuffled safely through the turnstile, man and wife were reunited, and I was able to make my way down the many steps to view the three bridges. What's unusual about Devil's Bridge is that when a new bridge was deemed necessary, it was simply built on top of the previous one. Thus, the modern bridge (itself over a hundred years old) was constructed above the stone bridge (1708), which was built on top of the original bridge (*c.* 1075–1200).

Legend claims that the original bridge was built by the Devil in return for the soul of the first living thing to cross the bridge. He was tricked by an old woman, who threw bread onto the bridge; her dog raced across in pursuit of the bread and so it came to pass that the Devil secured a canine soul instead of the anticipated human one. It would be a brave local who would refute the story – legends featuring the Devil tend to turn otherwise quite ordinary places into tourist honeypots (the exact same one is found in other parts of Britain and Europe).

After Devil's Bridge, it was off to photograph the Arch, which was helpfully marked on my OS map. The Arch isn't far from the Hafod estate and was built by its owner Thomas Johnes to commemorate the golden jubilee of George III in 1810, not long before the King became too ill to rule.

The crumbling stone arch now stands next to the B4574 road but until 2006 – when it was hit by a lorry and subsequently declared unsafe – vehicles still passed through it. In Harri's student days he would cycle here from Aberystwyth and he still recalls the thrill of whizzing along the single-lane road and straight under the Arch.

The Arch was my last stop before I joined Harri for lunch at Hafod, so, with a little time to kill, I decided to follow one of the waymarked routes from the car park. It wasn't long before my chosen path veered uphill and into woodlands; with no views to enjoy, a solitary walk seemed less appealing so I changed my mind and spent twenty minutes applying T-cut to the scratches on the rear wing of our car (as you do when you find yourself in a well-known beauty spot on a summer's day!).

I was busy polishing the car when Harri rang to confirm his anticipated arrival time at Hafod. He was going to get there earlier than expected, which was great. I'm so used to filling my hours with hiking, I was getting a little bored with normal tourist activities.

The final stretch of road to Hafod was narrow and a little hair-raising for this townie, but I arrived at Hafod's car park in one piece. By the time Harri materialised (a little later than the earlier time he thought), the weather had changed dramatically (this is mid Wales!), and we lingered over lunch *inside* the car as huge raindrops splashed onto the windscreen.

We'd explored very little of Hafod in June, but what we had seen had impressed us so much that Harri decided it was worth trying to incorporate more of the estate into 'O Fôn i Fynwy'.

Eventually it stopped raining, so we bought our £2 map (there's an honesty box in the free car park) and set off along the so-called Lady's Walk, one of two classic circular routes that Thomas Johnes created in his early years at Hafod. The woodland is really pretty here, with plenty of light weaving its way through to the valley floor.

We emerged from tall trees to follow a path alongside the stream, where we spotted the perfect dipping spot. It was idyllic, with a pebble beach and tempting, shallow waters. Had it been a little warmer, Harri would have been tempted despite the long walk ahead. And me? Water and air temperature must reach Mediterranean levels (at least) for me to be persuaded to dip even my toes in. This seldom happens in Wales, so I generally get to keep my feet dry.

Our curiosity piqued by the recently restored Mrs Johnes' Flower Garden, we stepped inside. It's not *yet* hugely impressive in terms of flora, but the walls and flowerbeds have been repaired and lots of plants have been added. It's just a question of time before everything is fully established and blooming. Trust me, this garden's going to look amazing in a few years.

The biggest disappointment was that Hafod's mansion is no longer standing. The original house Johnes built for himself, second wife Jane and daughter Mariamné in 1785 burnt down in 1807. Flames destroyed the library and much of the interior; priceless manuscripts on history, medicine, poetry and romance went up in flames.

'This fire is generally called the great fire of Hafod,' recounts George Borrow in *Wild Wales*. 'And some of those who witnessed it have been heard to say that its violence was so great that burning rafters mixed with flaming books were hurled high above the summits of the hills.'

Johnes rebuilt his mansion on the same spot, but the rebuilding project was costly and proved a constant drain on his resources. It was the second house – a 'truly fairy place' – which captivated Borrow in 1854. It looked, he wrote, 'beautiful but fantastic' and employed three styles of architecture, resulting in a Gothic tower at the southern end, an Indian pagoda at the northern, and a Grecian villa in the middle. By Borrow's own admission, this 'house of eccentric taste' filled him with admiration but also made him want to laugh.

By the 1940s the mansion had changed hands several times and was in a poor state of repair. Eventually it was bought by an asset-stripping company, and all fixtures and fittings were sold off; incredibly, the windows, stairs and even the floors were removed and exchanged hands for hard cash.

When the Forestry Commission took over in 1950, no one was interested in buying the shell of the mansion and the piecemeal demolition of the property began. What was left (presumably very little) was demolished with explosives in 1958, leaving only the stables still standing.

We wandered along the top of the sloping field, presumably once the magnificent sweeping lawn where Jane and the disabled Mariamné would have strolled while Thomas attended to business at Westminster. Photographs of Hafod before its decline reveal the grandeur of the isolated mansion house; regretfully, all that remains is a section of staircase and, nearby, a small pile of damaged masonry and sections of red brick.

All too soon, it was time for Harri and me to go our separate ways again. He was continuing along the river and walking to Pontrhyd-y-groes, while I headed back to the car to drive there. Rather than retrace my exact steps back to the car park, Harri suggested I followed another restored Hafod trail – the Gentleman's Walk – which, according to the leaflet, 'passed through wilder scenery and steeper ground than other walks at Hafod'.

Sounded interesting. The trail would be easy enough to navigate and my simple map numbered all the landmarks I'd be passing. I knew it was important I paid close attention to my whereabouts: not only was Harri relying on me to take photographs of those landmarks, but if I was ever to reach Pontrhyd-y-groes I had to first get back to our car.

'Just follow the map,' Harri assured me. 'Even you can't get lost here.'

I hate it when he says things like that. Because I can, and invariably do, get lost, frequently with or without a map and/or satellite navigation. And forgive me if I sound sexist, but I also do that female thing of turning my map upside down so that the route looks the same shape on the ground as it does on the map.

While I'd been waiting for Harri in the car park, I'd been completely baffled by the large graphic-style map on the interpretation board. Try as I could, I just couldn't work out how to get from the car park to a bridge we'd crossed in June (and would be heading for later). Of course, within a micro-second of glancing at the same map, Harri announced the designers had (inadvertently?) upturned it so that south faced north and vice versa. The £2 maps were laid out correctly, thank goodness, but you can see why people with no sense of direction – like me – frequently get lost in places like Hafod.

And of course, despite Harri's assurances, I did go off route ever so slightly, just the once or twice. I'd barely been walking alone for five minutes when the heavens opened and this time it wasn't light drizzle but the kind of torrential downpour where raindrops the size of golf balls bounce off the floor and your underwear and everything in your rucksack ends up soaked (this time round, anticipating decent weather, we hadn't bothered with June's elaborate regime of carefully bagging up every item carried).

I immediately panicked. Without my map I would be lost. Literally lost. So I did the only sensible thing and rammed it inside my waterproof and under my arm, figuring that if I walked with my arm tucked firmly against my side, my fragile little map might just survive the monsoon.

I was charging full pelt ahead along a high-level forestry track when I spotted Mrs Johnes' garden peninsula far below. My heart sank

– I'd gone too far. Soggy and morose, I reluctantly consulted my disintegrating map; there was nothing for it but to splash-backtrack until I reached the point where I'd gone wrong.

Back on track, I passed a landmark called 'Mossy Seat Falls' and the intriguingly named 'Tunnel', which turned out to be shorter and infinitely less exciting than its name suggested. I followed an always undulating and occasionally steep path through a moss-covered underworld that glowed green and surreal beneath dense woodland.

I had planned to go as far as 'Cavern Cascade' to take some photographs. It was marked as a significant detour from the main route, but, although I walked for a considerable distance in search of it, the terrifyingly steep drops into the gorge below eventually convinced me that this wasn't the safest terrain to be exploring on my own (with no mobile signal) and so I reluctantly turned back.

'Even you can't get lost here,' Harri had told me, but within minutes of leaving the woodlands, the footpath disappeared. It was there on my soggy map alright, but on the ground? Nowhere to be seen. This wasn't about being lost, it was about misrepresentation. The map showed a footpath right through the middle of this field, but there was no sign of a stile on the other side. How was I supposed to get out again?

It's at times like this that a little ingenuity is called upon. Spotting a locked metal gate, I clambered over it and quickly rejoined the original route. I soon passed the 'missing' stile; I hadn't been able to see it from the other side because it was completely obstructed by bushes.

At 'Dologau Bridge', I finally left the Gentleman's Walk (which was turning back on itself) and joined the Ystwyth Gorge Walk, which my leaflet described thus: 'This spectacular route takes the walker on a long, narrow loop up one side of the Ystwyth gorge and down the other.'

There's no denying the spectacular nature of the scenery here, though it's probably not the best terrain for vertigo sufferers; again there are extremely steep drops into the gorge. I thought at first the 'Gothic Arcade' pinpointed on the map referred to the massive irregular rock formations lining the chasm below, but it's actually the name for the man-made stone structure which stands on an earth terrace overlooking 'Chain Bridge'. Records suggest that the Gothic Arcade was originally a three-arched structure, and possibly a summerhouse, but all that remains is two 2.3-metre masonry 'piers' (one of which was entirely covered in plastic sheeting).

'Chain Bridge' bore a large sign suggesting that no more than two people should cross at any one time. Given the unnerving bouncing effect produced by this one, smallish person, I'd say that's pretty sound advice.

Ystwyth Gorge Walk eventually rejoined the Lady's Walk and the steep climb back to the car park. I breathed a sigh of relief. With a few little hiccups, I'd found my way around the convoluted walks of the picturesque.

Relaxing now I'd arrived back at my starting point in one piece, I decided to take a stroll around the graveyard of Hafod Church. Although a large notice stated the church was open (a metal grid erected to keep out birds gave the appearance that it wasn't), the main wooden door was most definitely locked (I've since found out it closes at 4.30 p.m.). Disappointed, I wandered around the graveyard looking out for interesting memorial stones. Headstone after headstone belonged to members of the Raw family who have lived at nearby Tyllwyd Farm since 1820 (and still do). This struck me as terribly poignant ... all those generations laid to rest side by side. Father and son. Grandmother and granddaughter. I didn't spot any headstones engraved with the name Johnes; they are, however, buried here somewhere.

The first church at Hafod was built in 1620 by Morgan Herbert, one of the early squires of the estate, but it wasn't elegant enough for the aesthetic tastes of Thomas Johnes, so in 1803 he commissioned James Wyatt to design a new church (Wyatt had previously restored Salisbury Cathedral and several extravagant Gothic houses).

Johnes got the outstanding Gothic church he desired complete with its sixteenth-century Flemish stained-glass window, but, sadly, a fire in April 1932 destroyed much of its interior, including furniture, fittings and paintings. A beautiful marble sculpture created in memory of his beloved Mariamné (she died in her twenties) was damaged beyond repair; however, the font, with its carved stone roses, the Johnes coat of arms, and figures representing the cardinal virtues, survived. The church was restored and fragments of the Flemish stained-glass window were salvaged and fitted into the chancel windows. Fire, it seemed, had blighted the life of Thomas Johnes and ultimately cost him his fortune.

When Harri and I caught up with each other at the Black Lion in Pontrhydfendigaid, I couldn't believe that he'd completely missed the downpour. His route had taken him away from the storm clouds, while mine had taken me straight into their path. I'd got a drenching, while he'd remained warm and dry.

Sometimes, life just isn't fair.

For photographs visit uk.pinterest.com/thewalkerswife

JULY 9: YNYS-LAS AND BORTH

There's something marvellously decadent about breakfasting in a dimly lit pub next to a vast stone fireplace. Breakfast in the Black Lion is something to get excited about – very excited.

Alyn is a trained chef and it shows; his peppered tomatoes are to die for. This morning our host was very apologetic about the (organic) scrambled eggs, insisting they weren't up to his usual standard. He clearly has lunar standards because, substandard or not, they tasted amazing. Having gobbled down a bowl of muesli, plus eggs, tomatoes and fried bread, I found a little extra space for several slices of buttered toast. Oh dear. In the just over two weeks since we returned from walking 'O Fôn i Fynwy', I'd been making up for all those missed meals. It had to stop. I made a mental note to skip elevenses.

The weather had done one of its typical British turnarounds since yesterday. Not that we were complaining: the sky was blue, the clouds white and unthreatening. The light breeze only added to the perfection of the day in hiking terms. Except that only one of us would be walking today. I found myself envying Harri his solitary eighteen-mile walk from Machynlleth to Ponterwyd but understood the only way he could research the proposed new route was if I dropped him off at Machynlleth and picked him up at the end of the day in Ponterwyd.

I'd miss the purposeful marching from A to B I had grown accustomed to; however, I had my own exciting plans. Today, I was taking a trip to the Ceredigion seaside.

I first discovered Ynys-las and neighbouring Borth on another chauffeuring occasion back in 2011 and had fallen in love with both places immediately. Borth is perhaps an acquired taste. Harri's father, who grew up in Aberystwyth a few miles down the coast, has less favourable views about this linear little town with its discordant houses and numerous timber groynes. Personally, I adore its quirkiness and, having got no farther than the single street that runs through the centre of town last time I was here, I was rather looking forward to trekking upwards and onwards to the exotically named Upper Borth.

But first on the agenda was Ynys-las, a twelve-mile drive from Machynlleth along the A487. This road used to be notorious for its slow-moving traffic, but one of the worst stretches near Glandyfi has now been widened and I sailed all the way to Ynys-las with no delays at all.

Ynys-las is not the place to be when the weather is bad. The wind comes off the Irish Sea and sweeps straight up the wide Dyfi estuary, whipping up random sand storms as it travels through. Once you're away from the sand dunes, there's very little shelter. And if you're thinking of heading towards those four-storey, pastel-coloured terraces in the distance, think again. Aberdyfi might be only a mile away as the crow flies, but the estuary is far too deep and fast-flowing to be safely crossed on foot.

The Dyfi estuary is considered to be a natural division between south and north Wales, and it was a crucial crossing point for centuries. Llywelyn the Great would have traversed the Dyfi when he was summoned to the Great Council of Aberdyfi in 1215.

Until a century ago, a ferry service connected Ynys-las and Aberdyfi. Always moored on the Aberdyfi side of the estuary, the ferry could be hailed to the other side by ringing a bell, which hung on a post on the rocky outcrop of Cerrig y Penrhyn on the Ynys-las side. Waiting passengers who became stranded by the incoming tide would clamber into a refuge tower erected on wooden piles to wait for their transport to arrive. It all sounds a little bit terrifying, if you ask me.

It's near impossible to imagine now, but there was a time when all manner of 'passengers' were bobbing to and fro between the two banks of the Dyfi on ferries: horses, cattle, carriages, people ... Such was the popularity of the route, that in the mid nineteenth century a railway bridge was also considered; it was eventually ruled out because of the difficulty of putting sound foundations down in the estuary.

Having ruled out a railway crossing, the railway company started operating a steam passenger service in 1861. The last of the vessels – the *Elizabeth* – was 121 feet long, but the six-foot draught of her hull meant she frequently went aground and the service was eventually abandoned for good.

Fast forward to 2015, and anyone in Ynys-las in Ceredigion wishing to travel to Aberdyfi in Gwynedd or vice versa now has no option but to embark upon a 23-mile road journey via Machynlleth in Powys.

It was just as well I had no intentions of visiting Aberdyfi today. On the contrary, my plan was to enjoy the Ynys-las National Nature Reserve for a while before heading down the Welsh coastline on foot to Borth.

When you first arrive at Ynys-las it can be slightly alarming to realise that you are expected to park at the top of the beach (or perhaps it's just me who prefers something a little more substantial under-wheel than shifting sands). YouTube is full of footage of parked cars disappearing under the waves while their owners – and crowds of onlookers – watch helplessly. I'm not aware of such a thing ever happening at Ynys-las, but you can never be too careful. In my book, cars and sand don't mix. I made certain I found a pebbly section as close to the sand dunes as possible and positioned my car so that I could drive straight off the beach – in a hurry if necessary.

There's a £1 parking charge which you're supposed to pay in the information centre (where the toilets are located); however, my arrival coincided with hundreds of school children who had formed a scrum around the cashier as they scrambled to blow their pocket money on pencils, rubbers and any brightly coloured bit of plastic they could lay their hands on. Impatient to get going, I decided I'd return just before 5 p.m. and explain the extenuating circumstances that had prevented me paying upfront.

It was time to go exploring. The nature reserve actually comprises three distinct areas: an internationally important peat bog, the Dyfi estuary, and the beach and sand dunes. No prizes for guessing where I was heading on this glorious, if ever-so-slightly breezy July morning.

Aberdyfi is one of the few places in Wales I've heard mentioned on my favourite soap, *Coronation Street*. Hairdresser Audrey once disappeared here for a weekend tryst with the suave but duplicitous love rat Lewis Archer (brilliantly portrayed by Nigel Havers). It's a popular and very pretty little seaside resort with house prices to match.

This is possibly the only seaside resort outside the Isles of Scilly where the fish and chip shop proprietor thinks it good business practice to close their doors at 8 p.m. prompt. Their punctiliousness means hordes of summer tourists who decide to postpone a bite to eat until *after* their evening stroll along the beach end up going hungry.

Not that I'm bitter about missing dinner on my 50th birthday. We'd been hiking the Cambrian Way most of the day and popped back to the rather posh Felin Crewi to freshen up before driving to the coast (jeepers, we must have had more energy in those days!). This being my half-centenary and all that, Harri decided to push the boat out and treat me to fish and chips in Aberdyfi … at 8.05 p.m. We weren't exactly burning the midnight oil but wanted to enjoy the idyllic setting before we looked for food. We had no chance – the local chip shop closed its doors at 8 p.m.

If, when visiting Aberdyfi, you fancy you can hear the sound of distant bells across the sea, don't be alarmed. You may be hearing the bells of the lost city of Cantre'r Gwaelod. Geological evidence supports local legends that areas now lying beneath the sea in Cardigan Bay were forested and probably inhabited 7,000 years ago. Cantre'r Gwaelod was said to cover much of this lowland area, and in his 1833 *Topographical Dictionary of Wales*, Samuel Lewis noted that at particularly low tides a collection of large stones and boulders could be spotted, seven miles off the coast at Aberystwyth. There's even a popular song – 'The Bells of Aberdyfi' – lamenting the sad loss of Cantre'r Gwaelod. It still makes an appearance in local pub sing-songs.

Follow the Wales Coast Path north from Aberdyfi and you'll soon reach the little seaside village of Tywyn, famous for what is believed to be the oldest inscribed cross in Wales. The words on the Cadfan Stone inside the church are thought to date back to the ninth century.

We've wandered tantalisingly close to Tywyn on several occasions, yet never quite managed to get there. I had been sorely tempted to put that right today. At low tide, it's easy enough to cover the four miles from Aberdyfi to Tywyn without leaving the beach. If I felt energetic and wanted to continue north past Tywyn, the new Tonfanau Bridge means you no longer have to walk inland around the Dysynni estuary.

So which was it to be? Tywyn or Borth? In the end, I chose to head to the Ynys-las side of the estuary, simply because it offered two for the price of one. Ynys-las and Borth combine the natural, windswept beauty of the estuarial nature reserve with the ramshackle, little town for which I retain an inexplicable fondness. Though, having given upmarket Aberdyfi the cold shoulder, I felt I should at least wave 'hello' from across the estuary.

Once you're away from the car park and visitor centre, there's a sense of being in a wild uninhabited land where all that exists is sea, sky and endless expanses of sand.

Ynys-las is all about sand. There are houses in the village, but they're set right back and you'd never know they were there as you weave your way through the extensive dunes, some of which are up to two hundred years old. I say 'some' because a sand dune system is ever-changing, and as new dunes form closer to the sea, the older ones are blown inland.

Sand dunes are one of the rare geological shifts that we can actually see happening with our own eyes. As I walked, head bowed, warm gusts of wind were lifting the tiny glistening particles of rock and dropping them someplace else. In another two hundred years the dunes that were now nearest the sea would have become the established 'old' ones.

I headed south along the long stretch of beach, taking my shoes off to enjoy the feel of damp sand under my feet. Two weeks before the start of the summer holidays it was all but deserted. The school children from the shop had headed excitedly towards the sand dunes, leaving the beach to strolling couples and the occasional dog walker. Several bare-chested young men sprinted towards the distant waves before confounding my expectations and putting on an astonishingly professional acrobatic display right there on the damp sand. I didn't like to stare *too* hard, but the hand-walking and somersaulting through the air was certainly impressive to someone like me who has never even mastered the simple cartwheel.

Eventually, the sand dunes were left behind and Borth's numerous (and mostly dilapidated) wooden groynes came gradually into view. Its unsheltered position on the coast has long made this little seaside town susceptible to flooding and erosion, the waves so beloved by surfers crashing directly onto its long beach and shingle ridge.

The timber groynes I was now approaching were part of coastal defences designed 50 years ago and were erected in the 1970s. They protected the shingle ridge admirably for many years, but their condition has badly deteriorated over the years, putting the beach (and low-lying town) at risk. With anticipated rises in sea level and the likelihood of fiercer storms in the future, the shingle bank was expected to diminish still further, leaving Borth with no protection from the sea. A report written in the year 2000 forecast that this sorry state of affairs would occur within the next ten to twenty years – urgent action was needed if this quirky little place wasn't to disappear altogether.

Last time I was in Borth, the new coastal defence scheme hadn't long been underway. The scheme included constructing rock groynes and breakwaters at intervals along the beach, plus one multi-purpose artificial reef near the Craig y Delyn cliffs, which would not only break the largest of the waves before they reached the shore, but would also encourage the type of waves beloved by surfers *and* provide a nesting ground for seabirds and a second more conventional reef. A win-win solution to Borth's fast disappearing natural coast defences.

Less popular was the addition of 200,000 tonnes of shingle to the beach, which would literally push the sea away from the town. I have to admit, back in 2011, the beach at Borth was not the most pleasant of landscapes, but needs must, and Borth survived the winter storms of 2014 in much better condition than its larger neighbour, Aberystwyth.

I got talking to two contractors after one noticed I was looking at my map and offered assistance. They told me that of the 70 plus houses that regularly flooded in bad weather, only two had suffered problems early in January 2014. The new flood defences were working!

In April 2014, the Welsh government announced more funding to complete the ongoing coastal defence works in Ceredigion, bringing the total amount spent in Borth to £17.7 million (from the Welsh government and the European Regional Development Fund).

But I'm getting ahead of myself. Well before I reached Borth there was something rather fascinating on the beach itself to explore – something I'd have missed had I not got talking to a solitary female dog walker who was on the lookout for it herself.

The storms that wreaked such havoc on Welsh seaside resorts in the winter of 2014 had also left an incredible legacy. As waves lashed the coastline, their sheer ferocity washed away the peat layer below Borth's sandy beach and dramatically exposed an ancient forest.

Right there on the beach and clearly visible at low tide are the stumps of oak and pine trees, preserved since the time of the Bronze Age more than 3,000 years ago. While some remains could be seen at extremely low tides prior to the storms, the catastrophic lifting of the peat had revealed hundreds of tree stumps that really *looked* like tree stumps.

I'd known nothing of this amazing spectacle so it was a happy coincidence that I was strolling along Borth beach when the tide was so low. Of course, since the forest's re-emergence from the peat there had been much speculation that it was part of the mythical kingdom of Cantre'r Gwaelod. For me, the sight of those tree stumps rising from the ocean was a scary reminder of the power of the sea and the permanent impact of rising sea levels.

I bade farewell to my friend and her by now very bored canine companions and headed into Borth, where the main street was sufficiently sheltered for the temperature to feel positively hot. There is some evidence that Borth existed in some shape or form as long ago as the sixteenth century. By the seventeenth century, fishing had become the mainstay of most local people, with herrings being one of the most popular catches. Some of the fanciful house names around here are the result of the town's seafaring men.

Borth first appeared on the map in the second half of the eighteenth century and grew rapidly when the railway arrived. Nowadays, the town relies on tourism and there are several caravan sites located between Borth and Ynys-las.

This being a Wednesday afternoon in the middle of July in Wales, many of the independent shops were closed, thwarting any desire on my part to inject some money into the local economy. I pushed ahead to Upper Borth, which presented itself as more affluent and less bohemian than its lower-lying neighbour. Despite the breathtaking views across the bay, I decided I preferred Borth proper.

Eventually, I joined the grassy footpath that led me to Borth's war memorial and here I settled down to enjoy my packed lunch. Its prominent position on the Wales Coast Path high above the bay means the memorial is a landmark for local people and sailors; it also means it is vulnerable to the elements. On 21 March 1983, the original war memorial was struck by lightning and destroyed. It is only thanks to a second round of public subscription that Borth has a new war memorial.

Despite the breeze, it was difficult to pull myself away from this scenic spot. I perched at the base of the memorial, mesmerised by the magnificence of the scene below, the tremendous power of the waves, and the stunning mountain backdrop.

By the time I picked up Harri at the end of the afternoon, I felt as though I'd had an enjoyable and active day. Perhaps I hadn't managed the full eighteen miles – nothing like it – but my day had been full of interest and delight. I'd explored a sand dune system, walked quite a long stretch of the Wales Coast Path and even wandered around a prehistoric forest. Not a bad day's work for a chauffeur!

For photographs visit <u>uk.pinterest.com/thewalkerswife</u>

Our accommodation

The Loft, Pen y Graig (www.holidayonanglesey.co.uk)

Trecastle Hotel, Bull Bay (www.trecastellhotel.co.uk)

Nant Bychan Farm, Moelfre (www.ukcampsite.co.uk)

Eryl Môr Hotel, Bangor (www.erylmorhotel.co.uk)

Y Gwydyr Hotel, Dolwyddelan (www.tripadvisor.co.uk)

Cae Du Campsite, Beddgelert (www.caeducampsite.co.uk)

Cae Gwyn B&B, Penrhyndeudraeth (www.caegwynbandb.co.uk)

Crystal House, Barmouth (crystalhouse-barmouth.co.uk)

Llanllwyda Farm, Bird's Rock (www.ukcampsite.co.uk)

The Maenllwyd, Machynlleth (www.maenllwyd.co.uk)

Bron y Llys, Dylife (www.bronyllys.co.uk)

George Borrow Hotel, Ponterwyd (www.thegeorgeborrowhotel.co.uk)

The Black Lion Hotel, Pontrhydfendigaid (www.blacklionhotel.co.uk)

Caravan & Camping Club, Rhandirmwyn (www.ukcampsite.co.uk)

The Level Crossing, Llandovery (www.booking.com)

National Showcaves Campsite, Dan yr Ogof (www.showcaves.co.uk)

Markets Tavern Hotel, Brecon (www.booking.com)

Cwmdu Campsite, Cwmdu (www.campingbreconbeacons.com)

Llanthony Treats, Llanthony (www.llanthonytreats.co.uk)

Ebberley House, Monmouth (www.ebberleyhousemonmouth.co.uk)

O Fôn i Fynwy: walking Wales from end to end

'In deciding upon a walking route across Wales, I was guided by the principle that the paths chosen should be walkable without undue difficulty or danger in all but the most extreme weather conditions. The basis for this decision was that one cannot choose what weather to walk in on a long-distance hike, and I didn't want to force users of this guide on to high mountaintops in unsuitable conditions. For this reason, the main route described avoids the highest summits of Snowdonia and mid-Wales, but without, I hope, sacrificing the scenic quality of these areas. In fine weather, experienced walkers are encouraged to take in as many summits as possible, and I have outlined alternative high-level routes across the Carneddau and Moel Siabod, as well as potential detours to the summits of Snowdon, Cnicht, Cadair Idris and Pumlumon.

This 364-mile route through Wales takes its inspiration from the traditional Welsh expression 'O Fôn i Fynwy', which literally means 'from Anglesey [Ynys Môn] to Monmouthshire', but is also used to mean the whole of Wales.

This guidebook gives detailed instructions on how to follow the undulating and frequently mountainous route from Holyhead to Chepstow, with details of maps, accommodation and refreshments included.

'O Fôn i Fynwy: Walking Wales from end to end' by Harri Garrod Roberts is available from Amazon's Kindle Store.

For photographs visit <u>uk.pinterest.com/thewalkerswife</u>

The Via Algarviana: walking 300km across the Algarve

'It must be human nature to find something to worry about, however, because no sooner had I leapt out of bed than I started to fret about the Ribeira da Foupana. Not that I was actually worried about the river – I'm sure it'll be flowing long after my own mortal soul leaves this world – but Harri had mentioned that this was one of the few Algarve rivers on our route which might pose difficulties in getting across. Almargem's Via Algarviana guide actually used the words 'an adventure' to describe crossing the Foupana, adding that the river was 'the most imposing river all along the route and that in times of heavy rain may become very dangerous or even impassable'. I didn't like the sound of that. Imposing? Did that mean the river was wide, or deep or fast-flowing? And what did they mean by dangerous? My imagination was now in overdrive.'

One week after completing the London marathon (her first), the author embarks on a long-distance backpacking trip across southern Portugal with Harri. She is confident she's fit enough to tackle the 300 kilometre Via Algarviana trail, but how will she cope when the temperature soars, no-one speaks English and drinking water is in short supply?

Follow Tracy as she hikes the tough, undulating route through depopulated villages and the beautiful mountains of inland Algarve, and gradually succumbs to the charms of a region that remains off the beaten track despite being so close to popular sandy beaches.

Away from the bustling resorts, the couple spent their days discovering a varied landscape of rolling hills, dry orchards, cork forests, and agricultural terraces. In the evenings, they enjoyed village life, traditional cuisine and the extraordinary kindness and hospitality of local people.

The Via Algarviana: walking 300km across the Algarve by Tracy Burton is available from Amazon as a paperback and an ebook.

For photographs visit uk.pinterest.com/thewalkerswife

The Via Algarviana: an English guide to the 'Algarve Way'

'Threading its way through the hills from settlement to settlement is the Via Algarviana ('Algarve Way'), a waymarked, long-distance trail stretching the entire length of the Algarve, from the Spanish border in the east to the Atlantic Ocean in the west. The 300km (186-mile) journey along this trail is an unforgettable experience and provides an introduction to an Algarve that few visitors ever get to see. This book describes the complete route from Alcoutim to Cabo de São Vicente (Cape St Vincent), as well as an alternative finish to the walk via Aljezur and the Rota Vicentina – another long-distance trail exploring southern Portugal's windswept Atlantic coast.'

Harri's guidebook also contains practical information for those who are contemplating walking the route, including when to go, how to get to the start at Alcoutim and the potential dangers en route.

The Via Algarviana: an English guide to the 'Algarve Way' by Harri Garrod Roberts is available from Amazon's Kindle Store.

For photographs visit uk.pinterest.com/thewalkerswife

Other books by Harri Garrod Roberts

Print books

Day Walks in the Brecon Beacons

Carmarthen Bay & Gower: Circular Walks along the Wales Coast Path

Carmarthenshire & Gower: Wales Coast Path Official Guide (Tenby to Swansea)

Day Walks in Pembrokeshire Coast National Park

Digital books

Circular Walks on the Gower Peninsula

Dylan's Welsh Walks

England Coast Path: Severn Estuary & Bridgwater Bay

Castle Walks in Monmouthshire

Castle Walks in the Marches of Gwent

Castle Walks around Newport and Cardiff Rhymney Valley Walks

For more information visit camau.co.uk

Printed in Great Britain
by Amazon